D0907103

NEIGHBORHOOD CONTROL IN THE 1970S

List of Contributors

James Davis
Norman I. Fainstein
Susan S. Fainstein
George Frederickson
Howard W. Hallman
Charles V. Hamilton
Ronald J. James
Victor Jones
Lewis Lipsitz

Michael Lipsky
Pepe Lucero
Judith V. May
David C. Perry
Jeffrey Pressman
Henry J. Schmandt
John H. Strange
Orion White, Jr.

NEIGHBORHOOD CONTROL IN THE 1970S

Politics, Administration, and Citizen Participation

George Frederickson, Editor
Indiana University

Foreword by
Howard W. Hallman
Center for Governmental Studies

Chandler Publishing Company
An Intext Publisher   New York and London

Chandler Publications in Political Science
Victor Jones, *Editor*

Library of Congress Cataloging in Publication Data
Main entry under title:

Neighborhood control in the 1970s.

   "Background papers for a conference sponsored by
the Center [for Governmental Studies in Washington,
D. C.] on the topic of 'Public administration and
neighborhood control' . . . held May 6–8, 1970 in
Boulder, Colorado."
   1. Decentralization in government—United States—
Addresses, essays, lectures. 2. Community power—
Addresses, essays, lectures. I. Frederickson, George,
ed. II. Center for Governmental Studies, Washington,
D. C.
JS341.N45   320.4   73–3044
ISBN 0–8102–0470–3

Chandler Publishing Co.
257 Park Avenue South
New York, New York 10010

Text design by Design 110

Contents

Foreword

If the just powers of government are derived from the consent of the governed, as the Declaration of Independence proclaims, how is this consent to be obtained. Through the popular election of public officials has been the traditional answer. Referendum and initiative were added by the progressive movement. Political parties and pressure groups are also important, as several generations of scholars have told us.

All these methods have met the test of time. All are valid, all are legitimate; but that does not settle the matter forever. Indeed, the last tumultuous decade has reopened the question of relationships between the governed and those who govern. A new slogan—participatory democracy—came into use in the early 1960s. A new practice—maximum feasible participation of the poor—began in the mid-1960s as part of the anti-poverty program. A new demand—community control—was heard as the 1960s ended.

Without a doubt, the issues raised by these new practices and demands will remain as the 1970s unfold. In spite of a conservative reaction which has tried to clamp a lid on greater citizen involvement, the movement for greater participation continues. I believe that this movement is fundamental to the further development of representative democracy. I also believe that it is essential, from the practical viewpoint, to make government work because the cities and metropolitan areas in which the majority of Americans now live will not be governable unless citizens participate more. Elected officials, professional administrators, and technicians cannot alone make our cities function properly.

Many in the generation now finishing college and entering public careers sense this. They are dissatisfied with the old ways and they seek new approaches. This collection of essays on politics, administration, and neighborhood control is written to assist them by defining the essential issues, analyzing the complexities, and advocating courses to pursue.

The essays should also be of use for the reeducation of political leaders and public administrators. Most of those now in the top ranks attended college in the period from about 1935 to 1955, as I myself did. We studied the reports of the President's Committee on Administrative Management dating from 1937. Efficiency, we were taught, is the primary objective of good administration.

We also followed the 1949 work of the U.S. Commission on Organization of the Executive Branch of the Government (Hoover Commission). The Commission stated: "Responsibility and accountability are impossible without authority—the power to direct. The exercise of authority is impossible without a clear line of command from the top to the bottom, and a return line from the bottom to the top." The holy law of hierarchy! Those on top command; those at the bottom respond.

Since then, the influence of the human relations approach has emerged. During the past twenty years students have learned about the needs of individual workers and about the work group as a social unit. Group dynamics, sensitivity training, and organizational development have become part of the curriculum. A major theme has been that by making employees more content, the organization will be more productive. Nevertheless, hierarchy and efficiency have remained dominant values.

But times are changing. The concern for participatory democracy, citizen participation, and neighborhood control now challenges the doctrine of hierarchy and affirms that there are values greater than efficiency. Might it be then, that political science and public administration theories need to be modified to respond to changing perceptions? A growing number of scholars seem to think so, many of them young but also some not-so-young. Some practitioners who confront changing situations—in the rare moments when they have time for reflection—think so too.

As a contribution to developing new ideas in political science and public administration, the Center for Governmental Studies in Washington, D.C. commissioned most of the essays in this book. The Center itself is engaged in a series of action-oriented studies on the decentralization of governmental programs and community participation. The staff consists primarily of persons with operating experience in public administration who are engaged in these studies because of a concern for strengthening practical implementation of new approaches. The Center sees the need for rethinking basic theory, and also for an interchange between scholars and practitioners.

The essays were written as background papers for the conference on the topic of "Public Administration and Neighborhood Control," sponsored by the Center. We focused on neighborhood control because it is the ultimate expression of administrative decentralization and citizen participation. The conference was held May 6–8, 1970 in Boulder, Colorado, and brought together about fifty persons, who met in two general sessions and in small discussion groups. Participants included authors and representatives of the major schools of public affairs, board and staff members of the Center, plus several public officials and businessmen. Afterward the essays were revised and updated for publication.

An idea repeatedly discussed at the conference was the hypothesis that the suburbs might serve as a model for neighborhood government in the central city. To develop that idea further, we arranged for David C. Perry to write an essay on the suburban model and we obtained from Victor Jones an essay that looks at neighborhoods and suburbs from a metropolitan viewpoint. As I reviewed the essays, I felt there was a need to place the neighborhood concept in a historical perspective, so I composed the essay that begins this collection.

The conference and the commissioned essays were made possible by a grant from the Ford Foundation. This effort and other programs of the Center are guided by the board of directors consisting of *Chairman:* Jose Lucero, President, Southwest Program Development Corporation, San Antonio, Texas; *Vice Chairmen:* Thomas C. Mayers, Director of Community Affairs, Olin Chemicals, Stamford, Connecticut; Norvel Smith, President, Merritt College, Oakland, California; John Ballard, Mayor of Akron, Ohio; John C. Donovan, Chairman, Department of Government, Bowdoin College, Brunswick, Maine; Ernest Estepp, Delbarton, West Virginia (former Director of Community Development, Southwestern Community Action Council, Huntington, West Virginia); Lauro Garcia, Jr., Director, Guadalupe Organization, Guadalupe, Arizona; Doris Graham, Executive Director, Dorchester Area Planning Action Council, Dorchester, Massachusetts; Charles T. Henry, City Manager, University City, Missouri; A. J. McKnight, Director of Southern Cooperative Development Program, Lafayette, Louisiana; William T. Patrick, Jr., American Telephone and Telegraph Company, New York, New York; S. H. Roberts, Vice President for Institutional Research, University of Tennessee, Knoxville, Tennessee; Con Shea, Executive Director, State Department of Social Services, Denver, Colorado; Hector Vazquez, Executive Director, The Puerto Rican Forum, New York, New York.

From the Center's staff, Alden F. Briscoe handled conference arrangements, Clementine Taylor provided secretarial services, and Everett Crawford, George J. Washnis, and James H. Ammons III served as recorders.

Howard W. Hallman
Center for Governmental Studies

Contributors

James Davis is Associate Professor of Political Science at Washington University, St. Louis. He received his Ph.D. from the University of Michigan in 1964 and taught at the University of Wisconsin—Madison, before joining Washington University. He has worked for brief periods in government agencies and in 1968–1969 was an advisor in the National Institute of Development Administration, Bangkok. He has published articles and books in the field of public administration and public policy, the most recent of which is *The National Executive Branch: An Introduction* (New York: Free Press, 1970).

Norman I. and Susan S. Fainstein did their graduate work at M.I.T. in political science. Norman Fainstein is Assistant Professor of Sociology at Columbia University. Susan Fainstein is Assistant Professor of Urban Planning at Livingston College, Rutgers University. They are both Research Associates at the Center for Policy Research. The Fainsteins have published several articles concerned with urban political sociology and social policy, as well as editing an anthology entitled *The View From the Bottom: Urban Political and Social Policy* (Boston, Mass.: Little, Brown, 1972).

George Frederickson is Chairman of Graduate Programs and Professor of Public and Environmental Affairs at Indiana University. Formerly Associate Director of Metropolitan Studies and Associate Professor of Political Science at the Maxwell Graduate School, Syracuse University, he spent the first part of 1972 as Fellow in Higher Education Finance Administration at the University of North Carolina. Elected to the National Council of the American Society for Public Administration in 1970, he is now a member of their Executive Committee and was Chairman of the Program Committee for the 1972 Annual Conference on Public Administration. He is Research and Reports Editor for the *Public Administration Review*.

Howard W. Hallman is President of the Center for Governmental Studies, a nonprofit research unit specializing in citizen participation and neighborhood government and manpower. His B.A. and M.A. are from the University of Kansas. He has worked in housing in Philadelphia, community action programs in New Haven, the Senate Subcommittee on Employment, Manpower and Poverty, and was consultant to the President's Task Force on Poverty. He is the author of over ninety articles, reports, and documents.

Charles V. Hamilton is Professor of Political Science at Columbia University, specializing in urban politics, political modernization and the politics of black Americans. He received his Ph.D. from the University of Chicago. His books include *Black Power: The Politics of Liberation in America* (co-authored with Stokely Carmichael) (New York: Random House, 1968) and *The Black Experience in American Politics* (New York: Putnam, 1972).

Ronald J. James is Special Assistant to the Director of the Office Opportunity. He has a B.A. from the University of Missouri and a J.D. from American University. He was a Lobbyist for the Urban Coalition Action Council 1969–1970.

Victor Jones is professor of political scence at the University of California, Berkeley. He has taught at the Illinois Institute of Technology and at Yale, Wesleyan, and York Universities.

Lewis Lipsitz is Associate Professor of Political Science at the University of North Carolina, Chapel Hill. He is the editor of a book of readings in American politics soon to be published. A version of his essay in this volume appeared in the December issue of *Dissent* magazine.

Michael Lipsky is the author of *Protest in City Politics* (New York: Rand McNally, 1972). He attended Oberlin College and received advanced degrees at Princeton University in politics and public affairs. He taught at the University of Wisconsin and was a staff associate of the Institute for Research on Poverty, before accepting his present position as Associate Professor of Political Science at the Massachusetts Institute of Technology. His essay, "Toward a Theory of Street-Level Bureaucracy," on which his contribution to this volume is based, was published in a somewhat modified version in *Urban Affairs Quarterly*, June 1971.

Pepe Lucero is President of Southwest Program Development Corporation, a Texas-based nonprofit organization doing work with Chicanos throughout the country. Mr. Lucero has served as a consultant to various private organizations and to the principal federal agencies. Five years in community action work in San Antonio as Executive Director of the Southwest Region's largest CAP agency gave Mr. Lucero a broad range of experiences in federal programs-local community work. The G.I. Bill and full-time work have seen Mr. Lucero through a B.A. in Government, twenty-seven hours in graduate work in the same area, and some work in law school.

Judith V. May is Assistant Professor of Political Science at Rutgers, The State University, Newark. The essay prepared for this volume appeared in *Politics and Society*, Fall, 1971.

David C. Perry is Assistant Professor, Department of Government, University of Texas, Austin. He is the author of articles in the field of law enforcement and police and the urban areas. He is presently co-editing a book on *Violence as Politics* (New York: Harper and Row, forthcoming), and is writing a book entitled *Police and Metropolitanism* (Columbus, Ohio: Charles Merrill, forthcoming).

Jeffrey Pressman is an Assistant Professor of Political Science at the Massachusetts Institute of Technology. His baccalaureate degree is from Yale, and his M.A. and Ph.D. are from Berkeley. He is the author of *House vs. Senate: Conflict in the Appropriations Process* (New Haven: Yale University Press, 1966) and "Preconditions of Mayoral Leadership" in the *American Political Science Review*. He is the co-author with Aaron Wildovsky of the book *Implementation* (Berkeley: University of California Press, 1973).

Henry J. Schmandt is Professor of Political Science and Urban Affairs at the University of Wisconsin—Milwaukee. He has served as chairman of the Southeastern Wisconsin Regional Planning Commission and as a member of the Advisory Council to the Wisconsin Department of Local Affairs and Development. He is co-author of *Metropolis: Its People, Politics, and Economic Life* (New York, Harper and Row, 1970) and *Milwaukee: A Contemporary Urban Profile* (New York: Praeger, 1971), and other works in the local and metropolitan political field.

John H. Strange Dean of the College of Public and Community Service, University of Massachusetts—Boston, recently edited *Blacks and Bureaucracy* (Crowell Co., 1972), and is the author of several articles on the political activities of black Americans. Currently a member of the Princeton, New Jersey Borough Council, he gained experience with community action and neighborhood groups while Director of Research, Planning and Program Development of the North Carolina Fund, a state-wide anti-poverty agency.

Orion White, Jr. is currently Associate Professor of Political Science at the University of North Carolina at Chapel Hill. He received his Ph.D. in political science from Indiana University in 1964. He has taught at the University of Texas and was Visiting Associate Professor at the University of California at Berkeley. His current research interests include politics and administration in post-industrial societies and theories of organizational change. At present he is completing a book, with Emmette Redford, on the post-Apollo program in NASA and is writing, with Robert Biller, an introductory public administration text.

Prologue

George Frederickson

This book is about American cities, those who govern them and those who are governed. Because those who govern our cities and their suburbs are increasingly "professional," public servants, this book is about public administration. Because the most common contact between the governors and the governed is in the form of citizen–bureaucrat relations, this book is about citizens and their participation in urban government. And, this book is about citizen politics and particularly political behavior in social and ethnic neighborhoods. Students of political science, urban studies, and public administration will find this book directed at them because the volume was designed to bridge the gaps between these subjects.

We were ill equipped socially, economically, politically, and administratively for the urban crisis. Both administrative and political thought had tended to focus on centralized massive political and administrative responses to social and economic problems. The reform-progressive era of American history had galvanized administrative and political thought to a preoccupation with hierarchy, centralization, merit system administration, nonpartisan local government, elections at large, efficiency, and economy and rational decision-making. While our interests were fixed on these concerns the cities deteriorated. They lost large chunks of their tax base, they absorbed the poor and the undereducated, their suburbs became middle and upper class enclaves, and their administrative apparatus separated into semiautonomous professional fiefdoms of educators, police-men, firemen, sanitation workers and social workers. In all of this one thing was clear, citizens were no longer directly involved in government, no longer in a participative role, and certainly no longer in control of local government.

In many ways this book is a response to these conditions. The thrust of the book is fourfold: (a) it argues that some degree of citizen participa-tion in ongoing urban government activities is an ethical requirement of any form of government which purports to be representative; (b) that some degree of citizen participation in the American city is an existential and growing fact, compelling the attention and examination of scholars; (c) that tension between the governors and the governed and their respective agents—bureaucrats for the former and "tribunes" of various sorts for the latter—is another existential and under-analyzed fact and, (d) that greater citizen participation, indeed the control of neighborhoods by citizens, must be taken seriously as a means of meeting the critical challenges of the survival of American cities.

This book is not neutral. The thrust of most of these essays is in the direction of increased levels of citizen participation and neighborhood control. There are cautions, caveats, and queries, to be sure, and indeed an antithesis essay by James Davis entitled "Participation in a Bureau-cratic Society: Some Questions and Skeptical Notes," which is an frontal attack on participation and control. In sum, though, the book argues the importance of nighborhood control as a fundamental means of bringing about more generally responsive, productive local government.

The control of local government functions at the neighborhood level is neither a new idea nor a new phenomenon. The concept of neighbor-hood control is as old as political theory, the earliest forms of government that are described and prescribed have to do with the city and the process by which the citizen interacts with his city government. The idea of neigh-borhood control in the American experience is traced by Howard Hallman in his opening essay, followed by Henry Schmandt's description of the various forms that political decentralization and neighborhood control can take. If neighborhood control is an old and honorable notion in American politics, David Perry contends that its contemporary manifestations can be most readily found by looking at the suburbs; and Victor Jones places the citizen participation and neighborhood control movement in the con-text of the wider metropolitan area.

If decentralized and locally controlled forms of government are to be preferred, as is argued here, what are the processes to be utilized to bring this about? Neighborhood control is rich in its implications for a public service which emphasizes professionalization, hierarchy, and merit. Both Michael Lipsky and Orion White formulate these implications, Lipsky from the perspective of his "street level bureaucracy" and White in his case study of the responses of bureaucrats to "Environmental turbulence." Jeff Pressman describes the changes wrought in local government as a consequence of patterns of fiscal federalism and argues that in many ways the national government relates to the neighborhoods of our great cities in much the same way as it relates to other nation states. Judith May sketches the "duel soverignty" that has resulted from federally funded inner-city programs. The political strategies for achieving neighborhood control are fomulated at the local level by John Strange and at the national level by Ronald James. Norman and Susan Fainstein consider the political evaluation of the decentralization of the education function and its local control in New York City. As a contemporary phenomenon, neighborhood control has special relevance to black and brown minorities. The implications of political and administrative decentralization for these minorities are described by Charles V. Hamilton and Jose (Pepe) Lucero.

The essays in this volume reflect major shifts both in the interests of social scientists and in their approaches to the study of government. The portrayal of poverty in Michael Harrington's *Other America,* the inner-city riots of the late 1960s, the dramatic emergence of public service unionism, the rise in lawlessness served to inform social scientists of the acuteness of the urban malaise. The result has been a fundamental rethinking of the politics, administration and economics of urban life in America. Economists have begun the shift from their preoccupation with the market model and its variances to a basic look at the economics of goods and services distribution and redistribution. Political scientists have begun to move from their preoccupation with interest group pluralism and voting behavior to a more fundamental concern for the roots of political apathy, the origins of legitimacy and illegitimacy in political systems, the sources and causes of political rebellion. The essays on black politics by Charles Hamilton and Mexican American politics by Jose Lucero and the explorations into power and legitimacy by Louis Lipsitz and David Perry all manifest these contempory concerns in political science. And, the essays by Jeff Pressman and Judith May represent the current interest in the distribution of both political power and economic resources in the city. Public administration specialists have shifted from their preoccupation with centralized hierarchic organizations which were presumed to be the most efficient, economic and rational decision making organs, to a concern for decentralized and locally controlled bureaucracies. Expressions of these concerns are especially apparent in my epilogue and the pieces by Mike Lipsky and Orion White.

The social sciences now more clearly recognize the extent to which their earlier theories were implicitly and in some cases explicitly supportive of an economic, political, and administrative system that severely disadvantaged large groups of American citizens, and often in the name of democracy. This recognition has caused a rapid and dramatic shifting of premises and theories in social science. We have seen in recent years the emergence of the Caucus for a New Political Science, the so-called New Public Administration, the Union for a Radical Economics, and similar groupings in other social sciences. Within each discipline fundamental challenges are being made to the premises and paradigms on which the social sciences are built.

This collection of original essays is designed to focus on a specific problem of the inner city—governance—from the newer perspectives of the social sciences. It is not addressed to an abstract or theoretical question but is, rather, dealing with the contours and texture of inner city government as it *now* exists and as it is likely, in the judgment of these authors, to take shape through the coming generation. The unit of analysis is not the city, but is rather the neighborhood; the preoccupation is not with voting behavior or interest groups, but with political strategies for achieving neighborhood control and maintaining power. These perspectives are particularly reflected in the works of John Strange and Ronald James. Rather than focus on the powers of community elites, it focuses on the political behavior of minorities, blacks, and Mexican-Americans. It is then very much in tune with the politics and administration of contemporary large city government in the United States.

An Introduction to Neighborhood Control and Citizen Participation

The Neighborhood as an Organizational Unit: A Historical Perspective

Howard W. Hallman

A confluence of ideas and social forces is currently focusing attention on the neighborhood as a unit for administrative organization and citizen action. Neighborhood councils, community corporations, little city halls, neighborhood health centers, community schools, and advocacy of neighborhood government are all part of this trend. This concern is not altogether new, for there has been a persistent interest in the neighborhood since the mid-1800s when American cities began to grow large. Like the relative emphasis on centralized and decentralized government,[1] this interest has waxed and waned; nevertheless, the neighborhood has always been the concern of some movement or another.

Municipal Government and Political Parties

City government grew in size and complexity as industrialization and urbanization proceeded. In the middle of the nineteenth century, when municipal functions began to expand, the city council was the dominant institution in urban government, and there was a general distrust of excessive centralization of power in a single executive. Thus, the new functions of government tended to be assigned to different boards and officials, some of whom were appointed by the council rather than by the mayor.

7

In our contemporary jargon, we would say that the accountability in such a system was weak.

At the same time vast numbers of immigrants were arriving in the cities. These people needed services and other assistance, but they found much of municipal government incomprehensible. The one who could most readily help them was the neighborhood political official, the precinct committeeman. He was a broker in votes and services, providing emergency food, influencing agencies on behalf of constituents, and doing other favors.[2] But, as Arthur W. Bromage writes, he was more than that.

> Sometimes the voter does not seek influence or favor. He merely wants to know how to approach city hall; what department to go to; how to apply for a job, a permit, a reduction in assessment, or public welfare assistance. The precinct committeeman will know, for he has long since learned these channels through day and night training.[3]

The committeeman, in his role as broker, was the foundation for the political machines that became entrenched in numerous cities. Corruption was the price of his personalized service and the other operations of the machine. Running the machine was the political boss, who, with his allies in business, government, and the party, grew rich and powerful. Nevertheless:

> Vicious as were his politics, the boss's method of operating provided the first real centralization of power over city administration. . . . It is a fact that the earliest concentration of the multifarious powers of cities grew up outside the formal governmental structure.[4]

This is ironic, for the precinct committeeman, who humanized municipal government and provided personal and decentralized services, was the power base for centralization.

But while municipal government was fragmented, individual departments were not decentralized in the sense that we use the term today. Schools, playgrounds, bath houses, fire and police stations were, of course, scattered around the city, but control was usually centralized. The one major exception was the police department, which, because of limits in communication and transportation, gave foot patrolmen and precinct stations more local discretion than they have today. By and large, in the last half of the nineteenth century, the political and governmental official with the greatest concern for the neighborhood was the precinct committeeman, not the public employee.

Settlement Houses and Community Centers

During the same period, the settlement house movement developed, representing another interest in neighborhood. The first settlement in the United States was founded in 1886, and by 1900 there were 103. According to Sidney Dillick:

> The settlement began as a center established by advantaged persons who desired to help the people of a deprived neighborhood, and developed rapidly into a significant social institution. . . . The settlement assumed a special responsibility for all families living within the radius of a few blocks of the settlement house. It also sustained a general relation to the larger district encircling about the immediate neighborhood. It was concerned with developing institutional resources suited to the needs of a working-class community. This included relief of distress, removal of unsanitary conditions, care of neglected children, and recreation.[5]

At first these settlements were private institutions, but after the turn of the century public schools were also used as community centers. After some experimentation a national conference on "Civic and Social Center Development" gave further impetus to this movement. By 1913, 629 school buildings in 152 cities were used for community purposes.[6]

In the decade before World War I, as settlement houses and school community centers grew in number, "a shift of emphasis occurred . . . from neighborhood organization covering a geographic area with a program of service to people in need, to neighborhood organization as part of a movement to revitalize communities."[7] In the 1920s this trend accelerated with the formation of community councils at both the neighborhood and citywide levels.[8]

The Neighborhood Unit and City Planning

One of the leaders in the school and community-center movement was Clarence Perry, who over a period of twenty years nurtured and evolved the concept of the neighborhood unit as a building block for city planning. In the influential 1929 "Regional Survey of New York and Its Environs," his description of the neighborhood unit included these features:

> The kind of housing required by child-rearing families is peculiarly and vitally dependent upon the resources and character of the immediate vicinity. The cellular city is the inevitable product of an automobile age.

> The area to be occupied by a residential community should be just what is required for the nice working of a school, playground and local shop services.
>
> The developer can surround a new home with a satisfying environment, but it can be preserved, after he has gone, only by the residents themselves. For this purpose, a voluntary property owners' association is an indispensable community mechanism.[9]

During the next decade these ideas were put into practice in such suburban developments as Sunnyside, Long Island; Radburn, New Jersey; Chatham Village, Pennsylvania; Mariemont, Ohio; and the three greenbelt towns constructed as a New Deal program in Maryland, Ohio, and Wisconsin.[10]

Eclipse of the Neighborhood

As the manifestations of the neighborhood idea emerged and developed, a counter trend toward centralization appeared and grew steadily stronger. The muckrakers attacked boss rule, and the reformers of the progressive movement instituted changes in local government.[11] In vogue for a while after 1910 was the commission form of city government, which usually included five commissioners, elected at-large, who combined executive and legislative power. Then the city-manager form, modeled upon the business corporation, was invented and, except in the larger cities, spread rapidly. It too featured at-large elections. Under both forms of government elections were nonpartisan; that is, candidates ran without the labels of national political parties.[12] The mayor-council cities strengthened the powers of their mayors and appointed chief administrative officers to manage the city departments.

These events undercut the political machine, diminishing the role of the precinct committeeman, but the reformers did not substitute any other neighborhood official to perform the brokerage and service roles. The centralization of power begun by the bosses was continued by city commissions, managers, and mayors.

In addition to city managers and chief administrative officers, other-professionals moved into top jobs in city government. The fundamental creed was efficiency and economy, and the basic practice was to centralize control of budgets and personnel. The flavor of this trend is illustrated by a passage in a book on police administration which discusses the dangers of decentralization by areas.

> This discussion should suggest to many cities the possibility of discontinuing stations which were established 20, 30, or 40 years ago, in the days

of horse-drawn vehicles, foot patrol, and word-of-mouth communications. This discontinuance of unnecessary district stations will result not only in financial savings, but in increased facility of control over the force, and increased manpower due to the release of inside men for outside duty.[13]

The trend toward centralization in the private social welfare sector also began during the early part of the twentieth century when the first councils of social agencies were formed. Next came the development of federated fund raising, which received impetus from the war chests of World War I and grew rapidly as community chests during the 1920s. By then the councils of social agencies acted as planning bodies and advised the community chests on the allocation of the funds they raised. Members of both the councils and chests have tended to be agency representatives and citywide leaders, which, like at-large municipal elections, allows only scant representation for poor neighborhoods.[14]

The New Deal accelerated the centralization process, not only from the states to the national government, but also from the neighborhood to city hall. Funds flowed to city government for various public works projects, enabling city planning commissions to implement ideas that had been on the drawing boards for years. After World War II, the urban redevelopment program gave cities additional funds, which were controlled by the central planning and redevelopment agencies. During the 1950s, the proportion of funds spent to improve central business districts, where real estate interests predominated, steadily increased.

Nonetheless, the neighborhood idea was kept alive. In Chicago Clifford Shaw's Area Project, which commenced in 1933, used a neighborhood base to combat juvenile delinquency.[15] Saul Alinsky and the Industrial Areas Foundation helped organize such groups as the Back-of-the-Yards Council in Chicago in the late 1930s and Mexican-American organizations in California in the 1940s.[16]

The settlement house movement continued, and most of what little neighborhood organizing there was in the fifteen years after World War II was accomplished by settlement workers. Suburban housing developers used some, though not all, of Perry's neighborhood unit ideas, and city planners brought them into the design of urban renewal projects. Neighborhood analysis was a basic component of planning undertaken in the 1960s under the federally financed Community Renewal Program. The neighborhood idea was down, but not out.

Revival

The revival of interest in the neighborhood as an organizational unit came about in several ways. The most obvious influence was the Community Action Program, which was launched under the Economic Opportunity Act of 1964. Its well-known requirement for "maximum feasible participation of members of groups and areas served"[17] made citizen involvement a national issue. The first year's struggle revolved around how much representation of the poor on the board of directors of the community action agency should be allowed and how this representation should be chosen. A legislative settlement in 1966 settled the issue of proportion by requiring at least one-third, and the experience of this led to selection by neighborhood groups. Even more significant to the neighborhood approach, program operations were based in the neighborhood, and sizable sums were expended in each for community organizers, multi-service centers, Head Start units for preschool children, and other neighborhood activities. Even rural dwellers commonly referred to their "neighborhood center."

The predecessors of the Community Action Program were the interlocking programs sponsored by the President's Committee on Juvenile Delinquency and Youth Crime and by the Ford Foundation. The Juvenile Delinquency Program was heavily influenced by the ideas of Lloyd Ohlin and Richard Cloward, who believed that delinquency was caused by lack of opportunity for the poor rather than by individual deviance and that the remedy was to change institutions in order to provide more opportunity for poor people.[18] They translated their ideas into a program for New York City's lower east side, proposing neighborhood organization and citizen action as major instruments of institutional change.[19]

When Ohlin went to work for the President's Committee on Juvenile Delinquency, these ideas were picked up by its chairman, Attorney General Robert Kennedy, and its executive director, David Hackett. Another person associated with this effort was Richard Boone, who was well-acquainted with Chicago's Area Project which had existed since the 1930s.

Although the Juvenile Delinquency Program was imbued with the idea of neighborhood citizen action and organizing, the local programs that it funded were governed by the same kind of coalition boards which had been running councils of social agencies for half a century, though with more representation for city and school officials and hardly any for the neighborhoods served. This was also true of the Ford Foundation's gray area project, which, in the early 1960s, under the leadership of Paul Ylvisaker, financed comprehensive social programs with components in education, manpower training, health, housing, and other services. Both these programs were exceptionally creative and originated most of the programs which the Office of Economic Opportunity (OEO) later packaged —Head Start, Legal Services, New Careers, and others. But neighborhood was more an administrative base than a means of citizen participation in policy making, something which came to the foreground only in the last half of the 1960s.[20]

These two programs had been in action for less than two years when the War on Poverty was declared in 1964. Their experience was quite limited, but their influence was significant, since Kennedy, Hackett, Boone, and Ylvisaker were among the chief architects of the new Community Action Program, a key part of the war on poverty.

Two years later the Model Cities Program was developed by the U. S. Department of Housing and Urban Development to treat the physical and social problems of the inner city. While its requirement for widespread citizen participation"[21] was intended to signal a lesser degree of involvement than that of the Community Action Program, it has actually induced greater citizen involvement. Moreover, this program was also based on the neighborhood approach and had neighborhood agencies and city planning commissions. This representation came about partly because some of the national administrators were from the urban renewal and city planning programs and others were from OEO and believed citizens deserved more opportunities to serve the city. But probably the main reason for the strong citizen element of the Model Cities Program was that by the time it was becoming active in 1967 and 1968, citizen involvement and neighborhood action were "blowin' in the wind."

Thus, the neighborhood idea reemerged not only because of books written on the subject and the several federal programs, but also because of strong social forces. As the civil rights movement neared its goals of legislation for equal employment, open housing, public accommodations, and voting rights, some of the more militant black activists began to demand black power. This demand led to an advocacy of black separatism or black control of the institutions serving black communities. Before long there were similar Spanish outcries.

But the demand for participation and control was a concern not only of minority groups. Persons on the ideological right, opposing many of the federal programs since the New Deal, advocated states' rights and local control. In the last half of the 1960s, university students, for different reasons, began to demand greater participation in the governance of the universities. While residents of white working class neighborhoods have not been as articulate with this kind of demand, voting patterns suggest that they too feel excluded and want more control over the events and institutions which shape their lives.

Expressions of this trend began to appear in reports of federal commissions. In 1967, the prestigious Advisory Commission on Intergovernmental Relations (consisting mostly of federal, state, and local officials) recommended:

the enactment of State legislation authorizing large cities and county governments in metropolitan areas to establish neighborhood subunits of government with limited powers of taxation and a local self-government with respect to specified and restricted functions including the administration of specified portions of Federal, State and local programs. Such subunits would be dissoluble by the city or county governing board at any time.[22]

The 1968 report of the National Advisory Commission on Civil Disorders (Kerner Commission) proposed that local governments

Develop Neighborhood Action Task Forces as joint community–government efforts through which more effective communication can be achieved, and the delivery of city services to ghetto residents improved.

Bring the institutions of local government closer to the people they serve by establishing neighborhood outlets for local, state, and Federal administrative and public service agencies.[23]

Establishment of neighborhood city halls was part of the second phase of action.[24]

Also in 1968, the National Commission on Urban Problems (Douglas Commission), in a chapter entitled "Urban Services: Steps Toward Neighborhood Regeneration" had two recommendations:

Accelerate improvement in poor neighborhoods by providing adequate city services.

Decentralization of municipal services to neighborhood city halls.[25]

These are not merely idle dreams. Many cities are moving in this direction. A 1970 survey by the Center for Governmental Studies and the International City Management Association identified seventy-two cities which report "little city halls" or multipurpose neighborhood centers operating under municipal auspices.[26] This means that mayors and city managers accept the neighborhood idea, at least as an organizational unit. Giving residents control over neighborhood services is another matter, but at least public officials accept the idea of "neighborhood."

But many leaders of city neighborhoods, particularly blacks, are now pressing to carry decentralization to its next step, neighborhood services control. This stage began in a number of cities in 1966, mostly under the Community Action Program, through the creation of community corporations, private nonprofit corporations which administer public funds.[27] It has spread under the Model Cities Program, which despite a commitment in Washington to act as a mayors' program, is also financing new community corporations. In a few places, residents have a much larger voice—

virtually a veto—in urban renewal projects. Community control has even entered the arena of public schools, not only in the well-publicized dispute in New York City, but also in demands heard in many places around the country.

Neighborhood operations and neighborhood control may not be panaceas to the enormous problems confronting cities, but, according to numerous responsible city officials and hundreds of thousands of citizens, they are part of the solution. For this reason, neighborhood has once again become an important topic for research and discussion as well as a focus for action.

NOTES

1   For further discussion of the cyclical tendency see Herbert Kaufman, "Administrative Decentralization and Political Power," *Public Administration Review,* 29 (Jan.–Feb. 1969), pp. 3–15.

2   J. T. Salter, *Boss Rule: Portraits in City Politics* (New York: Whittlesey House, 1935), p. 270.

·3   Arthur W. Bromage, *Introduction to Municipal Government and Administration* (New York: Appleton Century–Crofts, 1950), p. 245.

4   *Ibid.,* pp. 24.

5   Sidney Dillick, *Community Organization for Neighborhood Development—Past and Present* (New York: William Morrow & Co., Inc. 1953), pp. 34–35.

6   *Ibid.,* p. 65.

7   *Ibid.,* pp. 65–66.

8   *Ibid.,* pp. 67–94.

9   Clarence Arthur Perry, "The Neighborhood Unit: A Scheme of Arrangement for the Family-Life Community," *Neighborhood and Community Planning. Regional Survey of New York and Its Environs* 8:1 (1929), p. 17.

10   James Dahir, *The Neighborhood Unit Plan: Its Spread and Acceptance* (New York: Russell Sage Foundation, 1947), p. 91.

11   Richard Hofstader, *The Age of Reform* (New York: Alfred A. Knopf, 1955).

12   Bromage, *op. cit.,* pp. 339–393.

13   *Municipal Police Administration,* 5th ed. rev. (Chicago: International City Managers' Association, 1961), p. 53.

14   Dillick, *op. cit.,* pp. 71–76, 89–94.

15   Solomon Kobrin, "The Chicago Area Project—A 25-year Assessment," *Annals of the American Academy of Political and Social Science Inc.,* 322 (1959), pp. 19–29.

16   Saul Alinsky, *Reveille for Radicals* (New York: Random House, 1969).

17   *Economic Opportunity Act of 1964* (Washington, D.C.: U.S. Government Printing Office, Section 202 (a) (3).

18   Richard Cloward and Lloyd Ohlin, *Delinquency and Opportunity* (New York: Free Press, 1960).

19   *A Proposal for the Prevention and Control of Delinquency by Expanding Opportunities* (New York: Mobilization for Youth, 1961).

20   Peter Marris and Martin Rein, *Dilemmas of Social Reform: Poverty and Community Action in the United States* (New York: Atherton Press, 1967). For a comparison of the Ford Foundation's "gray area projects," a sample of the urban renewal approach, and a program

in Pittsburgh, see James B. Cunningham, *The Resurgent Neighborhood* (Notre Dame: Fides Publishers, Inc., 1965).

   21   *Demonstration Cities and Metropolitan Development Act of 1966.* Sec. 103 (a) (2), P.L. 89–754. U.S. Document Printing Office.

   22   Advisory Commission on Intergovernmental Relations, *Fiscal Balance in the American Federal System.* (Metropolitan Fiscal Disparities, 1967), Vol. 2, pp. 16.

   23   *Report of the National Advisory Commission on Civil Disorders* (Washington D.C.: U.S. Government Printing Office, 1968), p. 8.

   24   *Ibid.,* p. 153.

   25   *Building the American City* (National Commission on Urban Problems, 1968), pp. 349–350.

   26   George J. Washins, *Municipal Decentralization and Neighborhood Resources* (New York: Praeger Publishers, 1972), pp. 387–390. Also see Advisory Commission on Intergovernmental Relations, *The New Grass Roots Government?* (Washington, D.C.: U.S. Government Printing Office, 1972).

   27   Hallman, Howard W., *Neighborhood Control of Public Programs: Case Studies of Community Corporations and Neighborhood Boards* (New York: Praeger Publishers, Inc., 1970).

Decentralization: A Structural Imperative

Henry J. Schmandt

It is an interesting commentary that, despite our long standing commitment to local autonomy, the vast bulk of literature on city and school government for the past half a century or more has dealt almost exclusively with the process of centralization. Aside from a few planners, such as Clarence Perry, social engineers have given slight attention to the question of reducing large local units to neighborhood size. Now, however, the tide has started to flow in the other direction with neighborhood control, and decentralization, its structural equivalent, being swept into public prominence. Although it is easy to exaggerate the extent to which the movement for transferring power to the neighborhood has escalated, it has reached the point where it can no longer be ignored.[1] The motivating force is presently coming from black, and to a lesser extent Puerto Rican and Mexican-American, leaders. But the concept is also beginning to attract notice in white sections of cities, such as Cleveland, where the central organs of government are coming under black control.[2]

Decentralization in its contemporary usage is a term of variable content, at times almost a shibboleth for reconstructing the social and political order. Because everyone presumably knows what it is, little attention has been given to defining it operationally and even less to clarifying its goals. We read, for example, that it refers to the placing of authority in the hands of those who are affected by public programs and institutions and that it encompasses such terms as community control, neighborhood development, and citizen participation. But the kinds of authority to be exercised, through what means, and in what role the people are to be participants are seldom spelled out.

We read also that the neighborhood corporation, the most publicized form of decentralization, will liberate local settlements from outside power, develop the self-governing potentialities of the residents, and promote local self-sufficiency. All of these claims may well be valid, but on the basis of present evidence their acceptance requires a considerable leap of faith.

The objective here is not to argue the case for decentralization or neighborhood control—we assume its desirability in principle—but to approach it as a problem of organization and administration or, more precisely, as a structural variable of the local service delivery system. For this purpose we examine (1) the various forms (models) decentralization may take; (2) the likely impact of each on the behavior of administrators and constituents; and (3) the relationship of each to the stated goals of neighborhood control. These organizational aspects have been badly neglected in the current literature on decentralization, despite their importance to the issue.

The Concept of Decentralization

Decentralization is a highly respectable term with good historical credentials. Lying at the basis of federalism, states rights, local home rule, and grass roots democracy, it has long been part and parcel of the nation's political culture. In its more traditional usage it refers to the territorial distribution of functional authority among the national, state, and local governments and to the vertical allocation of power within each of these levels. In the contemporary era of the participation explosion, it has taken on new dimensions, and its meaning now includes the devolution of public power to local groups and organizations outside the normally constituted governmental structure.[3]

Decentralization is an apparently simple concept, yet considerable difficulty is experienced in moving discussions about it from generalities to specifics. Part of the problem, as James Fesler points out, is that this simplicity is deceptive, leading to treatments which either generalize too broadly or start from doctrinaire positions that predetermine answers to concrete situations.[4] These characteristics can be observed in the present tendency to romanticize the notion of decentralization and to transform it into an article of faith. Once this occurs understanding ceases and obfuscation triumphs.

A second source of difficulty is the wide assortment of forms that local decentralization can take, extending from district referral centers to neighborhood government. Mini-city halls, for example, may be established to bring the communications and information process closer to the citizenry; broad administrative discretion may be delegated to field officers; resident advisory councils may be created as an integral part of program planning; performance of various municipal services may be contracted out to community organizations; or jurisdictions over certain functions, such as public education, may be legally vested in neighborhood boards.

Decentralization is explicitly recognized here as a mechanism—an institutionalized governmental arrangement—for the achievement of certain end values. It involves the allocation of authority and responsibility to lower territorially based echelons of the established bureaucracy or to geopolitical levels lower than the large municipality or school district. Although the latter is what is now commonly referred to as neighborhood control, the less radical types are also included under this designation for purposes of analysis. The total array of forms is subsumed under five simplified models based on the degree of decentralization: exchange, bureaucratic, modified bureaucratic, developmental, and governmental.[5]

The Exchange Model

This model encompasses the decentralization devices for informing, advising, and interacting; in short, for communicating. Ideally, the process represents a two-way flow. Information about city plans, programs, and opportunities is made available to neighborhood residents through field offices, and feedback is passed upward to the relevant points in the bureaucratic structure. The same is true in respect to advice: both parties exchange views and ideas and make their feelings known. Decentralizing the information and advisory process to the locality has several consequences. It increases the likelihood that residents will acquire knowledge of their rights (this in itself is a form of power) and it provides them, through service on advisory committees, with the opportunity of communicating their views on programs and policies to relevant administrators.

Neighborhood outposts of local government, such as the mini-city halls proposed by Mayor Lindsay or the information and referral centers established under the poverty program, are examples of exchange mechanisms.[6] (The use of locality-based ombudsmen is another.) Although these devices may be helpful in acquainting people with sources of assistance and in giving them better access to the service delivery structure, the residents are still compelled to deal with the old-line agencies that many of them have come to distrust. Moreover, the personnel in the farreaches of city government are not likely to be aggressive in stimulating the deprived to take full advantage of the benefits to which they are legally entitled and of which they are unaware. Recruited through the regular civil service machinery which normally attracts individuals oriented toward traditional management philosophy and behavior, such employees tend to identify strongly with the organization and little with the client. Neighborhood centers funded under OEO do not suffer from these disabilities and hence can play an advocate role; but, as outsiders, their access to the established repositories of power is limited.

The mechanism most frequently proposed for solving the problem of citizen involvement in program planning and development is the advisory committee of representative residents. A wide gulf exists, however, between the administrators' conception and the constituents' conception of the role of such a body. The former, stimulated by the persistent threat of clientele insurgency, tend to look upon the role of an advisory committee as a device for winning consent and legitimacy from the target groups.[7] The latter, increasingly unhappy with what they regard as bureaucratic high-handedness, look upon it as a means of gaining access to the decisional process. They want to share not only the responsibility for power, as Selznick puts it, but also the power itself. The incompatibility of these two positions has, in the contemporary setting of urban unease, largely negated the potentialities of the advisory mechanism and led to considerable frustration on the part of both administrators and constituency groups.

The advisory committee technique is essentially a bureaucratic invention for facilitating program execution. It has worked reasonably well with groups and classes that identify with the goals of the established agencies. The advisory committee technique seldom produces salutary results when middle class administrators attempt to utilize it in connection with lower class constituents who suspect manipulation. In fact, it may even be counterproductive in instances where the attitudinal distance between the parties is particularly great, as, for example, in the case of a resident advisory council and the police in a ghetto precinct. Here contact between the two, instead of leading to greater understanding, is likely to reinforce the negative attitudes each has toward the other.

The Bureaucratic Model

The bureaucratic model involves the delegation of authority to subordinate civil servants in the neighborhood. This delegation may take two forms: functional and territorial. In the first instance, power is vested in locality-based officials along functional lines. For example, in a district police captain, health officer, or school principal, each of whom is directly responsible to his departmental superior at the city level. In the second instance, authority over a mix of functions is placed in a district or neighborhood manager, with personnel administering the individual services or programs reporting to him. He in turn is responsible to the citywide chief executive.[8] Many large industrial corporations utilize this latter form, establishing operating division under a general (nonfunctional) manager to whom subordinate functional units report. Such an arrangement balances the economies and quality of large-scale organization with divisional operations and permits programs and services to be adapted to local clientele or consumers.

Territorial decentralization in business and industry normally leads to better relations between the organization and its customers. The same results might be anticipated by localizing the administration of certain public functions on a neighborhood basis. Reorganization of this nature would make the structure more accessible to the residents and presumably more sensitive to their feelings, desires, and special needs. Several barriers, however, stand in the way to the realization of these objectives. One is the depersonalization demanded by public bureaucratic systems. As the Weberian model prescribes, officials approach their constituency in "a spirit of formalistic impersonality" in order to assure equitable treatment for all. Such an approach runs counter to the values and interests of lower class people whose tendency to personalize their relationships prevents them from understanding, much less accepting, the impersonal norms and operations of the bureacracy. Moreover, despite the ascribed norm of impartiality, administrators tend to enforce policy differentially both in response to clientele pressure and in response to the constituent's social class position. In both cases, the deprived neighborhoods are at a disadvantage. Relative to other sections of the city, they have neither the power to compete on equal terms for benefits nor the social status to attract them.

A second difficulty arises from the fact that this type of decentralization gives the bureaucratic subsystems no direct organizational ties or feelings of allegiance to the neighborhood. They remain oriented to central administration. Changing the bureaucratic power structure to give a neighborhood administrator control over the functional units would be a step in the right direction, but the effectiveness of such action would be severely circumscribed unless it was also accompanied by a modification of the reward structure. Under the present system, rewards (in the form of promotions and the like) are allocated to employees on the basis of their performance, judged by departmental norms and expectations rather than evaluated by the clientele or constituency they are serving. (Fear of the latter is one of the major factors behind teacher hostility to school decentralization.) When bureaucratic and resident norms correspond, as they generally do in middle and upper income neighborhoods, employee behavior is likely to be compatible with resident expectations. When these norms differ substantially, as in the disadvantaged areas, serious misunderstanding develops. The problem is to change the conceptions of public employees in these neighborhoods about their proper role behavior. Progress along these lines will be negligible until the assessment by residents becomes an important consideration in the evaluation process and is understood by the personnel involved.

A third source of difficulty involves the relationship between the top administrative personnel assigned to the locality and its residents. Both forms of the bureaucratic model, the district manager type in particular, theoretically offer the opportunity for greater interplay between administrator and constituents, opening the door for the consideration and negotiation of demands and needs on a more direct, more personal basis. These results can reasonably be anticipated when the local administrator is dealing with a friendly middle class constituency to which he can easily relate. Favorable results are less likely in disadvantaged areas where the administrator is brought face to face with a suspicious, if not hostile, clientele whose cultural values conflict with his own and whose tactical styles are often alien to his notion of proper behavior. There is strong likelihood that the pressure exerted by the residents, instead of leading to fruitful negotiation, would create considerable anxiety in the administrator, causing him to become overly protective of his position. As organizational research shows, an employee who directly faces challenges from clients tends to become more concerned with the defensibility of his own behavior than with solving the problem. A common technique in such instances is to fall back upon formal rules to prove that he has only been doing his duty. This reliance on regulations and their enforcement invariably results in a rigidity of behavior that serves only to aggravate the problem of developing satisfactory relationships with the constitutents.[9]

Modified Bureaucratic Model

In the previous model, the administrator with local powers is responsible to the same officials who delegated his authority, rather than to the constituents he serves. In the modified bureaucratic model his responsibility flows in two directions: to his superiors in the system and, to a lesser extent, to a neighborhood council representative of the residents. The latter might be empowered, for example, to pass on major personnel appointments, plan and approve renewal projects, and decide on the level of certain services, such as the frequency of refuse collection. A structural arrangement of this kind guarantees professional management, ensuring the continued flow of city resources into the area. At the same time, it gives the residents some control over the governance of their territorial haven.

The modified bureaucratic model, although it suffers from many of the disabilities of its bureaucratic counterpart, is a more advanced form of decentralization because it brings the neighborhood directly into the decisional process. Its potential depends on whether satisfactory relationships can be established between the locality-based administrator and the indigenous council. The probability of this occurring would be high in middle and upper class neighborhoods where the life styles and norms of the residents are similar to those of the administrator. It would be correspondingly low in lower class sections of the city where the social distance between the residents and administrator is great, their value orientations being substantially different. If, however, through a careful selection process, key personnel with a sympathetic understanding of the life styles and aspirations of the poor were assigned to these neighborhoods, the possibility of success would be measurably enhanced. For this to happen, municipal authorities must first become convinced of the necessity to share power with the localities in order to maintain an effective service delivery system. This stage of awareness has obviously not yet been reached, but the social dynamics of the present era are imperceptively pushing the bureaucracy in this direction.

Again, the drawbacks to the modified bureaucratic approach are numerous, although not necessarily insuperable. One of the more evident and typical problems is the difficult position of the neighborhood manager under such an arrangement. An administrator invariably operates within a set of varying expectations. His superiors, his subordinates, and the organization's clientele all perceive his role in different ways, each having different notions as to what his behavior should be. The greater the status or value orientation differences among the parties, the more differential are these expectations. Role conflicts arise in an administrator when his compliance with one set of expectations makes compliance with others more difficult or even impossible.[10] In the case of the bureaucratic official assigned to a neighborhood, the divergent expectations of the resident council and the service personnel could lead to severe role conflict. The police, to cite one example, would expect the administrator to support their concept of law enforcement and to back them against citizen complaints. The resident council, conversely, would expect him to take action against police practices that they considered degrading and insulting. Finally, his superiors at city hall would expect him to maintain an efficient and trouble free operation and keep both the employees and the neighborhood satisfied. Only a skilled individual, with the ability and temperament to cope with a high degree of role conflict, could withstand this pressure. Unfortunately, the present generation of municipal administrators, trained as they are in traditional bureaucratic practices, is generally not well equipped to play this role. The hope, such as it is, must lie in the new cadre of public service personnel who are being socialized in the politics of confrontation and conflict and in the new social ethics.

The Developmental Model

The experiences with resident participation in the poverty and model cities programs have resulted in considerable disillusionment among minority group leaders. Convinced that the poor cannot win over city hall and the established bureaucracy, many of them have turned to approaches that bypass the regular political and administrative institutions of the community and look at the neighborhood itself as a framework for control. One such approach is represented by the community development or neighborhood corporation chartered by the state, or federal government, and controlled by the residents.[11] Incorporating physical and civic development, the new structural mechanism encompasses both economic activities and service delivery functions. On the one hand, the neighborhood corporation is empowered to undertake rehabilitation projects, sponsor the construction of low income housing, and own and manage business enterprises, the profits of which are used to assist the financing of community social services. On the other hand, the neighborhood corporation is authorized to assume, under contract with the city and other agencies, the administration of such public functions as libraries, health centers, and day care nurseries. Prototypes of this model are the East Central Citizens Organization (ECCO) in Columbus, Ohio and the Bedford Stuyvesant Corporation in New York City.[12]

Unlike the preceding three models, the neighborhood corporation places both policy making and administration under resident control. This combination frees it from many of the contradictions and weaknesses inherent to the other structural forms. At the same time, however, the new mechanism has its own set of administrative disabilities that are, in one way or another, associated with the problem of decentralization. By taking on business and service functions, the residents in their collective capacity become the producers as well as the consumers of public and private goods. For those among them who direct and administer the affairs of the corporation, this role change also entails behavioral change. In their new capacity they take on the task of developing a viable organization and maintaining it as a going enterprise. The assumption of this responsibility necessarily places constraints on their freedom of action. For as board members and managers, they must relate not only inwardly to the constituents they serve but also outwardly to the established bureaucracies and funding agencies on whom they are dependent for cooperation and resources.

Despite its drawbacks, the developmental model offers distinct advantages to both the neighborhood and the municipal bureaucracy. It gives a locality based and indigenously created organization the legal tools to improve the physical conditions of the area along lines the residents desire and to fashion services in accord with their particular needs. Its success depends, of course, on the willingness of the city and other agencies to channel funds into the area and furnish it with technical assistance. The corporate device may actually enchance a neighborhood's possibilities of obtaining such resources and aid since it provides a more stable and effective structure for negotiation with the outside world than the existing plethora of special interest and ad hoc groups.

The development corporation model enables municipal authorities to turn over certain activities to the neighborhood without any substantial diminution of their own power. Through use of the contractual device for delegating a modicum of service functions, as well as through control over critical funding sources, they can shift responsibilities to locality leaders while still remaining in a strategic position to influence the latters' actions. Such an approach can, in other words, be a useful means of securing resident cooperation in achieving the goals of the larger community by giving neighborhood leadership some freedom in limited areas of concern. And if the arrangement fails, the city can conveniently withdraw its delegated powers and blame the local corporation for the results.

Governmental Model

The governmental model, the most radical of the five, embodies the devolution of legal powers on newly created political subunits of large central cities. In the case of municipal functions, this approach involves the formation of neighborhood entities with powers similar to those of suburban towns or villages. In the case of education, it pertains to the establishment of neighborhood boards with substantial authority over the public schools within their territorial jurisdiction. As some observers point out, the same logic that calls on suburbs to divest themselves of control over functions of area or regional concern argues for the transfer to central city neighborhoods of authority over matters of primary interest to their residents.[13]

The creation of sub-municipal entities or neighborhood school districts does not eliminate bureaucratization. It simply reduces the scale and permits the replacement of role incumbents with personnel better oriented to locality constituencies. The new government, no matter what internal structural changes may be made, still has essentially the same organizational maintenance, integration, adaptibility, and goal achievement requirements as its predecessor. It also has the same roles to fill, the same need for problem, policy, and program expertise, and the same necessity to foster stability and predictability in its operations. And beyond these functional requirements, it faces the same dilemma of establishing a working equilibrium between professional autonomy and community or political control.

At its inception, a neighborhood government can be expected to be more open in its recruitment policies, less formal and impersonal in its behavior toward constitutents, and more flexible in its procedures and regulations. However, if the evolutionary history of formal organizations is any indicator, a neighborhood government will become more concerned with its survival and enhancement needs and more bureaucratic in its operations as time passes. This phenomenon has already occurred among community action programs and agencies which have become increasingly institutionalized as they have evolved into social service bureaucracies. Similarly, whatever innovative potential the new structure may have, it is likely to be quickly submerged in the task of maintaining the enterprise. The inability of citizen self-help organizations of recent years to develop approaches to service needs and problems essentially different from the more traditional agencies attests to this likelihood.[14] Somewhere in the process of development, innovation and reform tend to become sacrificed for organizational survival, whether in the Peace Corps, a poverty agency, or a neighborhood corporation.

Locality control over the service delivery system would have several important advantages for the deprived areas. One is the opportunity it affords for the discovery and development of political leadership skills among the indigenous residents and, of equal significance, for the recruitment and training of a cadre of professional and technical personnel in the art of public management.[15] A second is the greater sympathy the "new establishment" would have for the feelings, life styles, and aspirations of its constituency. In the case of a locally controlled school district, for example, the indigenous board could tailor the curriculum to the particular needs and cultural norms of the people it serves. Finally, neighborhood government would provide an organizational structure or instrumentality, more legitimate in the eyes of the deprived than the existing bureaucracy, for taking advantage of and administering new social programs as they emerge from higher levels of public authority.

The Goals of Decentralization

Decentralization has been viewed here as a major goal (independent variable) in community functioning. The case for it must rest on the strength of its relationship to the results (dependent variable) that it is purported to further. These may be grouped for analytical purposes into three broad categories: therapy, service, and political. The first relates to the psychological effects of neighborhood control on individuals; the second concerns the responsiveness of the service delivery system; and the third involves the mobilization of political power. Although these goals are not necessarily incompatible with each other, they are conceptually distinct and governed by different standards of evaluation. It is important to know in assessing potentialities and results whether, for example, the primary objective of decentralization is the development of a political power base or the improvement of services. The first may well be a prerequisite to the second, but the argument can also be turned around.

Therapy

The analyses which support decentralization for therapeutic ends start from the assumption that residents in deprived neighborhoods are suffering from feelings of powerlessness and low personal and political efficacy. This pathology prevents them from obtaining and utilizing opportunities that are available through the institutions of society. Delegating governmental responsibilities to the neighborhood, so the argument runs, will stimulate participation in political affairs and self-help programs, and these activities, in turn, will give the residents feelings of confidence, individual worth, and power.

The therapy claim has little empirical support. Much of the research which is cited in its behalf deals with face-to-face groups, such as those that function in large corporate structures. The extended interaction and involvement induced by such settings have unquestionably proved beneficial to the participants. But to jump from a small group to a neighborhood of 25,000 or more people is an unwarranted conceptual leap. The kind of involvement that community government in any of its forms can realistically open to the bulk of residents, such as attending an occasional town style meeting or voting on issues and projects, is not likely to have much healing value.[16] This has been demonstrated by the experiences of the poverty and model cities programs. Virtually all available evaluations of these ventures stress the lack of interest on the part of the deprived in the participational opportunities offered them. They show that while a relatively minute portion of the target populations has increased its political awareness and skills, principally as employees and members of community action boards, the bulk of the hardcore and unaffiliated poor has not been reached.[17]

The belief that decentralization will significantly enlarge neighborhood participation rests, moreover, on tenuous theoretical grounds. With few exceptions, the literature on political involvement reports that an individual's social status, education, and organizational membership strongly affect the likelihood of his engaging in various types of community activity.[18] Political apathy, as numerous surveys show, tends to be greatest among the groups that are most poorly integrated into the reward structure of the society. Motivating them to take advantage of available political opportunities is an extremely difficult social undertaking.[19] The task is not independent of raising the educational level in these areas. To be participants in the political process, the residents must have the verbal skills necessary for communication and an awareness of the opportunities available.[20] Nor is the task independent of restructuring the political system to enable them to enter it and move up in its ranks. Neighborhood government can conceivably aid in a modest way in both of these respects. It can enlarge the opportunities for a small percentage of its residents to acquire sufficient skills and experience for active involvement, and it can facilitate their entrance into the local political system. These possibilities are by no means to be ignored but they are a far cry from the claim that decentralization is the answer to shaking the alienation and apathy of the deprived masses.

Service

Unlike the therapeutic goals of participational opportunity, the service oriented objectives to decentralization place the improvement of the delivery system first in the order of priorities. Underlying these goals is the belief that bureaucratic centralism has made the service structure dehumanizing, rigid, and insensitive. The evidence is clear that governmental programs administered by major urban departments have been distressingly immune to attempts by the poor to effect changes in either their content or procedures. Decentralization, as the preferred answer to this situation, would presumably give the residents of deprived neighborhoods better access to the delivery structure, make governmental programs more responsive to their needs and priorities, and enable them to be served by people who are attuned to their feelings and values.

Some social scientists, such as Herbert Kaufman, believe that these objectives can be attained by decentralization short of locality government.[21] It is their contention that the unrestricted warfare, which now exists between neighborhood spokesmen and agency bureaucracies, will resolve itself as administrative responsiveness to local desires is increased by delegating greater discretion to field offices. This, however, may be too sanguine an outlook. As noted earlier, bureaucratic structures are almost invariably oriented toward middle class life styles, socializing their role incumbents in such a manner that they are frequently incapable of understanding lower class clientele.

These attitudinal barriers were strikingly documented in a recent survey of public employees whose jobs involve direct contact with ghetto residents.[22] The study found that an overwhelming majority of the police held unfavorable images of the black population and strongly denied that they were treated more poorly than other groups (only 21 percent thought such inequality existed). The teachers were far more sympathetic but they too believed that considerable progress had been made in correcting whatever inequities existed. More telling, a large number of teachers subscribed to the cultural deprivation theory to explain the poor performance of disadvantaged students, and excluded any question of the quality of the schools or the competence of teachers. Social workers were by a wide margin the most sympathetic toward the deprived and the most critical of their own departments and the level of support supplied by the community. Even they, however, manifested elements of paternalism, viewing their mission as much to teach middle class ways as to help the clients help themselves.

The dominant tendency among bureaucracies in response to outside threats such as citizen protests is to seek to change the environment rather than to modify internal structures and procedures to accord with external changes. This tendency has been particularly evident during the last several years in the reaction of municipal and school administrators to constituency demands for more control. Decentralization, as perceived by the overwhelming majority of them, poses a threat to their power and professionalism. This fear, together with the attitudinal predispositions of the rank and file employees, militates against successful achievement of service goals through use of the bureaucratic or modified bureaucratic models. Should, however, the administrators become convinced of the inevitability of some form of control—and their increasing difficulties in program execution, due to resident hostility, will push them in this direction—they may be willing to reshape the service delivery system to make it more conducive to the neighborhood interests and aspirations.[23]

Adoption of the more radical forms of decentralization would theoretically eliminate many anomalies and difficulties associated with the lesser types of change by divorcing the neighborhood from the direct control of established bureaucracies. The unanswered question in such a case is whether the new forms would have access to the resources necessary for raising the service level and meeting the needs of the disadvantaged constituents. In considering approaches, therefore, it is important to weigh the potential ability of development corporations and neighborhood governments to respond to locality aspirations against the advantages of leaving primary responsibility for the service functions in the existing bureaucracies.

Political

In contrast to the service goals, which relate primarily to the output of the delivery system, those that are politically oriented involve mainly the input side of the structure. Their emphasis is on control rather than services. As such, they revolve around the mobilization of political power to enable residents of deprived areas to make effective demands on the service delivery and reward allocation system. Self-government, power redistribution, and neighborhood control over social programs are among the politically oriented goals most commonly attributed to decentralization.

A major problem for deprived groups is to build a viable power base which, over time, will significantly increase their influence in the community. Repeated experience has shown that crisis-oriented organizations seldom have a lasting impact because established centers of power control sufficient resources to fend off any attack, which ultimately plays itself out in a matter of months. In the past, the political parties provided a natural structure for building such a base but now have become objects of distrust among many of the disadvantaged. Neighborhood government, as conceived by some of its proponents, can serve this purpose. They see it as a mechanism to gain the adherence and loyalty of a fairly large number of people, to urge them to think of themselves as a political force.[24] When the goal of decentralization is viewed in this way, improvement of the service delivery system becomes secondary to, and a technique for, developing a power base capable of effectively pressuring the larger society for major institutional change.

Whether this objective can be achieved through the decentralization of service-related responsibilities to the localities is extremely doubtful.[25] The key question is whether a neighborhood government or corporation can administer service programs and at the same time foster broader political concerns, such as basic reforms in the national welfare system. By assuming responsibility for meeting functional needs of the residents, locality leadership necessarily circumscribes its freedom of action. As long as control rests with the traditional governmental agencies, neighborhood leaders are under fewer constraints to employ social protests strategies to wrest concessions from the establishment. However, once legal power devolves on them, they become, in effect, the new neighborhood establishment. They can no longer, in Alinsky's words, "rub raw the sores of discontent" in order to mobilize the residents. Instead they must negotiate and bargain with city hall and other outside agencies to gain sufficient resources for carrying out their assumed responsibilities.

Neighborhood government, in short, is based on the community development model, not the social action protests model. It tends to stress self-help neither encourages emotional deomonstrations nor engenders open hostility from or toward the larger community. Instead, it seeks to cooperate with the established bureaucracies and to draw on their resources to aid in the development of the locality. It is, of course, conceivable that neighborhood government could provide an organizational base with sufficient muscle to gain access to the regular political process channels of the city. Such a case would be analogous to that of an interest or pressure group in the traditional sense. This role is more compatible with the prevailing norms of the larger society than the social protest model and could therefore be productive. The risk incurred in following this path is the likelihood that organizing around social services could become an end in itself, displacing more fundamental political goals in the process. For if, as Arnold Gurin and Joan L. Ecklein persuasively argue, basic reform can come only through change-oriented social movements and not through governmental service programs, this consideration becomes an important factor in evaluating the more radical forms of decentralization.[26]

Conclusion

There are no fixed factors in the decentralization equation, as this analysis has attempted to show. The uncertainties which surround the issue give rise to doubts in even the most sympathetic observer. Differences of opinion among minority group leaders over the wisdom of the nieghborhood approach,[27] together with a lack of goal consensus among its supporters, continue to becloud the subject. Yet whatever its ambiguities and uncertainties, decentralization in some form appears inevitable. Recognition is growing among administrators and concerned citizens that the service delivery system in large urban areas cannot, as presently constituted, cope with the extremely pluralistic needs of a highly differentiated population.[28] In addition, a social dynamic to engage the public more directly in the decisional process exists, particularly in the deprived nieghborhoods. Set in motion largely by the anti-poverty program, decentralization has gained in appeal as the national mood has become increasingly one of intransigence, reaction, and even punitiveness toward efforts at large-scale social change.

Even if one accepts the need for decentralization, the question remains whether the existing bureaucratic structure should be made more responsive and accountable to locality needs through administrative deconcentration or whether this framework should be bypassed in favor of creating autonomous neighborhood institutions. A definitive answer to this question is not possible at this time, given the many contingencies involved and the small stockpile of relevant experience to draw upon. Much depends on the individual characteristics of each city and on the priority given to particular goals. A plan that may be desirable in Cleveland or Atlanta, for example, may be less appropriate in Los Angeles or Phoenix. Or, an approach that may be effective where the primary objective is improvement of the service delivery system may have little impact where the goal is political mobilization. Custom tailoring, not mass production, is called for. (See Table I.)

The analysis presented here suggests that if service responsiveness to ethnic and class sensitivities is the major goal, the more radical forms of decentralization appear to offer the best means for maximizing its ac-

TABLE I
THE IMPACT OF DECENTRALIZATION MODELS AND GOAL ACHIEVEMENT

Models	Goals				
	Efficiency	Responsiveness	Participation	Resident Control	Political Mobilization
Exchange	High	Low	None	None	None
Bureaucratic	High	Low	None	Low	None
Modified Bureaucratic	High	Medium	Low	Medium	None
Developmental	High	High	Medium	High	Low
Governmental	High	High	Medium	High	Low

complishment. The price to be paid in such cases is the risk of increased isolation from the resources and technology of the larger community.[29] If, on the other hand, improved and more extensive services are the goal, the modified bureaucratic model offers the distinct advantage leaving the primary responsibility for services to the established agencies while making them more open to locality influence. Adminstrative hazards and limitations on resident control constitute drawbacks under this arrangement, but the neighborhood would not incur the risks associated with governmental or corporate autonomy.

Finally, if either social therapy or political mobilization is the principal end, none of the models is particularly impressive. The forces that maintain deprivation and alienation, such as low income, unemployment, and discrimination are largely beyond the pale of neighborhood action. And while the establishment of locality government would bring into being a legally recognized political instrument for bargaining with municipal and other public agencies, the assumption of service responsibilities would tend to preeempt the time and energy of the indigenous leadership to the exclusion of broader political and social goals.[30]

The time has now been reached in the decentralization debate to move from the level of abstraction to the development of concrete plans for exploring the precise responsibilities that can be delegated to the neighborhood level and the machinery that can be used for administering them.[31] There is a need also to formulate a set of coherent strategies for translating these plans into action. Melville's Billy Budd died young because he could express his ideals only by an act of passion; to survive he needed a strategy with staying powers. In a sense, the movement for neighborhood government is in a similar position. To realize its appealing potentials it must sharpen its focus, zero in on a limited number of functions appropriate for locality administration and control, and begin to take on a clear-cut political form. The stakes are not only high; they are also crucial to the future of our large urban communities.

NOTES

1   Recent reports of the National Commission on Urban Problems, the Advisory Commission on Intergovernmental Relations, and the Committee on Economic Development contain recommendations for some form of decentralization to neighborhoods. The viability of the movement is also illustrated by the action of the Michigan legislature in mandating the division of the Detroit school system into seven to eleven districts with individual boards for each. The overall city board remains in existence with certain review powers over the district bodies (Senate Bill No. 635, 75th Legislature, 1969 Session).

2   See S. M. Miller and Martin Rein, "Participation, Poverty, and Administration," *Public Administration Review,* 29 (Jan.–Feb., 1969), pp. 15–25. The authors point out the issues that participation or neighborhood control raise today are primarily in terms of neglected and discriminated groups in the society.

3   This is referred to as "radical decentralization" by some writers. See, for example, Michael Lipsky, "Radical Decentralization: A Response to American Planning Dilemmas," a paper presented at Second International Symposium on Regional Development, Tokyo, Japan, September 17–19, 1968.

4   James Fesler, "Approaches to the Understanding of Decentralization," *Journal of Politics,* 27 (August, 1965), pp. 557–561.

5   A continuum of decentralization techniques is contained in "Decentralization to Neighborhoods: A Conceptual Analysis," An internal staff paper prepared for use of National Advisory Council on Economic Opportunity (Fall, 1968). A closely related categorization of participational forms is set out in Sherry Arnstein, "A Ladder of Citizen Participation," *American Institute of Planners Journal,* 35 (July, 1969), pp. 216–224.

6   The exchange model is essentially what the National Commission on Urban Problems recommended. As the Commission stated: "By decentralization we mean that the muncipal government would provide certain aspects (chiefly information, informal counseling, and referral) of certain municipal services through local offices set up in neighborhoods." *Building the American City* (Washington D.C.: U.S. Government Printing Office, 1969), p. 350.

7   See Elliott A. Krause, "Functions of a Bureaucratic Ideology: Citizen Participation," *Social Problems,* 16 (Fall, 1968), pp. 129–142. Also, Edmund M. Burke, "Citizen Participation Strategies," *American Institute of Planners Journal,* 34 (September, 1968), pp. 287–294.

8   See Guy Black, "The Decentralization of Urban Government: A Systems Approach," Staff Discussion Paper No. 102, Program of Policy Studies in Science and Technology, (Washington D.C.: George Washington University, August, 1968) for a discussion of the various forms of administrative decentralization.

9   Daniel Katz and Robert L. Kahn, *The Social Psychology of Organizations* (New York: Wiley and Sons, 1966), pp. 71–109. Also, Peter M. Blau, *The Dynamics of Bureaucracy,* rev. ed. (Chicago: University of Chicago Press, 1963), pp. 100–117.

10   Katz and Kahn, *op. cit.,* pp. 171–198.

11   Senator Gaylord Nelson of Wisconsin and others introduced in the 1968 Congressional session a bill entitled "Community Self-Determination Act," which provides for the issuance of federal charters to community corporations run by residents. The bill failed and the stance of the Nixon Administration through revenue sharring and other devices is to strip the neighborhoods of funding and other powers independent of city councils and mayors.

12   See Milton Kotler, *Neighborhood Government: The Local Foundation of Political Life* (Indianapolis: Bobbs-Merrill, 1969); Kenneth H. Miller, "Community Organization in the Ghetto," in *Social Innovation in the City,* Richard S. Rosenbloom and Robin Marris (eds.). (Cambridge, Mass.: Harvard University Program on Technology and Society, 1969), pp. 97–108.

13   See Richard F. Babcock and Fred P. Bosselman, "Citizen Participation: A Suburban Suggestion for the Central City," *Law and Contemporary Problems,* 32 (Spring, 1967), pp. 220–231.

14   See John B. Turner (ed.), *Neighborhood Organization for Community Action* (New York: National Association of Social Workers, 1968).

15   Manpower figures show the severe shortage of minority group professionals and technicians. In Wisconsin, for example, there was one black to every one hundred sixty-two whites in the professional category in 1968, and the shortage is increasing. In the city of Milwaukee where blacks and other minorities constitute approximately fifteen percent of the population, they hold only two percent of the jobs in the managerial, professional, and technical category. Only two and three-tenths percent of employed blacks and two and one-fifth percent of other minorities are in this category compared to twenty-one and three-tenths percent of employed whites. (*Equal Employment Opportunity Report,* 1968.) Department of Industry, Labor and Human Relations, State of Wisconsin.

16   One can legitimately argue that residents would be more likely to have confidence and trust in the government because of the predominance among the policy makers and administrators of those whose ethnic and class background is similar to theirs. This coincidence may have some therapeutic effect but it is not that to which decentralization proponents are referring.

17   See Ralph M. Kramer, *Participation of the Poor* (Englewood Cliffs, N.J.: Prentice Hall, 1969).

18   See N. H. Nie *et al.,* "Social Strcuture and Political Participation: Developmental Relationships," *American Political Science Review,* 63 (June, 1969), pp. 361–378 and (September, 1969), pp. 808–832.

19   See Frances Piven, "Participation of Residents in Neighborhood Community Action Programs," *Social Work,* 11 (January, 1966), pp. 73–79.

20   To say that socioeconomic status is an important variable in explaining the absence of participation by the poor does not mean they cannot be activiated without remaking their subculture. A persuasive case can be made that the most important stimulant to participation would be an enhancement of the economic well-being of the deprived, a task obviously beyond the purview of the neighborhood.

21   Herbert Kaufman, "Administrative Decentralization and Political Power," *Public Administration Review,* 29 (January/February, 1969), pp. 3–15.

22   Peter H. Rossit *et al.,* "Between White and Black: The Faces of American Institutions in the Ghetto," *Supplemental Studies for the National Advisory Commission on Civil Disorders* (Washington D.C.: U.S. Government Printing Office, 1968), pp. 71–208.

23   See Miller and Rein, *op. cit.,* for some of the problems involved. It would require the establishment of district services centers, the delegation of meaningful power to a resident council, and modification of civil service procedures to permit the direct recruitment of personnel from the neighborhood and the extended use of subprofessionals.

24   See Lee Rainwater ("Neighborhood Action and Lower Class Life Styles," *Neighborhood Organization for Community Action,* John B. Turner (ed.) *op. cit.,* pp. 25–39. Rainwater argues that lower class people, like most Americans, tend to think of the most direct route to a decent life as one that is pursued along highly individual lines. As a result, they often take the view that the best chance of getting what they want will come from disassociating themselves from those around them. If Rainwater is correct, and the evidence points in that direction, the difficulties of political mobilization in the neighborhood are compounded.

25   See John Kramer and Inge Walter, "Politics in an All-Negro City," *Urban Affairs Quarterly,* 1 (September, 1968), pp. 65–88. The experiences of instrumental organizations show that those whose potential constitutency is made up of individuals with limited resources are at a serious disadvantage. The costs are simply too great for the prospective participants in terms of time, money, and effort, as measured against the perceived returns. This was evident in Kinloch, Missouri, one of the few independent black suburbs in the nation where it was found that the low level of personal income of the residents compounded the difficulty of creating lasting political organizations. Similar results were also observed in the inner city of Milwaukee where low income was found to operate as an important constraint to participation in deprived neighborhoods. See Warner Bloomberg, Jr. and Florence W. Rosenstock, "Who Can Activate the Poor?" *Power, Poverty, and Urban Policy* Warner

Bloomberg, Jr. and Henry J. Schmandt (Beverly Hills: Sage Publications, Inc., 1968), pp. 313–354.

26 Arnold Gurin and Joan L. Ecklein, "Community Organization for What?: Political Power or Social Delivery," *Social Welfare Forum,* 1968. They maintain that mass movements in their goals and methodologies, as well as in their emotional climate, are more compatible with lower-class life styles than is participation in program planning and execution. See Peter Bachrach and Morton S. Baratz, *Power and Poverty* (New York: Oxford University Press, 1970). The difficulties of building a political power base in deprived neighborhoods is documented.

27 See Bayard Rustin, "The Failure of Black Separatism," *Harper's Magazine* (January, 1970), pp. 25–34, for a viewpoint opposing the neighborhood approach.

28 See Manfred Kochen and Karl W. Duetsch, "Toward a Rational Theory of Decentralization: Some Implications of a Mathetical Approach," *American Political Science Review,* 63 (September, 1969), 734–794. Aside from the commonly cited social gains, there are indications that cost-effectiveness considerations in the performance of social tasks call for a greater degree of decentralization in public and private services than what presently exists.

29 Decentralization must be viewed within the larger context of total community needs and problem-solving capabilities. Any extensive movement toward neighborhood government should also be accompanied by a centralization at the metropolitan or regional level of critical systems-maintenance functions such as transportation, environmental pollution control, and general land use regulation. It must also be accompanied by a major revision of revenue distribution policies so that the poorer neighborhoods are not left to their own fiscal capabilities.

30 See Martin Rein, "Social Planning: The Search for Legitimacy," *American Institute of Planners Journal,* 35 (July, 1969), pp. 233–244. He argued that organizing the deprived on a neighborhood basis cannot achieve very much fundamental change since its vision is limited to issues around which local initiative can be mobilized.

2

The Pros and Cons of
Neighborhood Control

A Better System of Prisons? Thoughts on Decentralization and Participation in America

Lewis Lipsitz

Social Science and Ideology

Looking back on it, who could have guessed ten years ago that we would now need to be talking seriously about issues of participation and decentralization? Or, at any rate, talk with the passion that men are talking with now. Reading much of the social scientific work with which the 1960s began, and which still dominates much of the field, one would have thought that popular government and certainly local government would soon be confined, as Engels said about the state in communist society, to the museum of antiquities along with the spinning wheel and the bronze axe.[1] I exaggerate, but how much? When we heard about the end of ideology, about the reduction of all the "great" issues to questions of technique, about the neutrality of social scientific knowledge and of bureaucratic expertise, about the successes of American polyarchy, about the virtues of an enduring apathy, we were hearing about the growth of a social order so satisfying that serious conflicts were no longer possible.

Stability was the rage in the 1960s, both explicitly and as an underlying orientation for research and interpretation. Questions of mass participation were related not so much to the quality of political life, or the responsiveness of governments, but to fears about political instability.[2] These anxieties, which grew out of the experience of the 1930s and of the McCarthy period, also blinded most social scientists to the deep inadequacies of our policy. We got in the bad habit of calling the United States a democracy when what was really meant was a competitive electoral system.[3] No doubt, America is a partly democratic society, but it is also partly undemocratic. Here is a rich arena for quantification and subtle analysis.[4] But we saw little such work. Instead, we saw democracy discussed as if it were an all-or-nothing quality; this often obscured the real issues. We forgot that democracy has many meanings, involving participation, economic and social well being, personal dignity hopefulness, as well as competing political parties and political rights. I do not mean, in the smallest way, to denigrate political competition or the right to dissent. What I mean to make clear is that the achievement and maintenance of these practices is not in itself enough; democratic values should require more of us. In addition, there are values beyond democracy itself, such as liveliness, compassion, culture, meaningfulness that ought also to be of concern to students of politics. Many of us forgot these things until recently. Preoccupied with the unforgettable horrors of the past, focused on the contrasts between ourselves and what we called totalitarian and developed societies, we failed to see the deprivation, restlessness, and oppression in our own society. Casting around for a model of the good state, we strangely could imagine none other than our own.[5]

During the 1960s the prevailing assumptions and style of our disciplines came under the scrutiny of men with an acute awareness of the conservative implications of these tendencies.[6] Intellectually, at any rate, the critics have won the field—incorporation of these intellectual victories into graduate education and professional life are another matter altogether.

The conservative assumptions about democracy are themselves open to many different interpretations. Noam Chomsky, for example, has seen them as the ideological weapons of a new mandarin class, a group of hired technicians who rationalized their own exalted roles as well as the existing social order.[7] Chomsky contrasts this role, that of the ideologist of power, with the role of the critical intellectual, the man who brings his analytical tools to bear on contemporary social life and who is willing to criticize his own society, openly and seriously.

The culmination of these conservative tendencies is perhaps the "end of ideology" argument because they doggedly refuse to imagine new conflicts and new forms of social life. There was and is much truth in the end of ideology position, but it is clearly not the whole truth. It limits our capacity for envisioning meaningful change. Moreover, "end" ideologists have not tried to develop exacting standards for judging our society and have tended to accept the prevailing pluralism as more or less satisfactory.

From this school, therefore, we cannot expect to get much help toward the clarification of the conflicts that the conservative theory itself fails to acknowledge or anticipate.[8] Perhaps more important than the existence of any group of mandarins, however, were the images of social life that lived in the minds of most professional social scientists and civil servants involved in social services. Looking back at Neustadt's *Presidential Power,* or Burns' *The Deadlock of Democracy,* we can see a strong liberal optimism about the utilization of federal power for equalitarian reformist purposes. Young people looked toward the federal bureaucracy as a leading source of social change and believed that enlightened management from the top could help to eliminate or reduce social inequities.

Now people are not so sure. For some, the national government pursues counter-insurgency at home as well as elsewhere. For others, bureaucracies, federal and other, are themselves a source of much oppression. For yet others, only grass roots organizing and widespread discontent can lead to more decent social order in the face of powerful conservative forces. It is not so simple any longer, and for good reasons, to locate institutions that are always to be trusted.

In addition to changed attitudes, there are other new realities. Particularly important is the growing self-consciousness of black communities and of young people. As more issues become more widely politicized, more groups attempt to influence outcomes, and pluralism multiplies with a vengenace. In my view, these new realities are potentially very hopeful, and also bring with them deep personal and political strains. And these strains are relevant to the issues of decentralization and participation.

Turning to the issues of decentralization, we find a number of obvious contradictions: popular participation versus expertise,[9] decentralized versus depersonalized bureaucracy,[10] and bureaucratic neutrality versus the creation of conflict.[11] There are others: the use of nonprofessionals in bureaucratic units[12] and the need for greater due process and tolerance for diversity within hierarchical organizations.[13] Beyond these, there is the question of the regulation of behavior itself and how much such regulation is necessary or desirable.

These issues in themselves need not be posed as dichotomies except that in practice they often are. The alternatives are seen as mutually exclusive, rather than complimentary. This is natural since behind these abstract issues are black versus white, people with considerable power versus people without much of it, students versus administrators, workers versus employers, clients versus agents.[14] The issues themselves could be solved, conceivably by philosophers, if only the poeple involved did not get in the way. Perhaps it was in part within such a perspective that Marx called on the philosophers to change the world rather than merely to interpret it. Our abstract solutions matter very little if we cannot put them meaningfully into practice. But of course it is the world that created such issues in the first place and that throws up new alternatives. And, of course, it is necessary for philosophers to interpret the world, and their interpretations, as Marx was himself aware, may carry some weight in the end; Marx's own example carries considerable weight.

The very existence of these issues, however, shows that we are admitting something to ourselves. We have begun to admit first, that power and wealth are inequitably distributed in our society; second, that bureaucratic styles can be deeply oppressive both to bureaucrats and their cleints; and third, that many poeple need and want greater knowledge of and control over the matters that affect them directly. Though these realizations do not answer any particular questions about institutional arrangements in specific areas, they do provide us with a predisposition. They provide us with receptiveness to change and a willingness to experiment with new forms and with alterations of habitual authority relations. But such a predisposition is not enough. Such a faint inclination for participation and decentralization gives us too little to go on. And a thorough embracing of decentralization, as a genuine solution to our contemporary problems, is not satisfactory. In fact, decentralization could easily become a placebo that provides the illusion of a solution by creating greater surface stability. We need a more reasonable setting for a discussion of these issues before we can decide how who ought to get what. Let us look first at the light political philosophy can shed on these issues and, second, at the American context within which these conflicts are being played out.

Political Thought and the Issues of Decentralization and Participation

Some of the problems of interpreting the meaning of democracy and of coming to grips with mass participation and control we have inherited from the ambiguities in the liberal tradition. Beginning with Locke, whose antipaternalism was quite clear, we see a reluctance to face the full implications of the principle of consent. Locke himself was not a democrat. And the liberal tradition has housed many a thinker who feared mass participation and increased democracy.[15] The notion of government by consent does have revolutionary implications. However, within the liberal tradition this notion has been viewed in two distinct ways: first, the line of thought that emphasizes popular participation and control, developed largely by the left; and second, the line of thought emphasizing liberty to include the possession of property, due process, and a tightly circumscribed sphere for government involvement, developed largely by the right.[16] From the left point of view, political democracy in itself is not enough. One would have to employ the principle of consent in discussing all institutional arrangements in a supposedly democratic society. Thus, the democratic theorist would be interested in popular participation and control not only in government, but also in economics, education, supposedly authoritarian institutions such as the military, and within the family as well. He does not necessarily have to conclude that the one man–one vote principle should apply everywhere and at all times. But he surely would no more accept the legitimacy of traditional arrangements in other spheres than he would in politics. From this point of view, democratic participation and control have only begun to reshape social life. We still see massive concentrations of power virtually immune to communal responsibility. Sometimes this aspect of democratic theory is characterized by emphasizing equality rather than liberty, but it should be made clear that this sort of equality ought to involve widespread participation and consent as well as the undermining of privilege.

Concentrations of power relatively immune to popular control have a classic defense other than in terms of property rights and liberty. This is the defense in the name of expertise and efficiency. There are just some functions, it is argued, that cannot be performed without a certain degree of autocratic power. There are just some forms of organization, it is maintained, that cannot operate without hierarchy. The well-known virtues of bureaucracies come under these headings. We hear such defenses employed to justify military hierarchies, educational autocracies, and the management of factories and of economic life. For the most part, despite the populist elements in their tradition, socialists as well as liberals have bought these arguments.

The socialists, seeking to attack private concentrations of power, looked toward political centralization as a solution. For them, men would participate through centralized party organizations. Here, contemporary liberalism finds itself in the same situation. While for the most part, socialists and liberal reformers have been centralizers who emphasized party organizations plus expertise in management at the top, there have been some exceptions. The Guild Socialists, for example, early in this century raised an issue that sounds strikingly contemporary. Here is G. D. H. Cole, writing in 1915:

> The State cannot, in the long run, be better than the citizens, and, unless the citizens are capable of controlling the government, extension of the powers of the state may be merely a transference of authority from the capitalist to the bureaucrat.[17]

The Guild Socialists, like the syndicalists and the anarchists, advocated forms of workers' control which, defeated in their own time, are only now beginning to be taken seriously.[18]

We are seeing now in our own country, as well as many others, a reopening of questions concerning a democratically organized and civil social life. First, blacks are demanding not just a vote, but a meaningful vote, which involves effective representation and some control over the matters that affect them most directly. Often, as we should know by now, the vote itself guarantees nothing, and, in addition, many governmental and nongovernmental functions must be subject to local influence because it is difficult to control them through the political process. Second, many are questioning the undemocratic functioning of major institutions: corporations, schools, and the military. Here we see calls for due process, equality, and opportunities for participation. No doubt some of these institutions cannot be suitably run as town meetings, but a good bit of change is justified despite opposition from those who cannot reassess habitual forms of authority relations. We see the democratic tradition alive then—in all its messiness, explosiveness, and optimism—in many contemporary struggles.

But neither liberal theory nor socialist theory can offer us much help in assessing any specific claims for decentralization and participation. Liberals and soialists have themselves been concentrating on efficiency and control for so long that they have little to contribute in these current debates. Only the anarchists and advocates of workers' control have tried to explore questions of localism and coordination of decentralized units. As a result, there is little richness in our tradition of theorizing that helps us come to grips with these issues.[19]

"A Better System of Prisons?" The Context of Local Control in Contemporary America

> Adieu Prince I have tasks a sewer project
> And a decree on prostitutes and beggars
> I must also elaborate a better system of prisons
> Since as you justly said Denmark is a prison . . .[20]
>
> from ELEGY OF FORTINBRAS, by Zbigniew Herbert

Fortinbras is the military man who appears at the end of Shakespeare's *Hamlet* and arranges the funerals. He also takes possession of state power. He has just returned from the field. There is a striking contrast between his character and Hamlet's. He is decisive where Hamlet was torn by inner conflicts. He appears capable of assuming power where Hamlet barely maintained control over himself. But then Hamlet faced a different series of problems: problems of the inner life, of murder, suicide, and salvation. Fortinbras faces the issues of organization and the exercising of power.

Zbigniew Herbert is a Polish poet. Perhaps he is telling us something about Poland in the lines quoted above. Perhaps he is telling us something about bureaucratic rule. Perhaps he is suggesting something about the inevitability of prisons: social arrangements which deform and punish our capacities for freedom. Perhaps he is asking us to face the boredom, craft, and tension which are a necessary part of rule. Perhaps he is speaking for the dignity of that reform which aims to obtain as much as it is possible to obtain. Perhaps he is communicating to us the emptiness of a politics that is without tragedy, without inner questioning, without poetry. Perhaps he is exploring the tensions implicit in the contrast between Fortinbras and Hamlet, neither one of whom represents a successful way of dealing with inner and outer realities, but both of whom command our attention.

Yet, after all, it is an elegy spoken by Fortinbras, not Hamlet, that Herbert has written. In this elegy, Herbert humanizes this soldier and shows us his own self-knowledge and troubles, as if he too is something of a Hamlet. But what sort of ruler will Fortinbras make? Is he the sort of man that Denmark needs? Or would Hamlet perhaps have made a better head of state, despite his limitations? Has Denmark been warlike and does it need to give more careful attention to domestic needs, and is there widespread discontent among the poor and a pressure for change? We do not know. And also, we do not know enough about Fortinbras or Hamlet and their likely advisors. And, of course, this is neither Herbert's interest, nor Shakespeare's. But it is our's. These are the sorts of questions we have to answer, when it comes to judging potential leaders, or potential forms of political organization. These are the sorts of questions that have not been adequately dealt with in most of the discussions of decentralization and participation.

Often the debate between proponents and opponents of decentralization and participation appears as if it were a debate over eternal truths. How much hierarchy is necessary? How much participation does it take to create a healthy personality? How fully should professional norms override popular preferences? Can poor people be rational? Can bureaucrats act like human beings? Can social scientists understand and love society?

A few of these, maybe, are real questions, but when they are brought to bear on the issues of participation and decentralization in America today, they often function as a disguise for normative preferences; they mask the real issues rather than unveiling them. They obscure the limits of what is possible by defining the possible without context. Other discussions of the issues focus too narrowly on the more immediate political considerations. We hear about the troubles caused in a particular town, or the pacification produced. We hear about a particular federal program undermined, or of small successes in making the bureaucracy knuckle under. Again, this is talk that needs to be aired, but it does not itself constitute a broad discussion of the issues.

Finally, trying to embrace both the specific problems and the underlying issues, Herbert Kaufman describes the cyclical shifts between centralization and decentralization in America, in an attempt to put the present upheavals in historical context. And although he notes that the cyclical nature of the pattern does not mean all remains the same, he does not pay enough attention to deeper issues that transcend immediate conflicts and immediate evaluations.

To make judgments about the issues involved in matters of decentralization and participation, we have to know more about the polity under discussion and the nature of the time. For example, if we know that corporate economic power is abusive and cannot be controlled locally, we might opt for national regulation. If we know that religious cleavage is acute and destructive and is being exacerbated by excessive central regulation, we might opt for greater local autonomy. If we know that libertarian principles opposed by the elete, are widespread, we might favor greater local lawmaking powers. If we knew that foreign policy commitments were overextending a society and leading to neglect of domestic needs, we might favor whatever measures, central and/or local, that were needed to alter these priorities. If we knew that many people felt powerless and frustrated in their attempts to get government to respond to them, we might, if we were prudent, try to open more avenues for influence, and give such groups more power. In all such cases, various mixes of central and local initiative might be worked out, depending on the circumstances.

How then do we establish a meaningful context for deciding about decentralization and participation in the United States today?

The first question we need to answer is: how effectively are Americans now participating in political life? I do not propose to attempt a full answer, but only to set out a few main issues for discussion. Ordinarily, in more or less democratic societies, political parties serve as the main forums for political discussion and the main vehicles for participation. In the United States, as Walter Dean Burnham has pointed out, the parties have not performed this function very effectively and, in fact, have deteriorated in these respects since the late nineteenth century. Burnham traces the relatively low levels of political participation in America to two primary factors: first, the growth of a one party system in many areas of the country after 1896 (a situation the New Deal did something, but not enough, to change); second, the failure of a major party of the left to develop in this country, leaving a hole in our political system. This last point is most significant, Burnham argues, because it means that no party is attempting to mobilize the poorest sectors of the population in any sustained way. Burnham's overview of the American party system looks like this:

the reality of American politics appears quite different from a simple vision of pluralist democracy. It is shot through with escalating tensions, periodic electoral convulsions and repeated redefinitions of the rules and general outcomes of the political game. It has also been marked repeatedly by redefinitions—by no means always broadening ones—of those who are permitted to play. And one other very basic characteristic of American party politics that emerges from an historical overview is the profound incapacity of established political leadership to adapt itself to the political demands produced by the losers in America's stormy socio-economic life. As is well known, American political parties are not instruments of collective purpose, but of electoral success. One major implication of this is that, as organizations, parties are interested in control of offices but not of government in any larger sense. It follows that once successful routines are established or reestablished for office-winning, very little motivation exists among party leaders to disturb the routines of the game. These routines are periodically upset, to be sure, but not by adaptive change within the party system. They are upset by overwhelming external force.[21]

Without a party that consciously aims to organize and politicize those with low incomes and little education, participation will remain low in these groups. Such people will be unable to relate their personal grievances to larger political questions, and they may also be attracted, when they are aroused, by demagogic or personalist appeals. We have then a long-term fact about the American political system: its failure to mobilize very fully that portion of the population most likely to support equalitarian social change. Related to this failure is a further difficulty: with low participation and the absence of a left wing party, many people may have political grievances and preferences which are unrepresented in the political arena. For example, although popular preferences may favor national health insurance, it will prove extremely difficult to overcome organized resistence by privileged minorities due to the absence of a major party that would mobilize the poor and the working class to support this measure.[22] There is nothing automatic, after all, about the translations of relatively inchoate popular preferences into public policy. The ability of the elite to quash a movement may be very great, especially when public sentiments have not been crystallized in a politically meaningful fashion.

Burnham's conclusions are extremely somber, since he does not see any persuasive evidence that a constructive realignment of our party system is in the offing:

American politics in its normal state is the negation of the public order itself, as that term is understood in politically developed nations. We do not have government in our domestic affairs so much as "non-rule." We do not have political parties in the contemporary sense of that term as understood elsewhere in the Western world; we have antiparties instead. Power centrifuges rather than power concentrators, they have been immensely important not as vehicles of social transformation but for its prevention through political means.[23]

The second point of reference concerns the rates and meanings of social change. What sort of change is taking place? Do people feel it is under reasonable control? Is the distribution of privleges and deprivations felt to be legitimate? On these scores, much has gone wrong in our society. At every turn, we are confronted with massive unplanned social changes with profound consequences: migrations from rural areas to cities, lack of adequate public services, deterioration of urban areas; environmental pollution. Here people experience, first hand, the impact of social forces beyond their control. Here people experience the destructive efficiencies of modern life and find alternatives lacking. Here the economically useless, or the marginally useful, find that their condition is a secondary consideration in a profit oriented economy. Most of these developments impinge most directly on the poor and the powerless who must bear the brunt of those changes they cannot halt.[24]

In addition, over the last twenty years, the distribution of wealth in this country has remained relatively unaltered. Again, it is those at the economic bottom of society whose condition has improved the least. Despite all of the talk about an affluent society, most Americans are far from economically comfortable.[25] Many, in all classes of society, feel the pinch and are not certain that the future will be better. In any case, it seems reasonable to assume that the lack of redistribution of wealth has produced in recent years feelings, though not consciously perceived, of discontent and a lack of hope.

Third and finally, we must ask about the legitimacy of authority structures in America. The 1960s was a time of questioning the legitimacy that social scientists believed was solid in the late 1950s. Schools, local governments, police, national bureaucracies, major corporations, the military, the electoral process have each had sharp challenges not only to aspects of policy, but also to the basic modes of functioning.

John Schaar has argued that what we are seeing is a general crisis of legitimacy in modern societies, a crisis which has multiple roots.[26] Without exploring Schaar's argument here, let me note that he criticizes the Weberian model of the rational-legal form of authority and maintains that the bureaucratic style cannot be a genuinely satisfactory form of authority. His critique of bureaucracy involves first an attempt to characterize what he calls the bureaucratic epistemology. He emphasizes the specific sort of rationality bureaucracies cultivate. This rationality involves: depersonalization, detachment of personal feelings, and interchangeability of individual bureaucrats. Finally, Schaar argues that bureaucracies deny personal responsibility. As he puts it, "All bureaucrats are innocent." In contrast to this bureaucratic conception of authority, Schaar describes what he calls natural or human authority. This sort of authority involves a "kind of knowledge which includes intuition, insight, and vision as indispensable elements. . . . One who possesses and values this kind of knowledge bases his claims to its validity on grounds which are quicksand to the objective and rational man. One of the foundations is strength of conviction. . . . The other ground is the resonance set going between leader and followers when communication 'makes sense'." In our time, Schaar writes, "the established processes and formal structures of control are at war with the conditions necessary for authority. In this battle, legitimacy is destroyed." In the end, however, while recognizing a crisis of authority, Schaar does not try to predict what new forms of authority may develop in the future.

There are many ambiguities here. It is possible, with opinion data, to prove that most Americans believe in the legitimacy of the national government. But it is equally possible to show that many Americans have a strong mistrust of local and national governments, courts, and political parties. All of these attitudes exist side by side, and to represent only one portion of them distorts both reality and the potentialities of the future.

To summarize then on the matter of a context for discussion: first, political participation in America is far from what it probably ought to be for a healthy democratic life; second, economic and social change and nonchange in recent years have shown the inability of our political institutions to cope with serious local and national problems; third, the legitimacy of many institutional arrangements is being challenged and, from the point of view of democratic theory, those challenges are often justified.

If I have established at least a portion of the context for a discussion of the issues involved in participation and decentralization, I have not shown how this context might help us come to some conclusions about these issues. I have already argued that participation is, no doubt, lower than it ought to be in America and that many widespread grievances are not mobilized. These two facts certainly warrant increased participation, but they do not tell us anything about the decentralization of bureaucracies or increased citizen involvement at the local level.

As a preliminary to answering these questions, let us turn briefly to some data on the attitudes of the poor in Durham, North Carolina.

How It Looks in Durham

Let's say we go to Durham, North Carolina, and ask some poor whites and blacks how they feel about the relationships between themselves and the various levels of government.[27] What do we find? First, we find an awful lot of ignorance, especially among poor whites. We find that nearly half of both racial groups have heard neither of the anti-poverty program, nor of Head Start. We find that approximately forty percent of the whites and approximately thirty percent of the blacks do not know about Operation Breakthrough, although this community action program was extremely controversial and made the papers frequently. We find that three-quarters of the whites and between forty and fifty percent of the blacks do not know whether or not there is a neighborhood council in their neighborhood. Finally, we find that when asked whether the poverty program would help most of the poor, or only a few of the poor, sixty percent of the blacks and three-quarters of the whites said they did not know.

Next, we find that most poor people do not feel that the government is helping them with their most important problems, which in their minds, are overwhelmingly financial—problems of food, clothing, shelter, and health care. When asked if the governments in Washington, Raleigh, or Durham had ever helped or hurt them, they responded as indicated in Table I.

TABLE I
HAS THE GOVERNMENT EVER HELPED OR HURT YOU?

	Washington		Raleigh		Durham	
	Helped	Hurt	Helped	Hurt	Helped	Hurt
Blacks	48%	21%	7%	21%	21%	14%
Whites	42%	15%	23%	11%	17%	4%

We can see here, first, a relative absence of a sense of connection with government. In no case do even half of them say that a particular level of government helped them, or hurt, them. Second, one sees a predominance of helping over hurting except in the case of the blacks' feelings about the state government. Much of this predominance results however, from the fact that these people see the government hurting them, not by what it fails to do, but only by the positive harm it inflicts—mostly in the form of taxes. Third, we see a sharp drop-off in the sense of receiving help from the government on the state and local level. On the whole, most of the help received from the federal government was seen in terms of social security, public housing, unemployment benefits, and jobs. If we look more carefully at the comments these people make about the government, we find mixed feelings, ranging from deference, cynical detachment, specific criticism, to a sense of loyalty. For example, here is a fairly typical, positive response, and an unusually revealing one:

Q   What are the biggest problems you face?

A   I don't have any too big problems to worry about right now. The biggest problem I have to worrying about health and things like that.

Q   Has the government in Washington ever done anything to help you?

A   Yes, my social security and the protection and all they give me in this country.

Q   Has the government in Washington ever done anything that hurt you?

A   Not that I know anything about.

Q   Has the state government in Raleigh ever done anything to help you?

A   Yes, not helped me directly, but they helped when my mother was an invalid. They helped me with that, with her care and upkeep. That was welfare and old age benefits.

Q   Has the state government ever done anything to hurt you?

A   Not that I know anything about.

Q   Has the city government here in Durham ever done anything that helped you?

A   I don't know anything specific, but they've never done anything to hurt me.

Q   They haven't hurt you?

A   No. In fact, I've never called on them to help me.

What is unusual is a certain self-awareness and sense of the citizen's potential activity that comes through in this last answer. Others have complaints beneath which one senses broader frustration:

Q   Has the government in Washington ever done anything to help you?

A   No they ain't never done nothing.

Q   Has the state government in Raleigh ever done anything to help you?

A   I don't ever want to talk about them crackers in Raleigh.

Q   Has the state government ever done anything to hurt you?

A   Yeh. . . . Too many taxes, raggedy streets.

Q   Has the city government in Durham ever done anything to help you?

Q   No.

Q   Has it ever done anything to hurt you?

A   They don't fix the raggedy streets either.

Often people have a sense of governmental inadequacies without being about to pinpoint their own recommendations or complaints. For example:

Q   Has the state government in Raleigh ever done anything to help you?

A   No, I can't say that it has directly. Just like everybody else, I go along with the state, the people in it.

Q   Has the city government in Durham ever done anything to help you?

A No, that's on the same footing. You can't find any one person that can come right out and say the state has done them any harm, any damage, but still, it looks like everything they do, everyone don't agree with it.

If we look in other ways at their attitudes toward political institutions, we find a heavy dose of mistrust and feelings of alienation. For example, we asked a series of questions about the political parties, the laws, and the relationship between rich people and the government. In Table II we compare the Durham findings with those of a national sample.

TABLE II
ATTITUDES TOWARD POLITICAL INSTITUTIONS[28]

	Durham Data		National Sample
	Blacks (%)	Whites (%)	(%)
Does the Government pay more attention to rich than the poor?			
Yes	28	60	
No	41	28	
Do not know	31	6	
Are the national parties controlled by the rich?			
Yes	45	51	32.1
No	41	40	
Do not know	14	9	
Are the laws rich man's laws?			
Yes	62	53	33.3
No	35	43	
Do not know	3	4	
Do elected representatives represent the citizen?			
Yes	53	52	43.7
No	21	24	
Do not know	26	24	
Are the parties too big?			
Yes	65	79	67.5
No	23	17	
Do not know	12	4	

In addition to the strong dose of mistrust seen in these responses, we also find that two-thirds of the people questioned believe that one-half or more Americans are poor. Close to ninety percent believe there will always be poor people. And close to one-half the blacks and two-thirds of the whites believe there will be the same number or more poor people ten years from now. Their picture of the world is not an optimistic one. They are resigned to the existence of poverty and to their own poverty as well. This attitude is more prevalent among blacks. Both groups have a heavy dose of distrust about government that has surely been thoroughly earned.

If we look at what happened in Durham in the 1960s we see a situation that has many parallels elsewhere. Since then, blacks throughout the country have become more organized and self-conscious and have been somewhat successful in pressuring local government and other local institutions. On the other hand, organizing among the poor whites has had only the most limited success, though these people are in no less need of better chances. Blacks have fought on such issues as desegregation, housing code enforcement, representation on local boards, welfare regulations, health care, employment. Only one white neighborhood group has been successfully organized. It has fought through a few small neighborhood issues.[29] Though blacks in the future may demand decentralization and greater control over local bureaucracies, it is the poor whites that are more in need of local organization and are more locked into the feelings of political futility.

Decentralization and Participation: Issues and Methods

There are many problems in America, not one. And there will have to be many solutions. Paul Goodman, long-time advocate of decentralization and citizen participation, has himself cautioned that the present movement toward local control and self-determination could well be a dead end and lead to the development of enclaves of neglect, such as the Indian reservations.[30] Looking at the problems of the poor in America we can see that local control and decentralization will not in themselves avail much. The changes needed are clear, and many of them, such as altering national priorities in such a way that health care, housing, education, apprenticeship training, and the like, have the resources necessary to help poor people, and others as well, restructure their lives, cannot be made locally.[31]

What local initiative and local conflict can supply, and have already supplied, is the beginning of political organization and self-help, a sense of potency and hope, and the possibility of correcting these priorities close to home. The poor in Durham, the white possibly more than the black, are in need of the effective national movement of the left that we have lacked for seventy-five years. In the meantime, localism can be a considerable virture if it does not lose sight of the larger issues. In terms of the problems of legitimacy discussed earlier, local control and participation can be a partial solution to establish more viable authority relations, especially for those groups of people who feel they are getting the rawest deal.

Calls for local control of education, however, will not necessarily mean better schools.[32] Calls for community control of police will not necessarily mean a more effective and intelligent police force, or a more honest one.[33] Calls for community control of local health facilities will not necessarily make these more adequate or more equitable in their distribution. Guerrilla warfare against targets close to home will assuredly not restructure the fundamental situation of the poor in most cases, and, additionally, such warfare often creates enemies of those who ought to be allies. Finally, emphasis on renovating the ghetto, must not distract us from the larger task of making the ghetto unnecessary. Moreover, it is clear that community control cannot, in many cases, mean total community control. Teachers must still retain professional standards of their own; so must police and other civil servants. Some policies, such as the notion of equal treatment itself, must be immune from local decision making. Community controlled policy, for example, should have no power to discriminate among citizens. Nor should school boards be capable of resegregating a system. Though these are obvious examples, they make clear a more general point: decentralized control cannot be complete control, and national standards ought to prevail, regardless of local sentiments, in many situations.[34]

But if we look back again at the Durham data we can see that local control is itself not simple to accomplish. For poor whites particularly, political activity is suspect and political ignorance is widespread. The blacks, though less fatalistic and better organized, face formidable barriers to effective access participation and have the problem of building a sustained movement. The problems then are different for these two groups. Blacks are attempting, with limited success, to get into the pluralistic ball game from which they have been effectively excluded for so long. They have found that pluralism was not plural enough. What they seek is both control and control over something worth having—which are not necessarily the same. Here considerable experimentation will have to be the rule, both for blacks and for the local bureaucracies with which they deal. Poor whites, on the other hand, have rarely demanded any local control since they accept their situation fatalistically and, despite deep resentments, are unable to organize themselves. The temptation then is to forget about poor white power. The question here is would not some local organization among poor whites, on a nonracist basis, help to create the preconditions for a better life for the poor in America? The answer is clearly, yes. How then can this be done? More specifically, the question is, what particular forms of local participation and control might prove interesting and effective.

Paul Goodman is again a good critic here.[35] He points out that many of the most promising avenues for local initiative have not been developed very effectively. For example:

... in both theory and practice, the liberty of occupation and function have been neglected. There has been little mention of workers' management and the kind of education and apprenticeship of the young that are necessary for this. Professional and guild autonomy has been readily sacrificed for narrow economic advantage. Producers' and consumers' cooperatives are in eclipse.

What Goodman is emphasizing here is that concentration on political forms of power and participation provides too narrow a focus. This criticism has most relevance to poor whites for whom workers' control and cooperatives might be a way out of passivity. Not only is it important that people be engaged in the issues that affect them, but also that personally experience the connection between themselves and larger social questions before they have a chance of becoming engaged. This is one of the reasons that participation where these people work might be fruitful and possible.

Bureaucracy has become a dirty word. This is only because it is associated with bureaucrats. But the bureaucrat is himself, oddly enough, a person and often finds himself in a position of great personal strain. He can respond to this strain, of course, constructively or destructively, depending on who he is and what the situation allows. The demands for participation and decentralization have commonly put considerable strains on bureaucrats who, starting with inadequate resources, have found their routines disrupted, their norms challenged, and their motives attacked. The question is how to deal with this?

The trouble is that teachers, social workers, police, and other civil servants get themselves locked into combat with militant local groups. Sometimes this combat is fruitful, but often it is not. From a bureaucrat's point of view, there are several things to be done. First, the bureaucrat's self-image, should involve a commitment to equality and dignity. Second, this means that the bureaucrat must try to transcend the conflicts and look for a common ground—often this must involve increased local decision making. Moreover, the bureaucrat needs to think carefully about the very programs he administers, the content of which he cannot simply take for granted. Some real innovation is called for within bureaucracies and, clearly, some of this is coming. Bureaucratic action can also take on a nonbureaucratic character where needed—like Danile Dolci's "reverse strike" which put unemployed men to work on socially constructive tasks and then called for payment and appropriate acknowledgement. Vladimir Mayakovsky, writing around the time of the Russian Revolution, talked about "crossroads crucifying policemen"—a line that conveys the implacable, tragic, and socially structured conflicts that set men against each other. It is only the consciousness of this dilemma that may make it possible to break out of it.

Summarizing, I would say that the current dilemmas of American politics are serious and that it is not easy to be optimistic. Increased participation and decentralization have certain obvious virtues, especially when they provide hope to those who have been hopeless and an arena for action to those who previously were fatalistic about their situation. But participation is never universal, nor is it neccsarily always the greatest value; nor is decentralization necessarily the healthiest or most significant method of solving political problems. We must face the fact that without a significant restructuring of national priorities, without altering our social system, much local work will be in vain. And, in recognizing this, we must see that many stand to gain by retaining our national life as it is.

NOTES

1   Frederick Engels, "Origin of the Family, Private Property and the State," *Marx and Engels: Basic Writings on Politics and Philosophy,* L.S. Feuer (ed.), (Gloucester: Peter Smith, 1965), p. 394.

2   See Bernard R. Berelson *et al., Voting: A Study of Opinion Formation in a Presidential Campaign* (Chicago: University of Chicago Press, 1954); Herbert N. McClosky, "Consensus and Ideology in American Politics," *American Political Science Review* LVIII (June 1964), pp. 361–382; J.W. Prothro and G.W. Grigg, "Fundamental Principles of Democracy: Bases of Agreement and Disagreement," *Journal of Politics* (Spring 1960), pp. 276–294.

3   See Seymour M. Lipset, *Political Man: The Social Basis of Politics* (New York: Doubleday & Co., Inc., 1959).

4   See D. Neubauer, "Some Conditions of Democracy," *American Political Science Review* (December 1967), pp. 1002–1009.

5   Gabriel A. Almond and Sidney Verba, *Civic Culture: Political Attitudes and Democracy in Five Nations* (Princeton: University of Princeton Press, 1963).

6   See especially C. Bay, "Politics and Pseudo-Politics," *American Political Science Review* (March 1965), pp. 39–51; C.C. Moskos, Jr. and Wendell Bell, "Emerging Nations and Ideologies of American Social Scientist," *The American Sociologist* (May 1967), pp. 67–72; Peter Bachrach, *Theory of Democratic Elitism: A Critique* (Boston: Little, Brown & Co., 1967).

7   Noam Chomsky, *American Power and the New Mandarins* (New York: Pantheon Books, Inc., 1969).

8   See Raymond Aron, *The Industrial Society* (New York: Praeger Publishers, Inc., 1967); Norman Birnbaum, *Crisis of Industrial Society* (London: Oxford University Press, 1969).

9   See S. M. Miller and M. Rein, "Participation, Poverty and Administration," *Public Administration Review* (Jan.–Feb. 1969), pp. 15–25.

10   See Paul Goodman, *People or Personnel* (New York: Random House, Inc., 1966).

11   Louis Gawthrop, "Toward a New Public Administration," paper, presented at the Annual Conference on Public Administration, Miami, Florida, April, 1968.

12   Arthur Pearl and F. Riessman, *New Careers for the Poor* (New York: Free Press, 1965).

13   W. G. Scott, "Organization Government: The Prospects for a Truly Participative System," *Public Administration Review* (Jan.–Feb. 1969), pp. 43–53.

14   See Robert Nisbet "Subjective Si! Objective No!" *New York Times Book Review* (April 5, 1970).

15   See R. Lichtman, "The Facade of Equality in Liberal Democratic Theory," *Socialist Revolution* (Jan.–Feb., 1970), pp. 85–125.

16 See, for example, M. D. Aiken, "Mill and the Justification of Social Freedom," *Liberty* Nomos Series, Vol. 4, Carl J. Friedrich (ed.) (New York: 1962), pp. 119–39; David Caute, *Left in Europe Since 1789* (New York: Mcgraw-Hill Book Company, Inc., 1966).

17 Quoted in S. T. Glass, *The Responsible Society: The Ideas of Guild Socialism* (London: Fernhill House, Ltd, 1966), p. 37.

18 See D. Armstrong, "Meaning in Work," *New Left Review* (July–Aug. 1961), pp. 16–23; Robert Blauner, *Alienation and Freedom: The Factory Worker and His Industry* (Chicago: University of Chicago Press, 1964); P. Anderson, "Sweden: Part II," *New Left Review* (May–June 1961) pp. 34–45; Georges Friedmann, *Industrial Society: The Emergence of the Human Problems of Automation*, H. L. Sheppard (trans.) (New York: Free Press, 1955).

19 Nor is most literature about developing nations much help, except perhaps for William McCord, *Springtime of Freedom: The Evolution of Developing Societies* (New York: Oxford University Press, 1963) and the writings of Gandhi.

20 *Selected Poems of Zbigniew Herbert* (London: 1968).

21 Walter Dean Burnham "The End of American Party Politics," *Trans-Action* (December 1969), pp. 12–22. See also "The Changing Shape of the American Political Universe," *American Political Science Review* (March 1965), pp. 7–28.

22 L. Lipsitz, "On Political Belief," *Power and Community* Philip Green and Sanford Levinson, (eds.) (New York: Pantheon Books, Inc. 1970).

23 Walter Dean Burnham, "The End of American Party Politics," *op cit.,* p. 22.

24 See Paul Goodman "Reflections on Racism, Spite, Guildt and Violence," *New York Review of Books* (May 23, 1968), pp. 18–23.

25 See S. Thernstrom, "The Myth of American Affluence," *Commentary* (October 1969), pp. 74–78; R. Parker, "The Myth of Middle America," *The Center Magazine* (March 1970) pp. 61–70; David M. Gordon, "Income and Welfare in New York City," *The Public Interest* (Summer 1969), pp. 64–88.

26 John Schaar, "Reflections on Authority," *New American Review* 8 (Jan., 1970), pp. 69–70.

27 The Durham survey, based on three four-hour interviews with fifty-three poor whites and twenty-nine blacks was carried out in 1966 and 1967.

28 The actual questions employed were:
1. Do you feel that rich people have a greater influence on government than the ordinary man?
2. Do you feel that both major parties in this country are controlled by the wealthy and are run for their benefit.
3. Do you feel that the laws of this country are supposed bo benefit all of us equally, but the fact is that they are almost all "rich-man's laws."
4. Do you feel that there does not seem to be much connection between what I want and what my representative does.
5. Do you feel that political parties are so big that the average member has not got much to say about what goes on.

Questions 2-5 were taken from McClosky.[2]

29 See Elizabeth Tornquist, "Standing Up To America," *New South* (Fall, 1969).

30 Paul Goodman, "The Limits of Local Liberty," *New Generation* (Summer, 1969), pp. 13–17.

31 Bayard Rustin, "The Failure of Black Separatism," *Harper's Magazine* (January 1970), pp. 25–34.

32 See for contrast David K. Cohen, "The Price of Community Control," *Commentary* (July 1969) pp. 23-32; Philip Green, "Decentralization, Community Control, and Revolution," *Power and Community* Green & Levinson, (eds.) (New York: Pathron Books, Inc.

1970); Sandra Feldman, "Decentralization and the City Schools," (New York: *League for Industrial Democracy),* occasional paper No. 12.

33 See Arthur Waskow "Community Control of the Police," *Trans-Action* (December, 1969), pp. 4–7. Waskow's discussion, which is highly favorable to community control, fails to explain how this can be more than an essentially defensive tactic to protect citizens against police abuse. More than this is needed and cannot be accomplished by community control alone.

34 We must consider finally whether the usual democratic optimism about decentralization is not altogether out of place. Theodore Lowi, for example, argues, in his book *End of Liberalism* (New York: W. W. Norton & Co., Inc., 1969) that the current press toward decentralization is only a further development of "interest group liberalism." From Lowi's point of view, such a development, like the rest of interst group liberalism, will serve only to fragment governmental authority, to create laws without standards, and to undermine the legitimacy of the political order. In addition, decentralization will lead to increased parochialism and, among blacks, to a focusing on the ghetto when it is the very existance of the ghetto that is the problem. I think Lowi's case is convincing. Decentralization will lead to a narrowed focus for protest; it will undermine the authority of governments and lead to differential applications of law in response to community pressures. It will increase chaos. Lowi proposes instead the recreation of a government of laws—the reimpositon of genuine standards in legislation: particularly, standards which would thoroughly and effectively provide Negroes with first-class citizenship. But here Lowi misses part of the point. His indictment of interest-group liberalism makes sense and one can apply such a critique, for example, to the poverty program. But the issues involved are more complex than his analysis permits him to acknowledge. He fails to see that it is precisely the failures of existing bureaucracies that must be remedied and that greater bureaucratization will probably not do. Moreover, he misses the significance of increased activism among the poor and its relationship to local protest. Lowi is correct, however, in regarding the vagueness of the poverty program as a kind of cop out, and he is right in arguing for clearer national commitments to justice. These standards are clearly necessary, but they will not in themselves recreate that rapport between governors and governed that he seeks. Stronger national policy making is not, therefore, antithetical to increased local participation and control.

35 Paul Goodman, "The Limits of Local Liberty," *New Generation* (Summer, 1969).

Citizen Participation in a Bureaucratic Society: Some Questions and Skeptical Notes

James Davis

Most of the literature and commentary on citizen participation is the product of good intentions, innocence, and sometimes political self-interest, but little else. One gets the impression that citizen participation is a good thing. Period. Such uncritical acceptance of, indeed devotion to, a phrase (concept) that may be either empty or loaded with political dynamite simply will not do. This essay is a reaction. Like many reactions it may go too far. Readers must, therefore, make the necessary corrections.

The essay does not report research. Rather it represents an attempt to synthesize reading, observations, and intuitions. It is intended to be only suggestive and provocative. If it succeeds in that it will have done its job.

The Bureaucracy and Public Policy

For many years citizen participation in one form or another has appeared in the administrative organizations of American government. Numerous government organizations have used citizen groups with only advisory powers. Some government organizations have used citizens to carry out programs, not merely give advice concerning them; the local boards of the Selective Service are an example. Civilian review boards for police, as has been suggested, might have powers of inspection and discipline as well as publicity. Sometimes citizen groups are used not only in the execution of a program, but in its planning as well—and sometimes only in the planning. Some citizens groups have been mainly symbolic and legitmating, while others have had substantial functions. Sometimes citizen participation has resulted simply from administrative decisions. Sometimes, as in the case of maximum feasible participation in the War on Poverty, citizen participation is required by law.

Citizen participation may be viewed as a goal, having valued consequences in itself. Citizens who see participation as a goal may equate it with power—having achieved participation, all else will follow. Citizen participation may be viewed as a method of increasing the self-respect of participants, perhaps increasing feelings of political efficacy. It may be a form of citizenship training, in which the stated purpose of participation —to give advice or administer a program—may be simply an excuse for the participation itself. From another perspective citizen participation may be a means to an end, the end being anything from a decreasing school dropout rate to popular acceptance of the draft.

From the preceding it must be clear that citizen participation means many different things and is manifested in many different ways, stretching from occasional advice to daily administration and from pure symbol to real substance. For all the difficulty with the phrase, citizen participation is more popular today than ever before. In recent years citizen participation in different forms has been a part of urban renewal, the war on poverty, and public education.[1] Neighborhood control (or community control)—surely a form of citizen participation in government—has been urged for institutions as disparate as the schools and the police.[2] From the popularity of the phrase one could easily gain the impression that a contemporary government program was not complete if it did not contain provision for citizen participation. Why is this so?

Bureaucracy is one of the most important characteristics of our age. Large organizations dominate our lives as never before, and increasingly we live in huge urgan complexes. Bureaucratic organizations play a critically important role in the planning and initiation of public policy and, more obviously, in the implementation of public policy. This is true in urban affairs, where we often find school systems, police departments, and welfare workers operating with a substantial amount of autonomy. It is also true at the national level. We find that the American political system contains an array of subsystems, or separate policy systems, in which bureaucratic organizations play important parts. Some years ago the political scientist Carl Friedrich observed that bureaucracy was the core of modern government; today that observation is even more accurate. In the face of such bureaucracy, the right to vote seems to lose significance. One could well argue that the power to control bureaucratic organizations directly is necessary to influence government. We can write our Congressmen, phone our city councilmen and subsequently vote against them. Presidents and mayors are subject to the same pressures. But the government bureaucracies are commonly staffed with career people who cannot be voted out. Career bureaucrats, secure in their agencies, may continue on their course unaffected by election results. They are impervious to change. Thus there has arisen an interest in and demand for direct citizen participation in bureaucratic agencies with the hope that direct participation will make it possible to affect agency programs and performance.

The frequent call for citizen participation in government can be viewed as one response to the high level of bureaucratization and urbanization. In times past, when government was of more limited scope and scale, and the number of participants and potential participants much smaller, citizen participation, may have been an easier and less pressing matter. It did not have to be planned and called for. Citizen participation, though it existed in some measure, was not an issue, not a matter of conscious public concern. Today, as government has grown beyond comprehension, citizen participation may be an attempt to reduce the scale of government.

The characteristics of bureaucracy are well known—hierarchy, specialization, expertise, impersonality, anonymity, and uniformity. Citizen participation as it is often understood—participation in administrative processes by volunteer laymen—seems to be the very antithesis citizen participation. Thus can be viewed as a means of qualifying or humanizing the bureaucracy. It may be a way of avoiding or shortening the hierarchy, of introducing other than expert or professional values, of avoiding impersonality and gaining familiarity, of reducing uniformity and enhancing individual adjustment. It can be viewed as a way of reducing the scale of large urban areas and making small areas comprehensible and responsible. In short, citizen participation, as policy and slogan, may be a way of coping (or appearing to) with the largeness of our time.

The current interest in citizen participation may represent an extension of the traditional American interest in and acceptance of interest group representation in government. Officials in the political policy process may favor a measure of citizen participation to their policy proposals in an attempt to attract an added increment of support. And once added to proposals, citizen participation language may be quite difficult to excise. What politician is brave enough to oppose it openly? One might as well oppose good health and education.

Administrative officials in government may propose or support their versions of citizen participation for several reasons. They may think that a citizen participation component is essential to gain sufficient public, group, and legislative support for programs they want to carry out. Providing something in the way of citizen participation may be a part of building a winning coalition, a way of gaining consent. In addition, it may be a way of creating a vested interest in government programs and a source of continuing support of them. Citizen participation may be understood as an administrative device, a source of environmental intelligence, and a source of assistance in problem solving. Citizen participation may be synonymous with feedback. It may be a way of drawing on knowledge, experience, or talent not otherwise available to an organization. And, finally, because it is fashionable, officials may add the language of participation to a program even though they may not be quite sure why or how they will exploit or control it.

Legislators may favor citizen participation for some of the same reasons. It may seem an agreeable addition to an otherwise questionable legislative package. It may be a justification for giving an interest group access into an administrative organization. A concern for citizen participation may be an expression of traditional values because citizen participation smacks of the grass roots. And, of course, the man who wears the shoe knows best where it pinches.

Citizen participants and would-be participants may espouse citizen participation for their own reasons. Demands for it may be an expression of frustration and dissatisfaction with the status quo, with the hope that participation will alter agency or bureaucratic behavior. Those not in official bodies may view citizen participation as a means of inserting their values into governmental or agency decision making. Participation may be viewed as a means of gaining and ensuring responsiveness to citizen wants and needs. In addition, the call for citizen participation in government may follow from the view that there is precious little link between voting and public policy; what counts are the decisions and activities of countless bureaucratic organizations. As suggested above, the current emphasis on citizen participation may be the result of the bureaucratization of our political system.

Citizen Demands for Participation

It is possible and perhaps fruitful to view administrators, officials, or bureaucrats (which word used does not matter a great deal) as member of their organization, as insiders. Nonmembers are outsiders. Demands for citizen participation may be made because outsiders, nonmembers, see that it is bureaucrats who exercise power, distribute resources, make choices. Moreover, it may appear to some outsiders that bureaucrats ignore their wishes and their needs and are generally unresponsive, arbitrary, and uninformed. Outsiders who feel this way may quite naturally demand a voice in the decisions that affect them, particularly if they do not view their condition as inevitable and think their demands for participation will be met in some degree. Their specific demands may be for community control, for a citizen planning body, for a civilian review board, for an advisory committee of some sort, or even for maximum feasible participation. All of these demands represent attempts to insert outside influence on the inside process of bureaucratic government.

Many demands for participation appear to be made in ignorance of the operations of bureaucratic organizations.[3] Outsiders who want in seem not to realize that citizens appointed to an organization (for purposes of advice, oversight, supervision, control, etc.) may not know how or not be able to do what they intended. Demands for citizen participation may be made without the realization that once inside an organization citizen participants may have little influence on its performance. Outsiders may participate only on a formal, surface level. Furthermore, they may become co-opted insiders, supporting what the organization has been doing all along, and thereby be diverted from their original aim.

A demand to participate in the decisions and programs of an organization is in effect a demand that power be shared or given up. Such demands are likely to be resisted by many who think that their position or influence would be detrimentally affected if the demand were met. First, those outsiders benefiting from the status quo will be disturbed when others propose change. Second, insiders will summon up arguments ranging from the need to maintain professional standards and organizational morale to the danger of proceeding precipitately toward unknown consequences. To be sure, opponents of change may not be able to oppose citizen participation directly, but they may be able to challenge lay interference with professional matters. And if citizen participation in some form is unavoidable, it may be so structured and restricted as to minimize any real impact on agency operations. Symbolic participation may indeed be a desirable compromise.[4] It may appear to meet legitimate demands while at the same time preserve a large measure of administrative autonomy.

The foregoing comments make clear that the demand for participation is a political tactic, a demand for power clothed in relatively acceptable language. Despite the language, a demand for participation from outsiders is a demand that the distribution of power and influence be changed, that some power in the hands of insiders be transferred to outsiders. Put this way, one's view of the matter may depend not on whether one favors citizen participation in general and in principle, but whether one favors the particular citizens' demand to participate.

Insiders such as police, social workers, and school teachers share several characteristics that may affect their acceptance of citizen participation. They possess something that they define as professional expertise and are, they believe, guided by professional standards. Insiders also share a common organizational ideology. Members of a bureaucracy are accustomed to its methods—reliance on rules and regulations, channels, hierarchy, continuity, predictability, and stability. An important goal of insiders is usually the defense and enlargement of the organization. Each member also values the maintenance and improvement of his own position. These observations are scarcely new, but they mean that some forms of citizen participation may be viewed by officials as intrusions, and uninformed intrusions at that, into organizational and professional affairs. To be sure, all forms of participation may not be viewed this way. Participation that appears likely to support organization goals may be welcomed and indeed encouraged; participation that appears to promote alterations in the locus of political power as well as organizational change may be resisted. And today many calls for citizen participation, especially in urban affairs, have precisely the latter goals.

Assuming some form of citizen participation is adopted, these are the two most likely consequences: first, after initial satisfaction, new participants may find that, because of their own ignorance of bureaucracy and law or because of their lack of influence in the larger political system, or both, they are still unable to get what they desire. They have come closer to the prize and it still escapes them. Dissatisfaction and frustration may then return and participants may then drop out, refusing to participate further in what they regard as a sham. Participants are likely to stay in only as long as they think they are benefiting. When they see that they are not, and perhaps not even contributing, they may quit.

Second, participants may have an effect on organization operations. They may achieve their purpose and make the organization responsive to their needs. But their very success may bring resistance and reaction from those who see their own world crumbling. Short-term success may bring long run reaction.[5] Effective citizen participation may even bring resistance from those who once supported it without realizing all its consequences—economic, social, and political. Citizen participation means bringing new people into the political system; this may have unanticipated, and for some unwanted, consequences.

Officials and Participants

Having briefly viewed citizen participation as a demand from outsiders, we may turn to citizen participation as a tactic of administrators. Administrators may have a variety of motives or goals for utilizing some form of citizen participation. At one extreme they may call upon citizen participation for legitimation of programs. In this case, a group of reasonably visible and docile citizens may be assembled solely to give their assent to programs designed by officials and intended only for official implementation. At the other extreme, administrators may use citizens for the purpose of economizing: citizens extensively carry out the work of the organization. Citizen participation may be used by administrators as a way for an organization to learn about its environment—a way of collecting intelligence and reducing the isolation of the organization. The intelligence failures of some organizations might be explained by the lack of timely and appropriate citizen participation. Participation then can be a means of increasing the permeability of an organization to outside forces, problems, and ideas. Citizen participation may also be a problem solving technique. Some people feel problems might be solved if those concerned, officials and citizens, could sit down together. And, finally, citizen participation is related to two common terms in the administrative vocabulary—delegation and decentralization. Responsibility and authority may be delegated by administrators to citizen groups, with the possible result of decentralization: many decisions made by smaller groups rather than all decisions made in a single headquarters. This use of citizen participation suggests that it may be a way of achieving some flexibility in administrative operations, a way of trying to ensure that administrative operations are responsive to varying conditions in different locales.

These uses of citizen participation by administrative officials for organizational ends can be illustrated by looking at the practices of particular government organizations. A classic example, of course, is the Tennessee Valley Authority (TVA), an organization famous for its grass roots democracy.[6] One notes in Philip Selznick's description of the TVA that the use of citizens in program administration was to some extent a survival technique—a way of making easier the accommodation of the organization to the interests of affected citizens. But citizen participation was also a communications device, a way of ensuring that citizens understood, appreciated, and cooperated with what the organization was trying to do. Citizen participation could also be understood as a technique for clientele mobilization; citizen participants are likely to be organization supporters. And, finally, it was clear that using citizens was one way of carrying out TVA programs.

The U.S. Department of Agriculture (USDA) uses citizen participation to carry out programs, communicate with clientele, mobilize support, and ensure adjustment to local conditions. While describing the TVA Selznick could write: "Especially in the field of agricultural administration, the TVA's methods have paralleled an emerging trend in the administration of the federal government. This is not often recognized within the Authority, but there can be little doubt that the USDA has gone much farther in developing both the theory and practice of citizen participation than has the TVA. The emergence of this trend accompanied the construction of a vast apparatus to administer an action program reaching virtually every farmer in the nation.[7] In particular, the farmer committees utilized by the Agricultural Stabilization and Conservation Service (ASCS) exemplify citizen participation to achieve organizational ends. The Agricultural Adjustment Act of 1938 provided that the Secretary of Agriculture should use local and state committees of farmers to carry out the provisions of the act. This committee form of administration is still in operation.

For a number of reasons the Selective Service System has used local boards of citizens to implement the draft.[8] The official view has been that implementation by local citizens was all that made conscription acceptable to the American people. In addition it was claimed that the use of local citizens was necessary to take account of local conditions and avoid undue disturbance to local manpower supplies. It was also clear that the use of citizen volunteers was more economical than a paid staff. One should distinguish the Selective Service local boards, however, from the forms of citizen participation appearing in TVA, USDA, and, to name another example, the World War II Office of Price Administration, whose local rationing boards were composed of local citizens.[9] Affected citizens, that is, young men of draft eligible age, have never been on draft boards. And, unlike the ASCS farmer committees, draft boards are not elected but rather appointed by the President on the advice of the state governor.

In reviewing examples of citizen participation some points stand out. First, citizen participation and decentralization go together. Even in national programs, some decisions, or some kinds of decisions, are made by local citizens or their representatives. A second point is that decentralization verges into disintegration and personnel structure becomes disorganized. A third point is that citizen participation and decentralization lead almost inevitably to variety in administration. Certainly this has been one of the complaints levelled most frequently against the Selective Service System. Steps taken to gain flexiblility and perhaps acceptability may open an organization to charges of variety, unpredictability, and inequity. And these charges may force more centralization and a reduction in participation.[10] The fourth point is that official decentralization and citizen participation have often been accompanied by racial discrimination practised by local units.[11]

The final point to be made is that when administrators want citizen particiaption it is usually for their ends and on their terms. When outsiders want it, it is for their ends and on their terms. That both official and citizen may want citizen participation does not at all mean that they want the same thing or will approve the same result. They may not even approve the same participants. On the other hand, recognizing the conflict of interest, it may be possible to design forms of citizen participation that will allow both sides satisfaction. Naturally, the more sides there are the harder this becomes.

Agency–Clientele Relations

To further understand the difficulties of implementing citizen participation it is useful to consider the different kinds of agency–clientele relations that may exist.[12]

First, there is no inherent community of interest between a government agency and the citizens either interested in or affected by what that agency does. There may be some community of interest, but there may also be substantial conflict. Examples of the latter situation are easy to find: local draft boards and potential draftees, police and criminals, and revenue agencies and taxpayers. The relationship between a welfare agency and a client may be a conflict relationship; so may the relationship between a regulatory agency and the group or industry being regulated. Assuming a conflict relationship exists between an agency and its clientele, officials would not be happy with a program of citizen participation that places the enemy in their councils. However, in the same circumstance citizens may want very much to participate and even try to get a legislative requirement to that effect. On the other hand, when there is a community of interest between agency and clientele, then, at least, informal citizen participation is all but inevitable. In any case the quality of the relationship that exists may effect the extent and purpose of any citizen participation. It would be unusual to find important citizen participation in an organization if the officials viewed the agency–clientele relationship as predominantly a conflict one. Consider, for example the likelihood of young men sitting on local draft boards. Or, consider neighborhood control of police. Obviously some neighborhoods might prefer it. Police opposition is equally predictable.

Public agencies have a variety of major purposes. Some provide service, such as welfare agencies, schools, and public health organizations; others, such as tax agencies, extract resources; others enforce laws, ordinances, and regulations. Agencies vary in the services they provide, the laws they enforce, and the people with whom they deal. This suggests that citizen participation is likely to have very different meanings, take different forms, have different consequences from organization to organization.

Organizations may service a variety of clienteles and a variety of citizens. Any organization is likely to have suppliers, supporters, customers, and perhaps inspectors. Each of such varied clientele has different interests in organizational performance. And each is likely to attach a different meaning to citizen participation. For example, a school system serves not only students who have diverse needs, but also parents, employers, employees, the immediate community and the country at large, and institutions of higher education. What can and should citizen participation in a school system mean? Since graduates of a school system may leave the area, should parents in the immediate neighborhood be the only ones to control or participate in school decision making? Neighborhood control of schools would make greater sense if graduates were sure to stay within their neighborhoods. But they do not. Any organization has a variety of clientele or potential clientele, which has implications for the understanding and execution of citizen participation. Who should participate? Should some groups be singled out? Do those who provide resources deserve less responsiveness than those who receive benefits?

Some Further Considerations

Federalism and intergovernmental relations bear directly on citizen participation. Almost all government programs involve several levels of government. Federal money is spent by state and local agencies according to federal standards. An act may be planned in a locality, reviewed in a state capitol, approved and finally authorized in Washington, implemented by local officials under they eyes of federal and state officials, audited by the U.S. General Accounting Office, and perhaps reviewed by the U.S. Bureau of the Budget as well. Where in this complex federal process can citizen participation be fitted? Can citizen participation at any level in this complex process be more than symbolic? Certainly the complexity of the government's administrative structure would militate against more than superficial citizen participation.

What physical area can logically be used to define citizen participation? We know very little , if anything, about the optimal area, or population, or tax base that may be associated with various governmental functions such as police, welfare, the control of pollution, and the like. But it is clear that different programs are administered over areas of different size. Some programs, such as pollution control, must be carried out on a metropolitan basis; others, such as five protection, might effectively be carried out in the smallest urban community. Some are funded (must they be?) at the state level and others on a national level. Can proper areas be specified for such varied programs? The answer so far is not clear, and it bears on the implementation of citizen participation. Given the growing interest in community or neighborhood control of various governmental functions, the problem becomes particularly important. Which functions can be appropriately controlled at the neighborhood level, and which cannot? Some observations are in order.

First, neighborhood control is not likely unless the neighborhood in question has a substantial tax base and is financially well-off. To expect neighborhood control with metropolitan or whole city financing seems unrealistic. Yet neighborhood financing, except in wealthy suburbs, is also unrealistic. Because of the financial exigencies, neighborhood control of major functions in cities is unlikely—especially if control means something more than advice. This does not mean that neighborhood control seems unlikely to corrur except in rare instances.

Second, the desire for neighborhood control is to some extent a product of social tension. It is not clear, however, that social cohesion can be achieved through the separation that may result from neighborhood control. Neighborhood control of major functions might well heighten differences and exacerbate tensions. Third, a major problem in the administration of public policy is the lack of continuity between many public programs and organizations. Uncoordinated efforts at problem solving are endemic in our urban areas. Neighborhood control could only lead to the profusion of uncoordinated and, worse, ineffective programs. Fourth, last and most important, the meaning of neighborhood control is puzzling. He can a neighborhood be defined? What is a community? How can the concept be operationalized? How durable or transitory is a community or neighborhood? And what is control? The connotation of control is surely stronger than the connotation of participation. Participation suggests, at least, the presence of many participants. Control somehow seems more unilateral, absolute, and unrealistic. Until such definitional questions are answered, neighborhood control cannot rise much above the level of a political rallying cry.

The expert–layman relationship is a further important consideration that may affect the implementation of citizen participation. Officials in an organization may consider themselves to be experts and professionals, who have access to and control over knowledge. If so, they may resist anything more than symbolic citizen participation as interference from uninformed persons. On the other hand, if citizens view officials as knowledgeable they may withdraw from active participation and simply accept the analysis and conclusions of experts that they trust or cannot question. Yet again, if officials are not trusted, important information and technical considerations may be ignored or rejected by citizen participants. Professionals or experts have different values and different world views from lay citizens and this may result in conflict. Professionals, for example, may be prone to think more generally and abstractly, while lay citizens more concretely and personally. Such differences in intellectual style may create tension. Experts may define problems that laymen are not aware of and do not understand. Laymen may find the expert's suggested solutions novel or unacceptable. More generally, citizen participation may be difficult, if not impossible, when administrators and citizens in effect speak two different languages. In an increasingly specialized and diverse world this may be increasingly common. The language of the ghetto is not the language of the lawyer or the bureaucrat.

Responding both to a demand for citizen administration and a demand for expert administration is not easy. True, experts may not be as wise or expert as they claim; the knowledge they possess may rest on quite shakey foundations. But the basic problem remains. In an increasingly information conscious society, what is the role, what can be the role, of the uninformed citizen? One course might be citizen advisory power. This might not satisfy those who feel that decisions being made by officials are adverse to them. Or citizens might participate in program execution rather than in program planning, although this also may seem superficial. In any event it is clear that problems associated with the expert–layman relationship warrant recognition and attention.

What are the anticipated consequences of citizen participation? Assuming that government organizations are, by and large, in the business of benefits and burdens, one can then ask, "How is their distribution affected by citizen participation?" Who gets more and who gets less? Participation may lead to special treatment for participating groups, and is this result equitable or acceptable? Active and influential participation by some citizens in an agency's operations will make the agency more responsive to them, which seems an admirable result. However, it is at least provocative to suggest that a welfare agency treating its clients in an uncritical way might be open to the same criticism to which some federal regulatory agencies treating industries uncritically have been subjected. Can we say that special responsiveness to one set of interests is permissible, but such responsiveness to another set is not? Are some groups more entitled to access and participation opportunities than others? If so, how should those groups be picked? And if not, then should the general public be represented in some special way? The particular arrangements made for citizen participation and its results are not necessarily admirable. They warrant careful analysis and thought. Uncritical acceptance of citizen participation may lead to everything from disappointment and frustration to conflict and corruption.

Conclusion

Two points need emphasis. First, bureaucracies operate in complex environments and are confronted with conflicting and competing demands on their resources and attention. Bureaucratic responsiveness to some demands, or the demands of some, may necessarily mean that other demands are not met. Because of limited resources, some demands may conflict with others. Bureaucracies must choose (or have chosen for them) which demands to satisfy and which to ignore. Citizens with unsatisfied demands sometimes complain about inadequate or nonexistent opportunities for consultation and participation. Such complaints are understandable, but they are not likely to be fruitful. For outsiders to gain meaningful participation opportunities in bureaucracies, insiders would likely have to give up influence, which is not likely to happen voluntarily. Furthermore, the impact of the bureaucratic environment on the citizen participant should be emphasized. It can stifle, frustrate, thwart, dilute, co-opt, and otherwise prevent citizen participation from having expected or desired results.

Second, participation may have important symbolic values and may also be a source of organizational intelligence. For innovation and modification to take place, feedback is an essential. For agencies to be responsive to their environments, and thus endure, they must know how they are affecting their environments. Citizen participation is one way of providing feedback. Because it is or can be beneficial to an organization, agency sponsored participation will continue to be used in various ways, as it has been in the past.

Because it is fashionable and perceived to be in the interest of agencies, participation may flourish as never before. But because of political and bureaucratic realities, participation demanded by outsiders is not likely to develop rapidly or have much impact. Citizen participation may indeed have been oversimplified and oversold. In a world where the citizen is uninformed and apathetic and the bureaucracy is rigid and unswerving can there be a place for citizen participation?

It may be that pressing directly for citizen participation may heighten political conflicts and, at the same time, delay progress toward important substantive goals: the reduction of poverty and discrimination, the improvement of housing and education, and the maintenance of order. It is these issues that are important. Compared to these substantive issues, citizen participation in bureaucracy is largely a peripheral issue that may divert us from more important matters. It may be argued that participation is essential to progress in the substantive areas mentioned, but it would be hard to demonstrate. It could be that rapid progress in housing, education, welfare, and civil rights is impossible—citizen participation or not.[13] If so, citizen participation can only be a symbol.

NOTES

*In preparing this paper I had much–appreciated bibliographical assistance from Sally Barker and Lois Hecht, both graduate students at Washington University. Miss Barker also let me read a provocative seminar paper she had written on citizen participation and gave me the benefit of her reading and reflection. Naturally, my errors are my own.

1   The bibliography in these areas is vast. For example see: James Q. Wilson, "Planning and Politics: Citizen Participation in Urban Renewal," *Urban Renewal: The Record and the Controversy* James Q. Wilson (ed.) (Cambridge: MIT Press, 1966), pp. 407–421; J. Clarence Davies, III, *Neighborhood Groups and Urban Renewal* (New York: Columbia University Press, 1966); "Note: Citizen Participation in Urban Renewal," *Columbia Law Review,* LXVI (March 1966), pp. 485–607; Daniel P. Moynihan, *Maximum Feasible Misunderstanding* (New York: The Free Press, 1969); Kenneth Clark and Jeannette Hopkins, *A Relevant War Against Poverty* (New York: Harper Torchbooks, 1970); Sar Levitan, *The Great Society's Poor Law* (Baltimore: The Johns Hopkins Press, 1969); Naomi Levine, *Ocean Hill-Brownsville: A Case History of Schools in Crisis* (New York: Popular Library, 1969); Marilyn Gittell, *Participants and Participation: A Study of School Policy in New York* (New York: Praeger, 1966).

2   For examples see Marilyn Gittell, "Community Control of Education," *Urban Riots: Violence and Social Change* Robert H. Connery (ed.) (New York: Random House, 1969), pp. 63–75; Arthur Waskow, "Community Control of the Police," *Transaction,* 7 (December 1969), pp. 4–7. For a general treatment of community control see Alan A. Altschuler,

Community Control: The Black Demand for Participation in Large American Cities (New York: Pegasus, 1970).

3   See Anthony Downs, For a review of organizational characteristic. *Inside Bureaucracy* (Boston: Little, Brown and Co., 1967)

4   See Murray Edelman, *The Symbolic Uses of Politics* (Urbana: University of Illinois Press, 1964) for use as symbols.

5   See Daniel P. Moynihan, *op. cit.*

6   Philip Selznick, *TVA and the Grass Roots* (Berkeley: University of California Press, 1949).

7   Philip Selznick, *op. cit.,* p. 221. The role of farmer committees in the Agricultural Stabilization and Conservation Service is discussed in Charles M. Hardin, *Food and Fiber in the Nation's Politics* (Washington: Government Printing Office, 1967); see especially pp. 55–140.

8   James W. Davis, Jr. and Kenneth M. Dolbeare, *Little Groups of Neighbors: The Selective Service System* (Chicago, Markham Publishing Co., 1968).

9   Emmette S. Redford, *Field Administration of Wartime Rationing* (Washington: Government Printing Office, 1947).

10   On this point it is worth quoting at length from an article by Herbert Kaufman, "Alienation, Decentralization and Participation," *Public Administration Review,* (Jan.–Feb. 1969), pp. 11–12 Kaufman writes: "Decentralization will soon be followed by disparities in practice among the numerous small units, brought on by differences in human and financial resources, that will engender demands for central intervention to restore equality and balance and concerted action; the factors underlying the movement toward metropolitan units of government and toward conditional federal grants in aid will, in other words, reassert themselves. Decentralization will stand in the way of other goals, such as school integration (as did states rights doctrines in other times). It will give rise to competition among the units that will be disastrous for many of them, which will find it more difficult to attract talent and money than others that start from a more advantageous position. In some units, strong factors may well succeed in reviving a new spoils system, thus lowering the quality of some vital services. Decentralization of public administration will not necessarily be accompanied by decentralization of the other public institutions with which public units deal, such as unions of public employees, so that the local units may find themselves at a serious disadvantage in negotiations and unable to resist the pressures of special interests. Economies of scale, which are admittedly overstated very frequently, nevertheless do exist, and the multiplication of overhead costs in local units will divert some resources from substantive programs to administrative housekeeping. Initially, all these costs will be regarded by those concerned with representativeness as well worth paying, but the accumulation of such grievances over time will inspire a clamor for unification and consolidation."

11   As Hardin points out, the ASCS farmer committees appear to have been guilty of discriminatory practices, especially in the south. And Davis and Dolbeare, among others, note the small number of blacks serving on local boards of the Selective Service System.

12   A standard brief treatment is Avery Leiserson, "Interest Groups in Administration," *Elements of Public Administration,* 2nd ed. Fritz Morstein Marx, (ed.) (Englewood Cliffs: Prentice-Hall, 1959, pp. 294–311. See also Bertram Gross, *The Managing of Organizations Vol. I* (New York, The Free Press, 1964).

13   See Edward Banfield, *The Unheavenly City* (Boston: Little, Brown and Co., 1970) Banfield says, "So long as the city contains a sizeable lower class, nothing basic can be done about its most serious problems." p. 210.

Representative Local Government: From Neighborhood to Region

Victor Jones

If we could recall the image that we held in 1959 of the challenge of the 1960s, and of the likely responses of local government, we would be chagrined to realize that we did not foresee the direction of the civil rights movement, the rise of black power, the upheaval among students and the beginning of reform in all parts of our educational system, the Vietnam War, the rising expectations and frustrations of millions of formerly quiescent people, the realization that public welfare is a degrading and humiliating way of life, the development of impatient leadership cadres among minority groups, and widespread postures on all sides of intransigency often accompanied by demonstrations and physical violence.

Looking backwards it is clear that the challenge of the 1970s is almost unchanged from the challenge of the 1960s: to develop a system of government and politics which will deliver goods and services and administer regulations efficiently, effectively, and justly, and at the same time provide, through representation and citizen participation, genuine popular control of the direction of governmental activity and a sense of communal membership.

I should like to raise several questions by making some more or less positive assertions.

1 We cannot put the disquietude of the past decade to rest and return to the status quo ante that existed when only a few professors questioned

the representativeness of local government, as it was organized the United States.

The 1960s was a noisy, impolite, violent irrational decade, a decade of "maximum possible misunderstanding." But out of it came a political agenda of basic issues we must address during the 1970s. Hopefully we can approach the task ahead with maximum mutual understanding, because it is a prerequisite for the institutional reconstruction, the policy decision, and the administrative actions we are facing.

We can also hope that nonnegotiable demands—except when used in the rhetoric of the hustings or as a ritualistic approach to reasoning together—will be replaced by open participation and negotiation, both by those out of power and those in power. Even so, the processes of politics, of getting attention, of securing and maintaining a following, of influencing the electorate, will frequently seem vulgar, threatening, and sinister to those who remember the 1950s.

The basic responsibility lies with people of power and influence to listen and to consider the goals, and means of achieving goals, that are pushed upon them from the outside. But again the responsibility is mutual —once those in power have been brought around to listening, demands must be translated into policies acceptable to a congeries of interests.
2 Nor can we return to the status quo ante that critics of municipal reform during the past fifty years would have us believe would bring government back—from the impersonal and ponderous bureaucracy and the power structure at city hall—to a warm and personal government in the neighborhoods.

In the first place, the current image of earlier machine politics in the ward and at city hall is highly romantic. Party bosses and party workers have had latent functions of social service, mediation between people and power, and coordination of fractionated government for both legal and illegal purposes. Most institutions, we now recognize, have latent as well as overt functions, and certainly the political machines around the turn of the century were not exceptional in this respect. But do we know that the older political machines maintained open channels of advocacy and protest?

In the second place, even if ward politics had all the virtues now retroactively ascribed to it, we must ask if it, and the administrative agencies which it controlled, would be able to deliver services today in a manner and a quality to satisfy the so-called politically deprived people of our cities. Furthermore, there is much historial evidence that corruption and personal self-serving were systemic.

It is necessary to return to a past that never existed, in order to provide means of political access to groups that do not, or think they do not, have such access under local government as it is now organized? As Alex Gottfried has written:

Machine politics is not yet dead, even in the invidious sense. There have been major transformations; there will be more. But the need for organizations, for leadership, and for political responsibility has increased in the contemporary world. Some promising new organizational forms are developing. They coexist side by side with the remaining weakened and modified older forms and with the still developing structures in the troubled Negro, Puerto Rican and Mexican-American ghettos. Perhaps we are now wiser than we were fifty years ago. Perhaps we can devise structures that will permit access and integration for those groups which are still dispossessed, without paying the enormous price we have paid for ineffective and often venal local governments.[1]

Finally, any attempt to restore machine politics based on the ward system is probably hopeless, because of changes that have occurred in American society since the heyday of machine politics.

3 Unless we have a revolution in the old-fashioned sense of the word, institutional changes will occur slowly.

This does not mean that changes will not be made quickly and abruptly, here and there, but nowhere will the whole system of local government be replaced by another whole system. Nor will any given modification of a part of the system be adopted simultaneously in all local communities.

In many instances social changes must first be made before we can even identify the consequences to the immediate participants and certainly to the innocent bystanders. It is desirable, therefore, to evaluate substantive changes, social institutions and practices before they spread widely and irrevocably.

There are so many uncertainties, for instance, in the decentralization of schools in New York City that all groups interested in educational decision making would be wise to wait for a short time, at least, to observe and analyze the New York City experiment. All elements of communities all over the United States can profitably learn from the results of this attempt to decentralize a school system in a city of eight million people. But such decentralization, as a movement to be universally embraced at once, can polarize the country, without negotiating the reform it seeks.

A plea for time, of course, can be a tactic to slow down or to avoid compliance, or even consideration of needed change. But recognition of this fact does not alter the other fact that time is an element of institutional change. The wisdom, if not indeed the necessity of "all deliberate speed" should not be rejected because so-called deliberation without perceptible movement has characterized other reform efforts.

4 Local government as it is now organized and as it now operates is being questioned and challenged from many sides.

Congressional committees, special Presidential commissions (e.g., the National Commission on Urban Problems and the National Advisory Commission on Civil Disorders), national organizations (e.g., the Committee for Economic Development and Urban America), governors and state legislators, and many special purpose advocacy groups (e.g., conservation groups), as well as civil rights groups, black power groups, and the professional neo-reformers associated with community action programs—all these and many others have doubts about the capacity or the willingness of local government to meet the problems of cities and suburbs. Many of them, black and white, rich and poor, government official and businessman, see local government as unrepresentative in structure, parochial in orientation, overly concerned with petty matters, unable to make hard decisions where the public interest is opposed to local interests (as defined by supporters of regional services and controls), or where justice and equality is opposed to private gain or prejudice.

I myself have heard state legislators in the San Francisco Bay Area speak in this manner of elected city and county officials. Strictures such as these may be deserved in some instances; they are certainly not deserved by most local officials. Many of them are equally applicable to state and federal officials, and to neighborhood leaders. In fact, they may be applied to any organized group of people. But the fact of life relevant to this discussion is that local government is widely criticized and that the criticism is growing, to the point of condemnation.

5 American federalism—and, of course, American politics—is changing in style, direction, and structure.

Such changes, but at a different rate and scope, may have been going on from the beginning of our national history. But the rate and magnitude of change now make the historical differences one of kind as well as quantity.

Local government has become one of three operational partners in the new federalism. Despite all efforts of state governments to return to a two level federalism, irreversible patterns of give and take, and sharing of functions and power are operating, for better or for worse, through frequent formal and informal relationships among state and federal and local governments and agencies.

This has been accomplished by local governments going to Washington, and by federal agencies going into the local communities. But more important, this intermingling has been supported, and at times demanded, by many collections of interests. As a consequence, federal constituencies have been built up in the metropolitan areas of the country, which overlap state and local constituencies.

The most startling and far-reaching change in American federalism is the emergence of the national government as the focus for discussion of urban and metropolitan affairs. It is now the leader in formulating urban programs, and in using the grant-in-aid to elicit intergovernmental cooperation among local governments in our metropolitan areas.

The political base of the active involvement of the national government in metropolitan and urban affairs must be emphasized. One could conclude from the cries of "home rule" and "states rights" that the state and national governments are hostile foreign powers. We should remember that from the beginning of our history, individuals and groups have habitually and constitutionally turned to other governments, and within a government to other branches and agencies, whenever they have been unable to get what they want from the particular level or agency with which they first dealt. In fact, there are interests within our local communities, such as organized labor, racial and ethnic groups, and many influential businessmen and professional people, whose orientation is typically national. They find it easier and more natural to look to state and federal governments to satisfy their interests directly or, at least, to influence local organizations of concern to them. Thus either the state or national government may, in their view, be closer to the people than local government. **6** Therefore, the governance of metropolitan America will be a mixture of the actions of public and private groups. Within the public sector, it will be a mixture of federal, state, and local governmental actions.

Under these circumstances, conflict and disagreement in metropolitan governance would not be eliminated, and neither would the need for cooperation and coordination, even if all local governments within each metropolitan area were consolidated. Furthermore, in most metropolitan areas, certainly for the larger more heterogeneous, multicounty, in some instances multistate, metropolitan areas such consolidation of local government is not likely to occur.

On the other hand, local government as now organized in metropolitan areas is unable to execute programs of the federal and state governments on a regional basis, much less to participate as an equal partner in formulating programs and in adapting them to local needs, desires, and conditions.

7 Concomitant with the thrust toward metropolitanization is another powerful thrust toward smaller areas where influence, control, and other objectives of political participation may be realized.

Although either neighborhood decentralization or metropolitan centralization of certain governmental activities (or both) may be undesirable, a movement in both directions at the same time is not necessarily contradictory. Movement in both directions at once is the essence of federalism —I say directions because we are certainly not compelled by federal principles to seek continuously for either smaller or larger units of political decision making.

The creation or development of either a regional agency or a number of neighborhood agencies, or both, will increase the decision making a system of metropolitan governance. A regional agency should reduce the dysfunctional effects of the governmental fragmentation of the metropolitan area. Neighborhood agencies, along with the continued existence of relatively small suburban municipalities, should reduce the dysfunctional effects of very large governments now existing or soon to be created. All this makes the problem of structural linkages among governments in and out of the metropolitan area very crucial.

8 Linkages between municipal government and neighborhood governments.

Some social reformers and activists want no link between the neighborhoods and city hall. Nothing less than the breaking up of the big city into many autonomous governments will satisfy them. Undoubtedly, others want nothing that suggests a division of authority between the city government and organized groups in subareas of the city. Neither of these will be satisfied with the changes that are already occurring in local government or with those that are beginning to be proposed.

Certainly, in some parts of the country there will be varying degrees of decentralization, but it will be done by, and not to, local leaders and municipal officials. We are still not out of the period of "maximum feasible misunderstanding," although it is now clear that change will have to come about through normal political means.

A new charter will be drafted in the next few years for New York City, and it is very likely that some form of neighborhood or community government will be created. It would be unfortunate if it were decided that New York City should be governed like London. There are no formal linkages between the London boroughs and the Greater London Council.[2] To use London as a model would destroy the only integrative force in New York City—the mayor. There are persons and groups who would like to do so —but without strong citywide leadership the communites would be helpless yet warring neighbors.

The problem is to devise an acceptable scheme of political and administrative decentralization that will operate within the context of a large city. Many proposals have already been made.[3] Two California proposals illustrate how linkages can be established between neighborhoods and city halls.

In 1969 the Los Angeles City Charter Commission provided in its recommended charter for

> the formation of self-initiating neighborhood organizations, [with populations between 5,000 and 30,000] with an elected board and an appointed neighborman, as a new institutional mechanism for communicating neighborhood needs and goals, involving citizens in city affairs, and reducing feelings of alienation.[4]

A neighborman would be the formal link among the elective neighborhood board, the residents of the neighborhood, and city hall. He would be selected by the neighborhood board, exempt from civil service, and paid by the city a salary no less "than the salary of a field deputy of a member of the [city] council."

The neighborhood board, of not less than seven members, elected by and from the registered voters of the neighborhood, could draw up bills of complaints and otherwise advise and recommend action to the appropriate public authorities. It would be the duty of the neighborman to follow up on the action of the neighborhood board.

There would be a formal linkage, then, between neighborhood and city hall. In addition, many informal relationships will develop not only between city hall and individual neighbormen, but probably among neighbormen and therefore between them as a group and city hall.

Another relevant proposal, lost for a dozen years on the library shelves, was made by the late Don Larson in his study of city–county consolidation for Sacramento. The feature of primary interest is the formal linkage, and the other possible informal linkages, between the general government of the area and the governments of subunits. The Sacramento proposal is illustrative of the many ways in which this might be done in a large city or complex metropolitan area.

Larson proposed to consolidate the Sacramento city and county governments under a metropolitan council of eleven members—six to be elected at large and five by districts or boroughs. In addition to serving as election districts for members of the Metropolitan Council, each borough would elect a Borough Council of five members.

> The Borough Council, as a unit, would be essentially a formal advisory link between the people of each area and the Metropolitan Council. To put teeth into this function, the charter should provide that any request or recommendation made by resolution of a Borough Council would have an automatic place upon the agenda of the next Metropolitan Council Meeting.[5]

The Borough Council would also provide another official bridge, in that the chairman of each council would serve on an eleven-member Metropolitan Planning Commission, and the other four members of each council would serve on one of the other metropolitan boards—Parks and Recreation, Health and Welfare, Public Works, and Public Safety.

The boroughs were also envisaged as administrative units, with sub-city halls or sub-civic centers, where agents of the metropolitan government could dispense services and as quasi-autonomous units to which government functions could be decentralized. Even in the 1950s, neighborhoods were not overlooked. Larson pointed out the possibility that even the boroughs might in time be broken up into neighborhoods with:

neighborhood councils which would be defined as smaller advisory or action organizations covering several square miles and a few thousand people.[6]

I have quoted from the Sacramento Report to help bring it down from the library shelves and once again into public view. Our organizational imagination is limited, and it is important that we not overlook a single proposal that addresses the problem of linking organizations in metropolitan areas.

If the ward or district system is used to elect members of the local legislative body, a link between the people living within the subarea and the central government is automatically provided. The desirability of making a district councilman a little mayor of his district is an open question. But if this approach is taken, it still will not provide for formally organized participation at the neighborhood level, unless the size of city councils is drastically enlarged.

9 Linkages among governments at the metropolitan or regional level.

During the past decade, with the open entrance of the national government into metropolitan affairs, and with increased interest in metropolitan planning on the part of local officials, the prospect of formal metropolitan decision making and execution is brighter than ever. Most local officials, but not all, insist that such governmental arrangements permit them to participate in the making and administration of metropolitan policies. On the other hand, some local officials in many metropolitan areas, and most local officials in a few metropolitan areas, favor a directly elected metropolitan body, with no formal linkages to city and county governments.

Insistence upon a directly elected regional government will make it impossible to develop a formal and workable scheme of metropolitan governance in most of our large and complex metropolitan areas. The Twin City Region in Minnesota is an exception—a referendum would probably not be required, and almost all local officials in that area favor direct elections.

In the San Francisco Bay Area the issue seems to be drawn sharply, with strong combatants who are now in agreement that there should be some form of multi-purpose but limited regional government.

The Bay Area has two large (or at least vocal) groups, heterogeneous in their make-up, one of which has taken a firm stand in favor of a directly elected regional government, while the other supports the creation of a regional governing body selected by and from elected city and county officials. Bills have been introduced in each session of the legislature since 1969 to create a multipurpose regional agency along each or both of these lines. In 1971 high political leadership in both the Legislature and in the Association of Bay Area Governments (ABAG) developed and sponsored a compromise bill to create a limited-purpose but wide-ranging regional agency. The governing body would have consisted of members directly elected by districts, members elected by and from city councilmen and county supervisors, and three members elected by and from the members of the boards of three regional special agencies.

I want to argue that, apart from the political realism of a compromise, the proposal to mix the two bases of representation—direct election, and representation of local governments—deserves consideration on its own merits:

(1) Mayors, city councilmen, and county supervisors should participate in regional policy making through membership on the governing body, because

a. They represent tough, ongoing, legitimate local governments with organizational and representational interests in metropolitan affairs;

b. Cities and counties are more likely to cooperate by willingly carrying out regionally adopted policies, if they participate in the formulation and adoption of regional policies; and

c. City and county officials can probably defeat any other proposal in a referendum.

(2) It is not true, however, that all interests within a metropolitan region such as the San Francisco Bay Area are represented by mayors, councilmen, and county supervisors. At least it is a matter to be inquired into. Otherwise, one must hold that everyone is virtually represented under whatever system is in effect.

(3) Direct election from districts, as a means of supplementing mayors, city councilmen and county supervisors on the governing body, can increase the representativeness of the regional agency. Not only is a combination of direct election with representation of local governments a means of obtaining the virtues of both systems, it is actually likely to increase the representation of various minority groups—such as blacks, Mexican-Americans, conservationists, and Democrats.[7]

In any event, the presence of city and county officials on the regional governing body would provide formal linkages to city and county governments. Steps should also be taken to link state and federal governments into the governance of the metropolitan region.

10 Minority representation may be enhanced by a mixed system of representation on the regional governing body.

A mixed system would provide representation of groups in the region that might not be represented among the city and county officials selected to sit on a regional governing body. Suggesting that the ABAG system of representation needs to be supplemented is, however, in no way an admission that it needs to be replaced.

But direct election alone is not likely to assure the widespread election of blacks and other members of minorities. The division of the Bay Area into thirty-six electoral districts would yield districts of 123,500 inhabitants. If the population of the Bay Area increased as projected, the average population of regional election districts will increase to 170,000 or more inhabitants within ten to fifteen years. Such districts would be small when compared with State Assembly districts, but they would still be relatively large. The problem of size is compounded by the unknown factor of where the district boundaries are to be drawn.

Based on districts of 123,500 people, one must conclude it to be unlikely that more than two blacks would be elected from the nine districts in Alameda County; or more than one, if any, in Contra Costa County. Perhaps one member representing Mexican-Americans would be found among the eight representatives elected from Santa Clara County. Probably two members of minority groups would be elected out of six in San Francisco. None would be elected in Marin, Sonoma, Napa, and Solano counties. Thus only six out of thirty-six directly elected members might be expected to be blacks and Mexican-Americans.

The number could be increased if there were also city and county representation on the regional governing body. Perhaps there would be no increase in the proportion of such members, but twelve out of seventy-two provide better representation than six out of thirty-six. There will be more voices to speak, more bodies to participate in committee work, and more hands to help or to listen to constituents.

Under a system where cities and counties were also represented, it would be possible to have minority group members, elected to the regional body by the city councils of at least San Francisco, Oakland, Berkeley, and Richmond. Such a selection from the Alameda County Board of Supervisors is not at all unimaginable. And the likelihood increases with time. Undoubtedly there would be already more Black representatives to the ABAG General Assembly and Executive Committee if black members of city councils and boards of supervisors had shown greater interest in participating in regional affairs.

11 Supreme Court decisions, agitation for neighborhood government, and widespread uneasiness about the quality and democracy of our system of local government, suggest the need for a systematic reevaluation of the theoretical bases of local governmental structure.

Regardless of whether Mr. Justice Frankfurter was correct or not in warning the Court that it was being asked by the plaintiffs in *Baker v. Carr* "to choose among competing theories of political philosophy—in order to establish an appropriate form of government,"—we outside the Court must face that choice in adapting local government from the neighborhood to the region to current expectations and perceptions of justice, democracy, effectiveness, security, and community.

12 This task must be approached with full realization that it is extraordinarily complex.

Local governments and politics are systems of social organization interdependent upon other overlapping social systems, some with territorial imperatives smaller than that of the local government, and with many spilling over into the larger and more inclusive society. Local government is not socially autonomous, if indeed any institution is, and its capabilities are often limited by the behavior of other institutions within its environment. Any conservationist should understand this ecological truism.

As an institution, local government is both tough and delicate. Its toughness has been demonstrated by the proliferation and survival of thousands of local governmental units, and by the slowness of structural reform. It is a delicate institution, however, that can be replaced or bypassed by impatient advocates of any given goal—hence, the easy creation of special districts for the special purposes of special groups. Given such pressures, governments could wither away, while remaining alive only in a most formal sense.

Even more terrifying is the possibility of destroying the important role of city governments, a role being assumed increasingly by county governments, of managing the resolution of conflict within the community—at least of providing a legitimate place for attempts to resolve conflict. This role has inestimable symbolic value.

The danger is present and great that local government and the associated local political system will be converted into an engine to stifle dissent and to manage conformity. It would then cease to be a general government and become in fact a very special kind of special authority. There is great danger today that extremists of either side could bring this about.

Under these circumstances, and with the full realization that structural reforms are important, but not all-important, we should pick up where the Supreme Court, perhaps properly and wisely, left off.[8] What kind of system or systems of representation do we want? What are likely to be the consequences of the continued use, or increased use, of discontinuance, or modification of the appointed executive, elected executive, small council, nonpartisan elections, local elections isolated from state and national elections? Do we know, for instance, that the manager plan is necessarily incompatible with a large partisan council elected by districts? How a responsive and responsible reevaluation can be staged is another matter. But clearly many features of local government and politics are being evaluated without reference to each other, or to the system as a whole. In the meantime local government as we have known it may actually be withering away.

NOTES

This is a revised version of a paper prepared while the author was a visiting scholar at the National Municipal League. Other versions have been published in the *Civic Review,* March, 1970, and in *Public Affairs Report* (Institute of Governmental Studies, University of California, Berkeley), April, 1970.

1   Alex Gottfried, "Political Machines," *International Encyclopedia of the Social Sciences* (New York: Macmillan and Free Press), vol. 12, p. 252.

2   Committee for Economic Development recommends *Reshaping Government in Metropolitan Areas* (New York, 1970) a combination of regional centralization and community decentralization. However, as in London, the regional governing body would consist only of elected persons directly and would have no formal linkage to community governments.

3   Donna E. Shalala, *Neighborhood Governance—Issues and Proposals* (New York: The American Jewish Committee, 1971). See for further examination of proposals.

4   *City Government for the Future* (Los Angeles: City Charter Commission, 1969), p. 19.

5   Don Larson, *The Government of Metropolitan Sacramento* (Chicago: Public Administration, 1957), p. 115.

6   *Ibid.,* p. 132

7   Stanley Scott and John C. Bollens, *Governing a Metropolitan Region: The San Francisco Bay Area,* (Berkeley: 1968), p. 158. The authors show that the city and county representatives in the Association of Bay Area Governments are "only thirty-seven percent Democratic, representing a population that is over sixty percent Democratic."

The Suburb as a Model for Neighborhood Control

David C. Perry

Recent patterns of urban politics exhibit an increasing emphasis on neighborhood control of central city ghettos as one of the basic strategies by which to achieve racial equality in the United States. This essay assesses the viability of the strategy of neighborhood control as a means for increasing the power of inner city residents over their own affairs. I argue here that such a strategy for central city ghettos implies, to a large degree, the shifting of the suburban model of community resources to the inner city. To put the argument most starkly, given the present alignment of the resources or determinants of control, neighborhood control is a viable option for suburbs but is, by and large, a potentially futile goal for most ghettos. The suburbs, in general, exhibit a much greater share of the determinants of neighborhood control. These determinants are: (1) cultural identity in order to exhibit racial and ethnic equality and acceptance; (2) economic resources in order to provide fiscal solvency and entrepreneurial competitiveness; and (3) governmental jurisdictions and structures that provide the potential for an efficacious articulation of resident demands.

Before proceeding any further, it should be emphasized that suburbs are not viewed here as universally affluent and racially secure communities. Suburbs do not present a uniform picture of racial assimilation,[1] and the fiscal landscape of the suburbs is characterized by recurring patterns of rich, poor, and middle income jurisdictions. In fact the surban rings of many metropolitan areas show fiscal disparities greater than those which exist between central cities and suburbs.[2] However, even with these "cracks in the suburban window"[3] the suburbs are much more capable of addressing the community problems of the 1970s than are the ghettos of the central city.

Cultural Identity

The suburban community, by nature, is an individual as well as a collective community of choice. For the individual it represents a preferable place of residence. Collectively it has been institutionalized as a goal of the middle class or upper class within the success structure of the euphemistic American dream pattern. As a result, this section of the essay cannot avoid describing the individual residents or groups of residents, who can escape from the ghetto and remove themselves to the suburbs, as having the ability of ultimate control over a neighborhood they do not prefer to live in. In line with this reasoning, if there is one word which best characterizes the growth of metropolitan areas in the United States, it is "spread." Suburban spread stands not only for the rejection of ghettos but also for the rejection of the central city municipalities which house ghetto communities. The ghetto, on the other hand, does not represent a community of choice. It is a place city dwellers move from but not a place to which suburbanites move. The 1970 census indicates that the white exodus to the suburbs and the migration of racial minorities to the center cities increased in intensity during the 1960s. The ghetto areas of our cities are becoming increasingly black. Recent studies in such diverse areas as Atlanta, Detroit, Los Angeles, New York,[4] Rochester,[5] and Austin[6] have found that seventy per cent or better of the residents of what has been termed the "ghetto" communities are nonwhite. Along with its black identity, the urban ghetto demonstrates an unemployment rate two and one-half times the national average and median earnings for its employed as less than $100 per week[7] which still makes the family income of the black family only sixty-three percent of the white median family incomes.[8] Even with the appropriate credentials can any person or group move to the suburbs? Can the black Americans living in the institutionalized deprivation of urban ghettos exercise the ultimate control over such communities by rejecting them and choosing to live elsewhere?

Urban scholars, such as Daniel P. Moynihan, have argued that "Outside the South, young husband–wife Negro families have 99 per cent of the income of whites! . . . Thus, it may be this ancient gap is closing."[9] Yet the credentials of income and education may not be enough to provide the ghetto resident with the credentials necessary to apply the ultimate element of control over his ghetto community, namely rejecting it. When the black ghettoite leaves the inner city he takes not only his income and his education, but he takes also his black identity. Thus while scholars such as Moynihan might argue that the income of blacks has increased relative to whites, the fact that suburbs are less black today than they were ten years ago cannot be escaped.[10]

Coupled with the ghetto being a depressed community of black identity is the reinforcing tradition of integration as it is practiced in the United States. It does not take a deep reading of American history to see that integration has been, for the most part, a substantial failure. Our spotty records in the areas of equal job opportunity, education, and housing can be explained from a variety of vantage points. However, the basic problem seems to be with what Anthony Downs would calls the tendency to maintain a kind of white "cultural dominance."

Such dominance does not mean ethnic purity. In fact, Downs points out that "(a) vast majority of whites of all income groups would be willing to . . . live in integrated neighborhoods, *as long as they were sure that the white group concerned would remain in the majority* in those facilities or areas."[11] Thus, while integration does not mean racial or ethnic homogenization, it does mean that white Americans

—like most other middle-class citizens of any race—want to be sure that the social, cultural, and economic milieu and values of their own group dominate their own residential environment and the educational environment of their children. This desire in trun springs from the typical middle-class belief of all racial groups that everyday life should be primarily a *value-reinforcing* experience for both adults and children, rather than primarily a *value-alerting* one.[12]

The drive for black identity runs at cross purposes to the value maintaining tradition of integration, which pointedly argues for equality for members of minority groups of different races based on a *lack* of recognition of their basic cultural differences: namely their color, their racial heritage, and (traditionally) their language. We have learned through the past decade of riots, busing controversies, court battles, and demonstrations that people continue to retain their eyesight, their hearing, and their cultures and, as a result, continue to play the politics of integration simply because they do see differences between themselves and other races. In short, it can be argued that the politics of integration has failed for both whites and blacks because, no matter how hard people try, they cannot deny their respective cultures and their desires to preserve their different identities.

Given the propensity for a kind of white cultural dominance,[13] it is highly unrealistic to assume that blacks residing in ghettos have the same potential as suburbanites to control their own communities, either by collectively rejecting them for the suburbs or by remaining and reshaping them on their own terms. The struggle for black community control at this level is far greater than the struggle for equal jobs or equal housing, or the like. It is a cultural struggle for community identity. The community in question is the ghetto, and the ghetto is the place where value altering black men can live. Whether or not black people will be allowed to control it is not simply black Americans' choice—it is also white society's choice.

As the next two sections will explicate, neighborhood control and the potential for such control rests in the suburbs. The suburbs, even though a diverse group of jurisdictions at best, are communities of choice and the product of cultural dominance as practiced in middle class America.[14] Here neighborhood control can be exercised without a basic threat to the maintenance of acceptable life style values because the residents in suburbs have proved by their mobility and their acceptance into the community that they are value maintaining. With these concluding comments, this essay will now move from the present discussion of the residential composition of suburbs and ghettos to the institutional composition of these communities—namely their economic resources and governmental structures.

Resources

This section sets out to demonstrate that white America has taken to the suburbs not only the dominant culture but also the political and economic power needed to sustain and protect its life style. In essence, it can be strongly argued that the suburbs provide the present day home and future potential for neighborhood control. On the other hand, the ghettos of the inner city, with its people's lack of tradition for self-control of their individual lives, much less their communities, and with a waning power base (political or economic), are not, with some notable exceptions, likely places for successful experiments in community control.

An elementary fact in economic life, which needs little explication here, is that a community dependent upon a stagnant or diminishing economic base is in serious trouble of maintaining itself, much less renewing itself. Between 1958 and 1963 the central cities of the thirty most populous metropolitan areas in the nation lost a net total of 33,000 jobs while the suburbs picked up a net total of 1.29 million jobs. (See Table I). Wilfred Lewis of the National Planning Association estimated that the fifteen largest central cities in the nation lost 195,000 jobs directly to their suburbs.[15] At the same time, as Table I indicates, the loss in manufacturing and wholesale jobs was almost made up by the increase in retail and service sectors.

Sar A. Levitan points out that the problem with these new jobs in the central city is that they

> are held by commuters from suburban rings rather than by central city residents. One explanation is that many low-skilled manufacturing jobs have moved to the suburbs, being replaced by white collar jobs for which the residents of central city are not qualified . . . [Another] . . . more valid explanation . . . lies in the qualitative deterioraton of the labor force. The inflow of poorly educated rural Negroes and the exodus of better educated middle class whites and blacks may have resulted in a lower quality labor force in the central city.[17]

Recent data seem to bear Levitan's thesis out. Sixty-two percent of all nonwhite families living in central cities reside in ghettos. Such areas contain fifty percent of all nonwhite unemployed and, more importantly, 716,000 qualitatively underemployed nonwhite residents.[18]

The measure of the nation's response to such a resource crisis in communities has been less than impressive and, at the same time, predictable given the existence of cultural dominance.

> Just before Richard Nixon was inaugurated President, his counselor Daniel P. Moynihan gave him a "Memorandum for the President on the Position of Negroes." The memorandum offered the President the following advice: "The Negro lower class must be dissolved by transforming it into a stable working class population." It is "the low-income marginally employed, poorly educated, disorganized slum dwellers," whom black extremists use to threaten white society with the prospects of mass arson and pillage.[19]

TABLE I
CHANGE IN EMPLOYMENT DISTRIBUTION IN THIRTY LARGE METROPOLITAN AREAS FROM 1958 TO 1963[16]

	Thousands		Percentage	
	Central City	Suburbs	Central City	Suburbs
Manufacturing	−263	393	−6.2	13.4
Wholesale	− 48	143	−3.8	47.5
Retail	108	556	5.1	45.7
Services	173	205	13.9	46.7
Total	− 30	1297	9.0	153.3

The answer to such a problem for Moynihan is to employ these people as "truck drivers, mail carriers, assembly line workers—people with dignity, purpose and, in the United States, a very good standard of living indeed."[20] What this position neglects to add is that the real wages of assembly line factory workers have declined relative to the price of the goods they buy. At the same time black residents of the inner city find themselves without the new or old jobs which provide an adequate income or resource base.

An even smaller number of blacks own their businesses. In urban areas exceeding 50,000 in population, blacks own approximately five percent of the businesses, although they comprise one-quarter of the population. In the ghetto the distribution of minority owned businesses becomes even more bleak. Here approximately three-quarters of the families are black and yet blacks own less than one-fourth of all the businesses. Of all black businesses

> a third . . . are single proprietorships with no employees and an equal proportion have less than ten employees. There are only a handful of larger black-owned businesses and few of these are located in ghetto areas.[21]

At the same time, central cities have not fared well in the service sector.

> Where the central cities of the 37 largest metropolitan areas accounted for 63% of all retail sales in the metropolitan area in 1958, they accounted for only 49% of such sales in 1967. During te 1958–1967 period retail sales increased at a real rate of 12.6% in the central cities . . . while their relative suburbs had retail sales increases of 105.8%.[22]

All this has occurred as high cost citizens, demanding more of the tax resources of the public sector, have increased the size of urban ghettos. There is strong evidence that the central cities have a much higher percentage of the urban poor than do the suburbs. A special study of the Bureau of the Census shows that of the 12.2 million persons at the poverty level and below living in all metropolitan areas, 8.3 million are in central city ghettos and 4.9 million live in the suburbs. Hence a full fourteen percent of the central city population are poor, high-cost citizens while only seven percent of the suburban population make similar demands.[23] The impact of such a concentration of poor in our central cities is reflected in seventeen of the emtropolitan areas where suburban family incomes exceed central city incomes by twenty-five percent.[24] The combination of lower incomes and higher demands for services in the central city has resulted in an increased tax strain on the central city income. In

1966–1967 taxes were six and one-tenth percent of personal income in the central cities of the thirty-seven largest metropolitan areas and only four and three-tenths percent of personal incomes in the suburbs.[25]

The data in this section lead the somewhat tautological conclusion that, compared to the suburbs, the lack of resources in the central cities, as evidenced by the increased significance of ghettos in general and black ghettoites in particular, leads to a relatively high demand for community renewal. The factors discussed here are increased evidence of the constant place of the ghetto as a community where people are allowed to live but whose needs preclude actual or potential control. The local resource potential they need to reject their community through renewing their life style, is to be whisked away to the suburbs. As such, the suburbs stand for much more viable places for cmmunity control than the ghettos. In sum, the present intercommunity reality will allow people to live in a ghetto and hence allow them a sense of community, but it allows the residents increasingly less potential and actual control.

Government: Jurisdictions and Structures

If it can be accepted that ghetto communities are by and large robbed of equal identities and resource bases, it can be asserted that the intergovernmental mix of jurisdictions and structures has not been helpful to the struggle for inner city community control. Neighborhoods in central cities do not possess a legal, jurisdictional identity and thus have little legitimate basis upon which to pin any real community control. By contrast, suburbs have legal entities with at least the potential for community control. The better off suburbs exhibit their control by exclusive zoning and first rate public schools, offsetting the need to raise local taxes by relying on their accustomed disproportion share of state aid. The capacity of the suburbs to control is also reflected in the pattern of governmental structures they select. The typical suburb, as contrasted with the inner city neighborhood, can be a council-manager system, a nonpartisan government, have elections at-large, civil employment on the basis of merit—in short, the reform or progressive local government package. The reform structure, as most analysts now agree, results in relatively low cost middle class, conservative, or protectionist government. The political conflict and rhetoric is low, except in unusual cases such as bond issues, fluoridation referenda, or tax increases. The government quietly and efficiently acts out the dominant ideology, the ideology that keeps the roads repaired, gets the kids into good colleges, keeps out the riffraff, and avoids trouble. Suburban government is responsive to the dominant middle class ideology. The suburbanites, thereby, do have a much greater level of community control than do central city residents.

By contrast, central cities are dominated by two primary interests: partisan political and bureaucratic. The partisan political pattern is characterized by patronage, ethnic coalitions, honest graft. The bureaucratic pattern is characterized by bigness, administrative centralization, professional and technical standards, and, most recently, public unionization. The combination of the partisan political and the bureaucratic patterns found in the central cities of the major metropolitan areas of the United States is such that large numbers of racial minorities living in highly concentrated areas view city government—as reflected by police, schools, welfare agencies, and hospitals—as unresponsive, unavailable, rule oriented, and repressive. If the city bureaucracies are controlled politically it certainly is not by the black, Mexican-American or Puerto Rican neighborhoods. These bureaucracies may be controlled by the partisan political system, as in Chicago, and be moderately responsive to the special concerns of the racial ghettos. The city bureaucracies may not be controlled by the political system and may simply be self-policing public service fiefdoms. For a variety of reasons the suburbs are better able to control their bureaucracies than are the central cities. It may also be that suburban middle class norms more nearly match public service bureaucracy norms, and therefore the bureaucracy appears more responsive. Either way, neighborhood control is more a suburban than a central city phenomenon. The difference can be characterized by the simplistic, though usually true, adage: In the ghetto Johnny steals a car, in the suburb Johnny borrows one.

Historically, the core city and suburbs can be depicted as a change from the relatively socially balanced center city municipality to the new lopsided municipality of the surburbs, comprised of narrow gauged socially select constituencies. The political leaderships have had to respond accordingly. This political transformation becomes even more ominous because our highly decentralized system of government historically has relied almost entirely on the cohesive powers of the municipality to hold together the highly segregated components of our urban populations. Moreover, the nation has leaned heavily on the local tax base in general and the property tax in particular for financing domestic needs.[26]

The dispersal of governmental jurisdiction has been primarily along geographic lines, but population movements have made it increasingly along income and race lines, which are most readily apparent in the Northeast and Midwest. At the same time it is not a visible pattern in the Southwest, where cities, such as Houston, San Antonio, or Austin, all show large sectors of middle class white sub-communities. The few successful annexation experiments of the Southwest cannot wipe away the plight of most central city municipalities and the relative jurisdictional affluence of most suburbs. The central cities, with tax resources increasing at a decreasing rate, are in no position to service the increasing numbers of high cost citizenry which compose their ghettos. Further evidence of the plight of central city municipalities and their

> . . . concentration of high cost citizenry . . . is dramatically underscored by public welfare statistics. For example, 27 per cent of Maryland's population is located in Baltimore, yet 72 per cent of Maryland's AFDC expenditures is to be found in that city. By the same token, Boston, with 14 per cent of Massachusetts' population, accounts for 40 per cent of that state's AFDC expenditure.[27]

This fact, coupled with such public service demands as the central cities' substantially higher public safety problems,[28] public transportation problems, and the like, has overburdened the resource base of the central city relative to the suburbs. As a result the

> central cities and suburbs continue to specialize in noneducational and educational finances respectively. Central cities only devote 34% of their taxes and expenditures to education while suburban areas devote 59% of their taxes and expenditures for educational purposes.[29]

The Federal and State aid complex has been far from responsive to this dilemma. For example, in the area of ". . . education central cities receive 38% of their total intergovernmental aid in the are of education while suburbs receive 64% of their aid for education."[30]

Suburbs can, by their nature, offer such luxuries as quality education, while central cities must provide for changing needs with decreasing resources. Central cities are always legally constituted municipalities and, as general service governments, are mandated within the guidelines of their respective states, to provide a broad spectrum, noneducational services regardless of whether the majority of the residents demand such a service or not.[31] Suburbs, on the other hand, demonstrate

> . . . considerable variation within metropolitan areas in the nature of local systems. In some, the areas outside the central city contains no municipal government; school districts and counties are the principal jurisdictions. In others, the landscape surrounding the central city is dotted with numerous incorporated municipalities. The existence of special districts, or the lack thereof, depends upon State laws and local opportunities.[32]

While the incorporation of central cities has helped states side step the political problems of the pressing social issues of the cities, the same option to incorporate has protected suburban communities from being annexed into the overburdened quagmire of the central city.

Since the turn of the century we have witnessed a sharp increase in municipalities in the suburbs. Up until World War II this increase was primarily due to tough state laws regarding annexation and extremely easy regulations regarding incorporation.[33] Thus, suburbs have been given substantial leeway with regard to the type of service tax structure they prefer, while central cities have been historically bound without similar structural options. The end results has been the incorporation of three-quarters of all metropolitan residents. Suburban municipalities comprise the vast majority of these metropolitan municipalities and have contributed to the tangled balkanization of the governmental structure of metropolitan areas. (See Table II) They stand as the end result of structural community control —as protective enclaves from the black and the poor of the central city. As Table II indicates, small and highly select numbers of suburban people (less than three percent of the total metropolitan population) have set up better than one-half of the municipal governments.

Whether this protective cafeteria of governmental options for community management will be the eventual downfall of suburban communities, as many policy analysts argue, is still open to question. What is not open to question is the fact that black ghetto enclaves within the municipal central city are largely foreclosed from similar formal structural options or choices in the suburbs.

Such an emphasis on suburban pluralism has been justified in a variety of ways. First, and most simply, some argue that the suburban special district or small government is critical to accurate decisions that could not

TABLE II
THE NUMBERS AND POPULATIONS OF METROPOLITAN MUNICIPALITIES IN 1967[34]

Population of Municipalities	Number and Percentage of Municipalities		Population and Percentage of Municipalities (1000)	
50,000 or more	314	6.30	64,044	72.58
25,000 to 49,999	212	4.25	7421	8.40
10,000 to 24,999	505	10.15	7805	8.84
5000 to 9999	586	13.77	4159	4.71
2500 to 4999	666	13.38	2356	2.66
1000 to 2499	1032	20.74	1675	1.90
Less than 1000	1662	33.39	783	.88
Total	4977	101.98	88,243	99.97

be reached by larger governments of a general purpose nature. In fact, it is argued that suburban localities are diverse, and the highly diffuse and specialized governmental complexes of the suburban rings are responsive to such community diversity.

A more complex argument for specialized structural identity in the suburbs is that "the multiplicity of local governments offers the opportunity for 'answers' of public services to exercise their sovereignty and to choose that locality which offers the public service-taxation package that best meets their individual preferences.[35] This argument sees suburban governments presenting a highly desirable shopping basket of public service tax rate offerings for people who are free to move. Thus local governments change their smorgasbord of services to accommodate migration flows and changing demands of the "consumers." This argument is of marginal utility when generalizing about the public service structures of communities because it pays no attention to the spillover effects of public services. Of the basic twenty services a central city municipal government provides, all but four exhibit observable spillover benefits to outside central city residents. (See Table III.)

TABLE III
PUBLIC PROGRAMS CLASSIFIED ACCORDING TO BENEFIT SPILLOVERS[36]

Public Program	Significant Spillover Effects	Insignificant Spillover Effects
Local Schools	x	
Transportation	x	
Public Welfare	x	
Health and Hospitals	x	
Police		
Basic Services		x
Special Services	x	
Fire	x	x
Water Supply	x	
Sewage Disposal	x	
Refuse Collection		x
Refuse Disposal	x	
Parks and Recreation	x	
Public Housing	x	
Urban Renewal	x	
Libraries		
Basic		x
Special	x	
Air and Water Pollution	x	
Urban Planning	x	

As a result, a move to the suburbs can usually mean retaining many desirable city services without having to pay directly for those services. The obvious upshot is that the city dweller, and high cost urbanite in particular, must provide not only for his own services without the option of structural choice, but he must provide also for the relatively more affluent suburbanite. Such added bonuses make the suburban community an even more desirable place in which to reside.

Neighborhood Control—Rhetoric or Revolution?

The deterioration and blight of America's great cities will not be solved soley by neighborhood control nor will they be solved in a decade or a generation. Their solution will require an inventive mix of new governmental structures, including neighborhood control. The effective implementation of the strategy of neighborhood control will demand a keener recognition and acceptance of value altering racial differences, the design of structures that compliment these differences, and the generation of vast new resources. All these things will need to be done if we are to employ neighborhood control in the task of rebuilding the cities and providing the services essential to improving the quality of life for the cities' residents.

The modification of governmental structure is central to the solution of the urban malaise, which, up to the present, has provided the potential for neighborhood control in the suburbs but not in the inner city. The structural design that allowed for separate jurisdictional status for the suburbs is the core of the problem. Structures will need to be devised that accommodate the pressing need for inner city neighborhoods to control, as do the suburbs, those public services which bear most directly upon them. The inner city must decentralize by neighborhoods, and these neighborhoods must exercise political control over the administrative apparatus that delivers services to it. This is hardly a revolutionary notion because it is essentially the suburban model transplanted to inner city neighborhoods. While certain public services, particularly education, law enforcement, health care, and housing, will need to be decentralized, other services will still require centralization. Major city rapid transit networks and metropolitan air and water pollution control systems must be centralized. The metropolitan area of the future could, for example, resemble the design set forth in the recent report of the Council on Economic Development, which suggested a three tier urban structure somewhat on the format described here. It is also likely that some cities will opt for a decentralized inner city with a contracting format such as is found in the Lakewood Plan used in southern California. Other cities will adopt the matrix or project form of organization. The central conclusion here is that cities must invent new structural ways to meet the demands of all of their residents.

The form of decentralization and neighborhood control described here is simply a means of recognizing the legitimacy of differences in race, culture, and life-style. If the black man or the Mexican-American cannot move to the suburbs (he may not want to) he may design city services that meet his neds most directly. This may mean that city schools offer courses in black history, but that is no more unusual than suburban schools offering courses in Russian to fifth graders. City public bureaucracies will be required to modify their traditional public administration approaches to such procedures as budgeting and personnel management. Budgeting routines will be changed to deter not only how much is spent for what, but in what neighborhoods. Personnel rules and regulations will be modified to broaden the capacity of the poor and undereducated to take public service positions. Exaggerated and superfluous requirements for public employment will be modified so as to enhance the capability of government to hire and train racial minorities.

The most difficult problem to solve in urban America is financial. If inner çity neighborhoods had political and administrative control but adequate resources were not available to support their needs then political freedom would be the most hollow of victories. The most likely solution to the cities' financial problem will be based on centralized revenue gathering capacities, either at the county level or at the level of special resource gathering districts established by the state and in some cases by two or three states in combination. If revenues were gathered on a regional basis, they would have to be distributed on a neighborhood basis for those services that are highly decentralized. This will require the construction of complex formulae based on per capita and need criteria. These formulae will no doubt be the center of great political controversy, for no well-off suburb is anxious to pay for the spillover benefits they have been receiving. Thus areawide revenue gathering and neighborhood-specific distribution will probably have to be imposed either by states or the national government.

The problems of urban America are solvable. Some cities are already beginning the structural and fiscal alterations necessary to cope with their problems. The renewal of American urban life will depend on the capacities of our governments to invent and construct a future in which every neighborhood can control those public services most essential to it.

NOTES

1   The term suburb is coming to mean more than it has in the past. "... by 1968 there was a higher percentage of Negroes in poverty in the suburbs (28%) than in the cities (26%). And per capita income for Negroes in the cities was higher than in the suburbs." Gail Miller and Donald Canty, "Where the People, the Power, and the Problems are Moving: A Profile of Suburban America," City 5: 1 (Jan.–Feb., 1971), p. 13.

2   "For example, elementary school districts in Cook County, Illinois, reveal a range of about 30-to-1 in their property tax base per pupil in 1964 and various studies have reported ranges of 10-to-1 or more in the per capita tax base of municipalities within metropolitan areas." Advisory Commission on Intergovernmental Relations, *Urban American and the Federal System*, M-47. (October, 1969), pp. 10–11.

3   *Ibid.*

4   Sar A. Levitan, Garth L. Mangum, and Robert Taggart III. *Economic Opportunity in the Ghetto: The Partnership of Government and Business.* (Baltimore: The Johns Hopkins Press, 1970), p. 2.

5   David C. Perry. "Police Service in a Dual Society: A Study of the Urban Context of Police Service and its Problems in the City of Rochester, New York," Dissertation, 1970, p. 120.

6   *U. S. Censuses of Population and Housing, Austin, Texas,* U. S. Bureau of the Census. (Washington, D.C.: U. S. Government Printing Office, 1962).

7   Levitan, *op. cit.,* p. 3.

8   *Ibid.,* p. 7.

9   *Ibid.,* p. 6.

10   ACIR. *Fiscal Balance of the American Federal System: Vol. 2. Metropolitan Fiscal Disparities.* (Washingron, D.C.: U. S. Government Printing Office, 1967), p. 39. This study points out that "between 1950 and 1960 the Negro proportion of the central city rose from 12.3 to 16.7 percent but actually *dropped* from 5.2 to 4.5 percent of the SMSA population outside the central cities." These figures represent demographic trends for the 37 largest metropolitan areas in the United States.

11   Anthony Downs, "Alternative Futures of the American Ghetto," *Daedelus* (Fall, 1968), p. 1338.

12   *Ibid.*

13   Louis Knowles and Kenneth Prewitt, *Institutional Racism in America* (Englewood Cliffs, N.J.: Prentice Hall, Inc., 1969), p. 7–14. They argue that "Some form of white supremacy, both ideology and institutional arrangement, existed from the first day . . . English immigrants . . . considered themselves culturally superior to the natives they encountered." This tradition of superiority became a part and parcel of our religion through "manifest destiny" and the "white man's burden" and economically through slavery and then the rejection of the freed slaves as a viable labor force in favor of European immigrants after the Civil War. See also *Report of the National Advisory Commission on Civil Disorders* (New York: Bantam Books Inc., 1968), p. 278.

14   Downs, *op. cit.,* p. 1338 ff.

15   Levitan, *op. cit.,* p. 2–3.

16   *Census of Manufacturing, 1963* Area Statistics, U. S. Bureau of the Census, (Washington, D.C.: U. S. Government Printing Office). *Census of Business, 1958 and 1963 Wholesale Trade, Retail Trade and Surveys* U. S. Bureau of the Census (Washington D.C.: U. S. Government Printing Office).

17   Levitan, *op. cit.,* pp. 2–3.

18   *Report of the National Advisory Commission on Civil Disorders* (New York: Bantam Books, 1968), pp. 264–265.

19   William K. Tabb, *The Political Economy of the Black Ghetto* (New York: W. W. Norton and Co., Inc., 1970), p. 5.

20   Daniel P. Moynihan, "Memorandum for the President," *New York Times,* 1 March 1970, p. 69.

21   Levitan, *op. cit.,* pp. 5–6.

22   *Ibid.,* pp 5–6.

23   "Trends in Social and Economic Conditions in Metropolitan Areas," *Current Population Reports Series P-23.* Special Studies No. 27,U. S. Bureau of the Census, Washington, D.C., 1969, p. 52.

24 ACIR, *Information Bulletin,* op. cit., p. 5.

25 *Ibid.,* p. 30.

26 ACIR, *Urban America and the Federal System,* (Washington, D.C.: ACIR, October, 1969), p. 9.

27 *Ibid.,* p. 10.

28 "Central cities tend to be much more dangerous places to live in than their respective suburbs. Crime rates in the central cities (of the 37 largest metropolitan areas) were, on the average, 100% greater than those in the suburbs . . ." ACIR, *Information Bulletin, op. cit.,* p. 1.

29 ACIR, *Information Bulletin, op. cit.,* p. 1.

30 *Ibid.*

31 ACIR. *State Aid to Local Government* (Washington, D.C.: U. S. Government Printing Office, 1969), p. 8.

32 ACIR. *Fiscal Balance in the American Federal System, op. cit.,* pp. 58–59.

33 See John C. Bollens and Henry J. Schmandt. *The Metropolis: Its People, Politics and Economic Life* (New York: Harper and Row, Inc., 1965), p. 156ff. "A considerable upsurge in municipal annexation has taken place in the post-World War II years. In large part, however, its usefullness has been confined to the absorption of neighboring unincoporated urban fringe areas, many of which had developed serious service and regulatory deficiencies having repercussions both locally and elsewhere in the metropolis." p. 157.

34 *Governmental Organization,* U. S. Bureau of the Census, Census of Governments, 1967 (Washington, D.C.: Government Printing Office, 1968), p. 11.

35 ACIR. *State Aid to Local Government, op. cit.,* p. 8.

36 George F. Break, *Intergovernmental Fiscal Relations in the United States* (Washington, D.C.: Brookings Institution), p. 176.

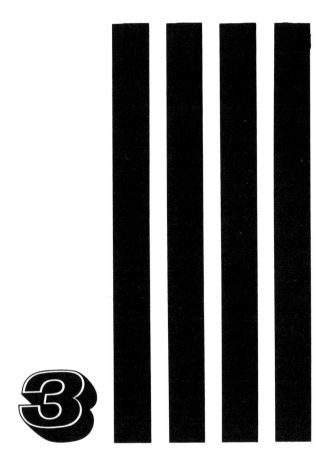

New Public Administration, the Neighborhood, and the Citizen

Street Level Bureaucracy and the Analysis of Urban Reform

Michael Lipsky

Street Level Bureaucracy

In American cities today, policemen, teachers, and welfare workers are under siege. Their critics variously charge them with being insensitive, unprepared to work with ghetto residents, incompetent, resistant to change, and racist. These accusations, directed toward individuals, are transferred to the bureaucracies in which they work.

Men and women in these bureaucratic roles deny the validity of these criticisms. They insist that they are free of racism and that they perform with professional competence under very difficult conditions. They argue that current procedures are well-designed and that it is only the lack of resources and lack of public support and understanding which prevents the successful performance of their jobs. Hence bureaucrats stress the need for higher budgets, better equipment, and higher salaries to help them do even better what they are now doing well, under the circumstances. These urban bureaucrats, are by their own testimony, the heroes of the city, performing as best they can, at considerable personal risk and under psychological strain, thankless tasks others will not do. They claim familiarity with the conditions of the urban poor that few of their critics possess and hold that they serve fairly and adequately under adverse conditions.

How are these diametrically opposed views to be reconciled? Do both sides project positions for advantage alone, or is it possible that both views may be valid from the perspective of the policy contestants? Is it possible that critics of urban bureaucracy may correctly allege bias and ineffectiveness of service, and, paradoxically at the same time, that urban bureaucrats may correctly defend themselves as unbiased in motivation and objectively responsible to bureaucratic necessities?

What is particularly ominous about this confrontation is that these street level bureaucrats, as I call them, represent American government to its citizens. They are the people citizens encounter, or are controlled by, when they seek help from the American political system. While it is true in a sense that the Federal Reserve Board has a greater impact on the lives of the poor than, say, individual welfare workers (because of the Board's influence on inflation and employment trends), it nonetheless remains that citizens perceive that it is the public employees who are most influential in shaping their lives. As ambassadors of government to the American people, and as ambassadors with particularly significant impacts upon the lives of the poor and of relatively powerless minorities, how capable are these urban bureaucrats in providing high levels of service and responding objectively to individual grievances and needs? It is one conclusion of this paper that both perspectives has some validity.

In analyzing the contemporary crisis in bureaucracy and the conflicting claims of urban bureaucrats and their nonvoluntary clients, I will focus on those urban bureaucrats whose impact on citizens' lives is both frequent and significant. Hence the concentration on street level bureaucrats: those government workers who directly interact with citizens in the regular course of their jobs whose work within the bureaucratic structure permits them a wide latitude in job performance, and whose impact on the lives of citizens is extensive. Thus, the analysis would include, for example, the patrolman on the beat, the classroom teacher, and the welfare investigator. It would be less relevant to the public school principal, who deals primarily with subordinates rather than pupils, or to the traffic cop, whose latitude in job performance is relatively restricted.

Further, I want to concentrate on ways in which street-level bureaucrats respond to conditions of stress imposed by their work environment, where such stress is relatively severe. Analytically, three kinds of stress may be readily observed in urban bureaucracies today.

1 INADEQUATE RESOURCES Street level bureaucracies are widely thought to lack sufficient organizational resources to accomplish their jobs. Classrooms are overcrowded. Large welfare caseloads prevent investigators from providing all but cursory service. The lower courts are so overburdened that judges may spend their days adjourning but never trying cases. Police forces are perpetually understaffed, particularly as the scope of alleged crime and demands for civic order increase.[1]

Insufficiency of organizational resources increases the pressures on street-level bureaucrats to make quick decisions about clients and to process cases with inadequate information and too little time to dispose of problems on their merits. While this may be said about bureaucratic decision making in general, it is particularly relevant to the problems of street level bureaucracy because individual bureaucratic behavior is subject to the influence of urban institutions. The stakes are often high—to both citizen and bureaucrat.

2 THREAT AND CHALLENGE TO AUTHORITY   The conditions under which street level bureaucrats work often include distinct physical and psychological threats. Policemen are constantly alert to danger, as are other street level bureaucrats who function in neighborhoods alien to them, or which are generally considered dangerous or characterized by high crime rates. Curiously, it may make little difference whether or not the probabilities of encountering harm are actually high, so long as people think that their jobs are risky.

Even if the probability of actual physical harm is somewhat remote, street-level bureaucrats experience threat in their inability to control the potential work related encounter. Teachers especially fear the results of loss of classroom discipline or their inability to manage a classroom. Policemen have been widely observed to ensure the deference of a suspect by anticipatory invocation of authority.

3 CONTRADICTORY OR AMBIGUOUS JOB EXPECTATIONS   Confronted with inadequate resources and threats that increase the importance of work related results, street level bureaucrats often find their difficulties exacerbated by their uncertainties concerning expectations of performance. Briefly, role expectations may be framed by peers, by bureaucratic reference groups, or by public expectations in general, or by a combination of all three.[2] Consider the rookie patrolman who, in addition to responding to his own conceptions of the policeman's role, must accommodate the demands placed upon him by (1) fellow officers in the station house who teach him how to get along and try to correct the teachings of his police academy instructors; (2) his immediate superiors who may strive for efficiency at the expense of current practices; (3) police executives who communicate expectations contradictory to station house mores; and (4) the general public, who in American cities today is likely to be divided along both class and racial lines in its expectations of police practices and behavior. One way street level bureaucrats may resolve problems related to their jobs without internal conflict is to drift to a position consistent with dominant role expectations. This resolution consistent with dominant role expectations. This resolution is denied bureaucrats working under conflicting role expectations.

Controversy over schools, police behavior, or welfare practices exacerbates of the job expectations stress conditions because it places in the spotlight of public scrutiny behavior that might otherwise remain in the shadows. These stresses result in the development of psychological and behavioral reactions that seem to widen the already existing differences between street level bureaucrats and spokesmen for the nonvoluntary clienteles. Three such developments may be mentioned here.

First, it is a common feature of organizational behavior that individuals in organizations need to develop simplifications, or some kind of shorthand by which they can make decisions quickly and expeditiously. A policeman develops simplifications that suggest to him that crimes are in the process of being committed. Teachers develop simplifications to allow them to determine which pupils are good students and which are threatening troublemakers.

This is a cliché of organizational behavior.[3] But it is highly significant and not trivial, when we recognize the conditions under which these simplifications tend to be developed in stereotypic ways with racist orientations. When a black man driving through a white neighborhood is stopped by a policeman merely because the man is black and therefore (according to the policeman's mode of simplification) suspiciously out of place, he has been stopped for good reason according to the policeman, but for racist reasons according to the aggrieved citizen. Teachers may select students for special attention or criticism because of their manner of speech, mode of dress, behavior in class, parental background, or other characteristics unrelated to their ability. Policemen, judges, and welfare investigators may be significantly influenced by symbols of deference or defiance to themselves or their authority. These signs may be related to general and generational responses to the enforced passivity of the past and unrelated to the bureaucracies or bureaucrats themselves.

Race-oriented simplifications are particularly explosive even if only a few street-level bureaucrats engage in racist name calling. Those subject to bureaucratic abuse understandably engage in the same kind of simplifying of the world that bureaucrats engage in. Thus it takes only a few racist incidents to develop and sustain the impression that overall police behavior towards blacks is discriminatory. We are truly in a crisis because greater black community solidarity and greater willingness to object to police behavior create the very conditions under which race-oriented simplifications are increasingly invoked, leading to an escalation of tension and hostility. The greater the tensions and the images of conflict in the minds of street-level bureaucrats, the more likely they will be to invoke the simplifications they think provide them with a measure of protection in their work. This increase in discrimination under tension occurs above and beyond the move overtly discriminatory attitudes that are sanctioned by the larger community and society.

The second development heightening the existing bureaucratic crises is the tendency on the part of street level bureaucrats to develop defense mechanisms that result in a distortion of the perceived reality and permits accommodation and resolution of stress tendencies.[4]

One such reaction is the tendency to segment psychologically, or fragment conceptually, the population they consider their clienteles. Some police bureaucracies have regularly dealt with black crime through this technique.[5] If one can think of black people as outside the community, then one can perform according to community standards without experiencing the stresses exerted by diverse community elements. The police riots during the 1968 Chicago Democratic Convention,[6] and more recently in various university communities, can only be understood by assuming that long-haired, white college students are thought by the police to be outside of the community that can expect to be protected by norms of due process.

Similarly, teachers reduce their own sense of stress by defining some students as uneducable or marginally educable. Early selection of some students for higher education, based upon such characteristics as the ability to speak English and class background, permits the educators to perform in their expected roles according to a more limited definition of the population to be served. Tensions in city schools and overassumptive police practices in ghetto neighborhoods are not only a function of the apparent foreignness of teachers and policemen to blacks, as Nathan Glazer has suggested.[7] The process of determining foreigness did not begin yesterday with black people. If nothing else, the labeling of whites as foreigners by blacks has been reinforced, if not inspired, by bureaucratic processes of categorizing nonvoluntary clients.

The development of tracking systems in public schools illustrates the development of institutional mechanisms for segmenting the population to be served to insure teacher more success through population redefinition.[8] This is the latent function of tracking systems. It should be noted that population redefinition, as I have described it, must find support in general community attitudes, or else cross-pressures will emerge to inhibit this development. The growing cleavage in American cities between whites and blacks may never result in the apartheid, predicted by the Kerner Commission. But subtle psychological apartheid, resulting from redefinitions of the populations served by public programs and institutions, is equally ominous and may be already accomplished.

A third development in the bureaucratic crisis is the way in which the kind of behavior described here may work to creat the very reality that people either fear or want to overcome. For example, in categorizing students as low or high achievers—in a sense predicting their capacities to achieve—a teachers may create the very simplifications of a student's potential with which he has been labeled. Recently, evidence has been presented to demonstrate that on the whole, students will perform better in school if teachers think they are bright, regardless of whether or not they are.[9] Similarly, the propensity to arrest black youngsters for petty crimes, the increasing professionalization of police forces (resulting in the recording of more minor offenses), and society's concern for clean arrest records as criteria for employment may creat a population inclined toward further illegal activity perforce if not be choice. Our society's penal institutions have been characterized as schools for criminal behavior rather than for rehabilitation. Thus we creat a class of criminal types by providing them with informal vocational training.

Not only individual teachers but schools themselves communicate expectations to students. Increasingly, educators communicate expectations to students. Increasingly, educators of disadvantaged minorities are convinced that the achievement of high-school students is directly related to the extent to which schools communicate expectations of high potential to their students. Various street academies that have grown up in New York, Newark, and other cities, the Upward Bound program, and other experimental programs for poor and ghettoized youth, are premised on the assumption that if educators behave as if they think college—and hence upward mobility—is a realistic possiblity for their students, high-school dropouts and potential dropouts will respond by developing motivation currently unsuspected by high-school personnel.

In their need to routinize and simplify in order to process work assignments, teachers, policemen, and welfare workers may be viewed as bureaucrats. Significantly, however, the work load of street level bureaucrats consists of people, who in turn are reactive to the bureaucratic process. Street-level bureaucrats, confronted with inadequate resources, threats and challenges to their authority, and contradictory or ambiguous role expectations, must develop mechanisms for reducing job-related stresses. These mechanisms, with their considerable impact on clients' futures, deserve increasing attention from students of urban affairs.

Public Policy Reform in Street-Level Bureaucracies

Although much more could be said about the stresses placed on street-level bureaucrats, the remainder of this paper will focus on the implications for public policy and for public perceptions of urban bureaucracy, by an analysis of the ways street-level bureaucrats react to problems related to specified work conditions. Where does this kind of analysis lead?

First, it may help bridge the gap between, on the one hand, allegations that street-level bureaucrats are racist, and, on the other hand, insistence by individuals working in these bureaucracies that they are free from racism. Development of perceptual simplifications and subtle redefinitions of the population to be served—both group psychological phenomena—may be undetected by bureaucracies and clientele groups. These phenomena will significantly affect both the perception of the bureaucrats, and the reactions of clienteles to the bureaucracies. Perceptual modes that assist bureaucrats in processing work and, though not developed to achieve discriminatory goals, result in discrimatory bias and may be considered a manifestation of institutional, as opposed to individual, racism. So there must be a distinction between insititutional routinized procedures that result in bias and personal prejudice.

Second, we may see the development of human relations councils, citizen review boards, special equal opportunity units, and other community relations bureaus. They may provide increased marginal access to the system for citizens. But equally important, they inhibit institutional change by permitting street-level bureaucrats to persist in behavioral patterns through their creation of special units to handle "human relations problems." These insititutional developments do not fundamentally affect general bureaucratic performance. Instead, they insulate bureaucracies from having to confront behavioral factors which results in what appears to be racist work performance. These observations particularly obtain when, as if often the case, these units lack the power to impose on the bureaucracy decisions favorable to aggrieved citizens.

Third, tracking systems, vocational schools with basically custodial functions, and other institutionalized mechanisms for predicting capacities should be recognized as a means to ease the bureaucratic burden at the expense of equal treatment and opportunity.

Fourth, the inherent limitation of human relations training (sensitivity and T-group training) for street level bureaucrats should be recognized as inadequate to their fundamental behavioral needs. Basic bureaucratic attitudes towards clients appear to be a function of the worker's background and of socialization on the job. Training designed to improve relationships with black communities must be directed toward helping bureaucrats improve performance, not toward classroom lessons on equality, which are soon forgotten.[10] The psychological forces that lead to the kinds of biased simplifications and discriminatory behavior mentioned earlier appear sufficiently powerful to suggest scepticism over the potential for changing behavior patterns through human relations training efforts.

Fifth, just as training should be encouraged that relates to job performance needs, incentives should be developed that reward successful performance, utilizing indicators of clientele assistance. While performance standards can be trivialized, avoided, or distorted through selective use of statistics, the potential utility of statistics has hardly been explored. For example, it would be entirely appropriate to develop indices for teacher success and to develop appropriate merit rewards based upon adequately assessed performance indicators. For teachers, pay raises and promotions might be based upon average reading score improvements in relation to the school or citywide average for that grade level. In some ghetto schools, this index might initially reward those teachers who minimize the extent to which their students fall behind citywide averages. Public employee unions, of course, would oppose such proposals vigorously. There is every reason to think such proposals would be strongly endorsed in experimental educational units.

To improve public bureaucracies, the American political system has moved from public service as patronage to public service retruitment through merit examination. But in American cities today administrators are frustrated because of the great difficulty in bringing talented individuals into government at high levels and introducing innovation at lower levels. Mobility in the civil service is based too little on merit. Deadwood is built into the systems, and the least talented public employees remain in public service.

These conditions have prevailed for some time. What is new to the discussion is that black educators and critics of police forces now argue that (1) merit examinations do not test abilities for certain kinds of tasks that must be performed in ghetto schools and ghetto police surveillance; and (2) on the basis of the records of ghetto schools and ghetto law enforcement practices, in many cases civil service protection cannot be justified. The society cannot afford to continue to protect civil servants, or the natural allies of the bureaucracies, at the expense of their clientele. The criticism and reevaluation of bureaucratic standards that have accompanied demands for community control are supportive of these proposals.

Sixth, this analysis is more generally supportive of proposals for radical decentralization and neighborhood control. Advocacy of neighborhood control has recently revolved around five kinds of possible changes in the present organizational arrangements. It has been variously held that neighborhood control would (1) increase loyalty to the political system by providing relatively powerless groups with access to governmental influence; (2) increase citizens' sense of well-being as a result of greater participation; (3) provide greater administrative efficiency for overly extended administrative systems; (4) increase the political responsibility and accountability of bureaucracies currently remote from popular influence; and (5) improve bureaucratic performance by altering the assumptions under which services are dispensed.[11]

The analysis of street level bureaucracy presented here has supported neighborhood control that would create new standards by which to judge improved bureaucratic performance. Specifically, it has been proposed, among other things, that the performance of policemen, teachers, and other street level bureaucrats is significantly affected by the availability of personal resources, the sense of threat which is experienced, the ambiguity of role expectations, and the diversity of potential clientele groups. Most community control proposals here are addressed to these considerations.

Recommendations for the decentralization of police forces provide an opportunity to demonstrate the applicability of these ideas. For example, it has been proposed that the police function be divided into maintaining order (such as traffic control, breaking up domestic quarrels, parade duty, etc.) and fighting crime. The former is said to be a function that could easily be performed at the neighborhood level; whereas, fighting crime, requiring both weaponry and greater technical training, might continue to be a citywide function. Such a redefinition of tasks would restore the cop to the beat and would replace city policemen by neighborhood residents who would be more sensitive to community mores and would relieve the city police of some of its least rewarding and most aggravating duties.[12] Such reorganization might reduce the stresses, resulting from the variety of duties policemen are currently asked to perform, as well as increase the resources available to the individual policeman.

Radical decentralization is also commended by this analysis because the increased homogeneity of district populations would permit greater uniformity and responsiveness on the part of the police toward its neighborhood clientele. The socioeconomic of range the new clientele would be narrower and could be coped with with greater confidence. The system would not be so constrained by competing definitions of appropriate bureaucratic methods or by competing demands on the conceptualization of service. Citywide performance standards and appropriate regulations concerning nondiscriminatory behavior could be maintained with the expectation that they would be no less honored than currently.

This analysis is further supportive of proposals for radical decentralization so that minority group employment under community control would be increased through changes in recruitment methods and so that civic employment would offer greater attraction. Increasing minority group employment in street level bureaucratic roles is not suggested here for the symbolism of minority group inclusion or for the sake of increasing minority groups opportunities (although these reasons are entirely justified). Rather, this analysis suggests that such people will be less likely to structure task-performance simplifications in sterotypic ways.

Potential clients might also have greater confidence and trust in individuals with whom they can relate and who they can assume have greater understanding of their needs. However, it is not clear to what extent such predictions are reliable. Black recruits to police bureaucracies as currently designed would undoubtedly continue to be governed by the incentive systems and job perceptions of the police force. Black patrolmen today may even be the objects of increased community hostility. But in systems encouraging increased community sensitivity, black patrolmen might thrive. The benefits of community control, perhaps like most political arrangements, may ultimately depend upon the development and arousal of political consciousness. Voter turnout is low when community participation is introduced through elections in which people have previously developed little stake or involvement (such as elections for Community Action Agency boards and school elections in New York City).[13] Similarly, the potential for greater rapport between street level bureaucrats and clients may ultimately depend upon the extent to which community involvement in the issues of community control precedes the transfer of power. Without such prior arousal, community control may provide only unrealized structural opportunities for increased community participation with greater bureaucracy–client rapport should community groups seek to influence public policy in the future.

These comments are made in full recognition that they are supportive of structural and institutional changes of considerable magnitude. If the analysis developed here is at all persuasive, then it may be said that the bureaucratic crises that I have described are built into the very structure or organizational bureaucratic life. Only structural alterations, made in response to a comprehensive analysis of the bureaucratic crisis, may be expected to be effective.

Conclusion

Let me conclude and summarize by indicating why the current situation, and this analysis, point to a continuing crisis in city politics. It is not only that antagonisms between bureaucracy and clients will continue to deepen or that black separatism will continue to place stress on street-level bureaucracies, with which they are poorly equipped to deal. In addition to these factors, we face a continuing crisis because certain modes of bureaucratic behavior effectively shield the bureaucracies from the nature of their own shortcomings.

Street level bureaucrats, by perceiving their clients to be fully responsible for their actions—as do some policemen, mental hospital workers, and welfare workers—may absolve themselves from contributing to the perpetuation of problems. Police attribution of riots to the riffraff of the ghetto provides just one illustration of this tendency.[14]

On the other hand, attributing their clients' performance to cultural or societal factors beyond the scope of human intervention also works to absolve bureaucrats from responsibility for their clients' futures.[15] While there may be some validity to both modes of perception, the truth (as it often does) lies somewhere in between. Meanwhile, both modes of perception function to trivialize the interaction between bureaucrat and client at the expense of responsibility.

Changing role expectations provides another mechanism that may shield street-level bureaucrats from recognizing the impact of their actions. This may take at least two forms. Bureaucrats may try to influence public expectations of their jobs in order to convince the public of their good intentions under difficult conditions. Or they may seek role redefinition in such a way as to permit job performance according to role expectations in some limited way. The teacher who explains that "I can't teach them all; so I will try to teach the bright ones," is attempting to foster an image of fulfilling role expectations in a limited way. While this may be one way to utilize scarce resources, and deserves some sympathy, it should be recognized that such tendencies deflect pressures away from providing for more adequate routine treatment of clients.

But perhaps most significantly, it is difficult for street level bureaucrats to acknowledge the impact of their behavior on clients because their very ability to function in bureaucratic roles depends upon routines, simplifications, and other psychological mechanisms to reduce stress. Under such circumstances, attacks upon the substance or content of these reactions to job stress may be interpreted as criticisms of the basic requirements of job performance. As such, the criticisms are interpreted as ignorant or inaccurate.

Even if street level bureaucrats are prepared to accept the substance of criticisms, they are likely to view them as Utopian in view of the difficulties of their jobs. They may respond by affirming the justice of criticism in theory but reject the criticism as inapplicable in the real world. Because they (and we) cannot imagine a world in which bureaucratic simplifications do not take place, they reject the criticism entirely.

This inability to recognize or deal with substantive criticism is reinforced by the fact that street level bureaucrats find the validity of their simplifications and routines confirmed by their selective perception of the evidence. Not only do the self-fulfilling prophecies mentioned earlier confirm these operations, but also street-level bureaucrats affirm their own judgments because they depend upon routines that offer a measure of security and because they are unfamiliar with alternative procedures that might free them to act differently. That fact that street level bureaucrats are in some sense shielded from awareness of the impact of their job-related behavior insures the crisis between street level bureaucrats and their clients will continue even while administrators in these bureacracies loudly proclaim the initiation of various programs to improve community relations, reduce tensions among clientele groups, and provide token measures of representation for clientele groups on lower level policy making boards.

The shelter from criticism may contribute to the conservative tendencies of street-level bureaucracies, widely commented upon in studies of bureaucracy generally. For our purposes they may help to explain the recourse of community groups to proposals for radical change and their recognition that only relatively radical alternatives are likely to break the circle of on-the-job socialization, job stress, and reaction formation.

An illustration of relatively drastic changes is shown in the recent recruitment of idealistic college students into the police and teaching professions.[16] These individuals are not only better educated, but are presumed also to approach their new jobs with attitudes toward ghetto clients quite different from other recruits. What higher salaries, better working conditions and professionalization were unable to accomplish is being achieved on a modest level by the Selective Service System, the War in Vietnam, and the unavailability of alternative outlets for constructive participation in reforming American society. Higher salaries (which go mostly to the kind of people who would have become policemen and teachers anyway) have not previously resulted in recruitment of significantly more sensitive or skillful people, although it has been the (somewhat self-serving) recommendation for bureaucratic improvement for many years. On the contrary, the recruitment of college students, whose career expectations in the past did not include this kind of public service orientation, may accomplish the task of introducing people with the desired backgrounds to street level bureaucratic work independent of (or even in spite of) increased salaries, professionalization, seniority benefits, and the like.

It is obviously too early to evaluate these developments. The new breed of street-level bureaucrat has yet to be tested in on-the-job effectiveness, his ability to withstand the pressures and resentments of his peers, or his staying power. The example illustrates the importance of changing basic aspects of the bureaucratic systems fundamentally instead of marginally. If the arguments made here are at all persuasive, then those who would analyze the service performance of street level bureaucracies should concentrate their attention on components of the work profile. Those components discussed here—resource inadequacy, physical and psychological threat, ambiguity of role expectations, and the ways in which policemen, teachers and other street level bureaucrats react to problems stemming from these job-related difficulties—deserve particular attention.

NOTES

The following works, among others, have proved useful in providing an analysis of bureaucracies from which many generalizations concerning street-level bureaucracy have been drawn.

Howard Becker, "Social Class and Teacher–Pupil Relationships," *Education and the Social Order* Blaine Mercer and Edwin Carr (eds.), (New York: Holt, Rinehart, and Winston, 1957). David Bordua (ed.), *The Police: Six Sociological Essays* (New York: John Wiley, 1967). Marilyn Gittell and Allan G. Hevesi (eds.), *The Politics of Urban Education* (New York:

Praeger, 1969). Erving Goffman, *Asylums* (Chicago: Aldine Publishing Company, 1961). Michael Lipsky, "Is a Hard Rain Gonna Fall: Issues of Planning and Administration in the Urban World of the 1970's" paper delivered at the Annual Meetings of the American Society of Public Administration, Miami Beach, Fla., May 21, 1969. Michael Lipsky "Toward a Theory of Street-level Bureaucracy," paper delivered at the Annual Meetings of the American Political Science Association, New York, N.Y., September 206, 1969. Arthur Niederhoffer, *Behind the Blue Shield* (New York: Doubleday, 1967). President's Commission on Law Enforcement and the Administration of Justice, *Task Force Report: The Police* (Washington, D.C.: U.S. Government, 1967). David Rogers, *110 Livingston Street* (New York: Random House, 1968). Robert Rosenthal and Lenore Jacobson, *Pygmalion in the Classroom* (New York: Holt, Rinehart and Winston, 1968). Jerome Skolnick, *Justice Without Trial* (New York: John Wiley, 1967). James Q. Wilson, *Varieties of Police Behavior* (Cambridge: Harvard University Press, 1968).

1   See Allan Silver, "The Demand for Order in Civil Society," *The Police: Six Sociological Essays,* Bordua (ed.) (New York: John Wiley, 1967) pp. 1–24.

2   See Theodore Sarbin and Vernon Allen, "Role Theory," *The Handbook of Social Psychology,* 2nd. ed. Gardner Lindzey and Elliot Aronson (eds.), (Reading, Mass.: Addison-Wesley, 1968), pp. 498–99, 532.

3   See Anthony Downs, *Inside Bureaucracy* (Boston: Little, Brown, 1967), pp. 2–3, 75–78, for a discussion of conditions affecting bureaucratic decision making.

4   For a general discussion of psychological reaction to stress, see Richard Lazarus, *Psychological Stress and the Coping Process* (New York: McGraw-Hill, 1966). This work is particularly useful in providing conceptual distinctions for various phenomena related to the coping process. See especially Ch. 1; pp. 266–318.

5   See James Q. Wilson, *op. cit.,* pp. 157ff.

6   Daniel Walker, *Rights in Conflict* (New York: Bantam Books, 1968).

7   Nathan Glazer, "For White and Black Community Control Is The Issue," *The New York Times Magazine,* April 27, 1969, p. 46.

8   See the decision of Judge Skelly Wright in *Hobson v. Hanson,* June 19, 1967, 269F Supp. 401 (1967); also Kenneth Clark, *Dark Ghetto* (New York: Harper and Row, 1965), p. 128; Rosenthal and Jacobson, *op. cit.,* pp. 116–118.

9   Rosenthal and Jacobson, *op. cit.*

10   See John McNamara, "Uncertainties in Police Work: The Relevance of Police Recruits' Backgrounds and Training," *The Police,* Bordua (ed.), *op. cit.,* pp. 163–252.

11   See, for example, Alan Altshuler, *Community Control: The Black Demand for Participation in American Cities* (New York: Wester Publishing Co., 1970). See also Milton Kotler, *Neighborhood Government* (Indianapolis: Bobbs-Merrill, 1969).

12   See, for example, Arthur Waskow, "Community Control of the Police," *Transaction,* 7, 2 (December 1969), pp. 4–7; also James Q. Wilson, *op. cit.,* Ch. 9.

13   A number of writers have commented on the low turnout for elections to CAP and Model Cities boards. See, for example, Alan Altshuler, *op. cit.,* pp. 138–139. On decentralized school board elections, see the *New York Times,* February 19 to March 22, 1970.

14   See Peter Rossi, *et. al.,* "Between White and Black, The Faces of American Institutions in the Ghetto," *Supplemental Studies for the National Advisory Commission on Civil Disorders* (Washington, D.C.: U.S. Government Printing Office, 1968), pp. 110–113.

15   *Ibid.,* p. 136.

16   See, for example, the *New York Times,* February 13, 1970.

The Problem of Urban Administration and Environmental Turbulence

Orion White, Jr.

Introduction

It is a commonplace observation that our cities have reached an acute crisis. The amount of emotion, research, and rhetoric that has been spent defining urban problems and recommending solutions has probably not been surpassed in our national history.[1] Yet little progress seems to have been made towards settling the crisis. The stalemate may be a result of our tendency to conceptualize the problem in political rather than adminis- trative or institutional terms. While much has been said about how urban bureaucracies have contributed to the problem, the solutions offered for changing their behavior have usually been political rather than administra- tive. It is being increasingly recognized that our political processes are simply the techniques that express more deeply rooted patterns of alloca- tion: political decisions merely reflect underlying economic and social distributions of power based on class.[2] No doubt, in the long run fully, complete solutions to the urban crisis must be based on radical revisions in political structure and process from the national level down to the urban area, but it does not seem likely that immediate solutions to this problem can be political. Never having experienced any truly basic political reform, our nation will probably need a protracted period of adjustment in order to reshape its political patterns into a form more appropriate for our future —which it appears, will be different from anything that man has experienced heretofore.[3]

If the problem of urban reform for the immediate future must be one of administrative or institutional revision, what specific aspect must be the focus of attention in such a revision—advances in administrative technology, designed to increase economy and efficiency, or the development of the power technique to confront urban bureaucracies, which have been recently attacked as the oppressors of the urban disadvantaged and the opponents of constructive change? Neither of these seems to be the answer. Administrative technology, many argue, is already too far developed; and confrontation is a political solution to an administrative problem —just the type of error which has hindered attempts to meet the crisis up to now. Rather, the answer to this question seems to be that we must develop ways of making urban public organizations more sensitive to and more effective in dealing with the human, social, economic, and political contexts in which they operate. This answer will require that the incremental political reforms that do seem feasible or probable, such as plans for neighborhood control of various urban administrative programs, be matched by administrative reforms to facilitate the political revisions. Instead of seeking change through confrontation, we could seek it through renewing the capability of public organizations to cope with political changes.

The implication of this definition of the problem upon the intellectual consideration of public organizations is profound. It means that those who study administration must shift the focus of their theoretical orientation away from the internal dynamics of organizations. Instead, they must center their attention primarily on the interactions between public organizations and their environments and view internal dynamics as an aspect of this process.[4]

Happily, the theoretical orientation of the field of public administration has recently begun moving toward the interaction perspective. The politics–administration dichotomy of the early orthodox literature of the field virtually prevented analysis of the environmental relationships of public agencies. Even after theorists rejected the traditional dichotomy, there were few contributions to a theoretical understanding of how agencies interact with their environments. When Pendleton Herring and Paul Appleby defined administration as including policy formation, students of the traditional school of administration generally interpreted their definition to mean that administration involved the art of politics, and their research under this paradigm produced, for the most part, descriptive analyses showing that when policy is formed in government, it involves the close interaction of administrators and a variety of political actors.[5] Hence, no theory of administrative politics was developed. The two outstanding exceptions to this generalization are, of course, *TVA and the Grass Roots* by Philip Selznick, which analyzed the interaction between organization and environment in terms of the notion of cooptation, and *The Political Process: Executive Bureau-Legislative Committee Relations* by Leiper Freeman, which analyzed the political interactions of the Bureau of Indian Affairs.[6]

In the modern literature of organization theory, however, the interface of organization and environment became, rather early, a main focus of attention, primarily as a result of the ground breaking work of James Thompson and others at the University of Pittsburg Center for Administrative Science.[7] Thompson's theoretical concern was how organizations set goals in interaction with their environments—particularly environments that were composed of differing or heterogeneous sets of demands. A sbustantial addition to the conceptualization of organization–environment relationships was the publication of F.G. Emery and G.L. Trist's classic article defining and analyzing turbulence of environments as a major theoretical variable.[8] While, as yet, little research has been carried out to explore these conceptualizations, another aspect of concern with the interactions between organization and environment seems to be emerging. It is the result of the growing emphasis on organizational development as a theoretical concern and strategy for problem solution. This concern involves the strategic question of the environment's impact upon internal organizational development efforts. However, this concern is only part of the broader objective of developing means for organizations to be pro-active, both in regard to their internal structure and in relation to their environments.[9] Viewed in this perspective, the organization is a strategic base for positive goal oriented change, as opposed to reactive problem oriented change. It seems obvious that such a perspective will depend critically upon the analysis of the relationships between organization and environment.

In addition to all these concerns, which demand that attention be given to organization and environment, the newly emerging conditions in the cities are increasing the urgency of this shift in attention. We live in an increasingly existential and phenomenological age, and nowhere is this face more evident than in our cities. We have seen in urban areas in the 1960s the beginning stages of the postindustrial, affluent, service economy that has rendered our culturally dominant middle class lifestyle irrelevant to many of the young. With the breakdown of this lifestyle, we have begun to see in some urban areas the development of true social pluralism, with a wide diversity of individual and group lifestyles, unprecedented heterodoxy in religious and political philosophy, and the consequent outmoding of even the most basic categories by which social reality is defined. Truly, we are beginning to experience in a quite real way the phenomenological condition of multiple realities, where people literally live in different psychological worlds within the same society.[10]

The implications of this emerging condition are so profound that coping with this condition may very well override the traditional and standard categories of problems the urban administrator has faced, such as poverty, crime, dissent, and physical decay. Furthermore, it will mean that the administrator must begin to view his job from the perspective of the organization–environment interface. In the past, an urban school administrator, for example, could concern himself mainly with the internal management processes of the school system, because he faced a relatively constant environment of upper class, middle class, and lower class families, who were all living and aspiring approximately to the same economic and personal life-style values. But now, in some areas, an urban school administrator faces such a diverse environment members as radicalized middle class blacks, young blacks in the Black Panther Party, disaffected affluent middle class youths, whose parents may be organized into groups ranging from the John Birch Society to the Peace and Freedom Party, and children being raised in urban communes, who may not have the usual legal identity. And all of this is overlaid with the burgeoning movement for the use of illegal drugs, with consequent damage to the legitimacy of the general legal order.

Under such conditions, all of the types of theoretical concerns mentioned above concerning the interface between organization and environment become real and urgent to the practicing urban administrator. He must know how to cope with an environment that makes heterogeneous or conflicting demands and which is highly turbulent and thereby threatening. Increasingly, it appears that he will not solve any problems by attempting merely to react to them but that rather he must move pro-actively toward a complete redesign of the conditions out of which the problems emerge. Also, he is finding that, because of the increasing number of realities or worlds which the people in his environment are experiencing, he must devote more and more effort to mediating between these worlds and parts of his own institution or between them and some other institution.

The changing nature of the urban administrator's task therefore demands that he develop an understanding of how public organizations interact with their environments. The first step in developing this understanding is to analyze the dynamics of organizations as they are currently structured and as they interact with complex, turbulent environments. Using this understanding as a starting place, we may be able to develop ways of restructuring these organizations so that they have highly permeable boundaries and can perform the tasks of survival and pro-action that are required of them in emerging urban environments.

The Turbulent Environment

In 1965–1967 I conducted an exploratory field study of three public administrative agencies in an attempt to develop an empirically based conceptual framework for the study of organization–environment interaction. The general purpose of the study was to examine the relationship of environmental conditions to the outputs of the agencies—specifically to see how, if at all, relationships between client and agency personnel at the organizational boundary (i.e., in the field) were affected by environmental conditions. For this purpose, four agencies were selected for study. The environmental context surrounding each agency presented a continuum ranging from a very low to a very high level of turbulence and political threat. After access was gained to the agencies and the field research had started, one agency withdrew its consent to participate in the research. However, this agency was in the mid-range of the turbulence–threat continuum; hence the full range of environmental conditions was maintained as in the original research design. In all agencies, interviews were conducted at all levels with as many personnel as would consent. In all agencies the chief focus was on field units that interacted directly with clients, and, in each of the units, almost all the field personnel were interviewed with a structured interview schedule. Field personnel were also given a questionnaire to complete. The questionnaire and schedule provided a base for comparison of the agencies in terms of the major variables being examined. Upper level administrative personnel were interviewed on a semistructured or open-ended format, depending upon the contingencies of the field research situation.

The theoretical premise around which the study was designed was that high levels of environmental threat would produce internal organizational consequences, resulting in high levels of role stress, consequent anxiety or insecurity, and, on the part of field personnel, a rigid response in the client interaction situation.[11] Three categories of variables were defined to suggest how, if at all, environmental threat conditions linked through organization structure and process produce an impact at the client face-to-face interaction level. The first group of variables, termed external system factors, included the perceived legitimacy and consistency of the agency's goals, the perceived contingencies and extent of the agency's dependency on the environment in the resource-input process, and a group of role factors such as adequacy of authority, effectiveness of role socialization, structural ambiguity, and effectiveness of demographic processes for recruitment to the role. Internal system factors, the second group of variables, included such things as the extent and nature of any group or clique conflicts within each agency, the degree of cohesiveness and supportiveness of work groups, the extent of the individual's integration into his work group, and the congruency of informal group norms with formal structural norms. The third group of variables defined relevant conditions stemming from individuals. This group was named latent structural factors and included such conditions as an individual's personal status congruency—the compatibility of his previous career background with his current job, his level of psychological anxiety, his personal psychological rigidity, his self-esteem, security, and his level of professional commitment to his role.

The first two groups of variables were measured through the structured and unstructured interviews, while the third group was assessed through a questionnaire that included background data questions and a number of psychological scales.[12] Also, a short version of the Hall Organizational Inventory was included as a quantitative or objective check on the interview data regarding the structural variables.[13] While the interview and questionnaire data were regarded as an important part of the study, in that they provided a base for comparison between the agencies, much more important data were gained through the research strategy of field observation and "anthropological" or interpretive note-taking. A detailed research log was kept that described all interactions between the researchers and the agencies being studied.

The analysis presented here is drawn from the larger comparative study. The one agency that was experiencing the highest level of environmental turbulence and political threat has been selected as the basis for a case study analysis of the relationship between organization and environment, internal organization dynamics, and outcomes at the client-interaction level.

Specifically, the case analysis will be used to illustrate the theoretical assertion that the more turbulent and threatening an environment, the more likely that an organization will respond maladaptively. This assertion is based on the theoretical premise that organizations must possess a repertoire of response capabilities for environmental interaction and that the responses must be matched appropriately to varying environmental conditions if optimal survival potential or capacity for pro-active action is to be maintained. A scheme for conceptualzing varying environmental conditions, levels of environmental threat, the repertoire of organizational responses, and the appropriate linkage between the environmental condition and the response pattern is shown in Table I.

The meaning of the categories used in this scheme should be relatively clear to those who have experience in administration or who know the organization theory literature out of which the catagories have been synthesized.[14] In terms of the chart, the theoretical premise that will be explored here is simply that, as environmental threat rises, the response of the organization is more and more likely to be of a type described at the left of the horizontal axis rather than at the right, where it should be for purposes of optimal adaptation. The causal linkage behind this mal-

TABLE I
**SCHEME FOR CONCEPTUALIZING ORGANIZATION – ENVIRONMENT INTERAC-
TION**

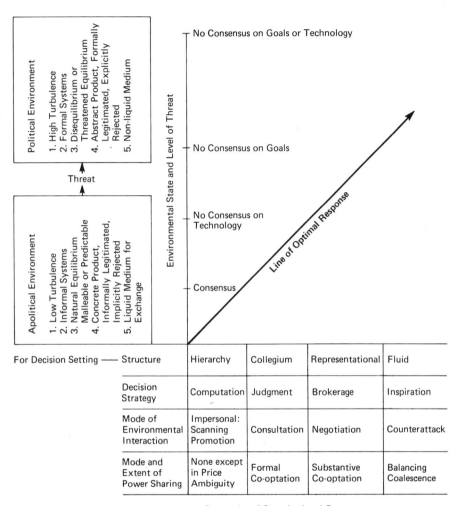

Repertoire of Organizational Response

For Decision Setting —— Structure	Hierarchy	Collegium	Representational	Fluid
Decision Strategy	Computation	Judgment	Brokerage	Inspiration
Mode of Environmental Interaction	Impersonal: Scanning Promotion	Consultation	Negotiation	Counterattack
Mode and Extent of Power Sharing	None except in Price Ambiguity	Formal Co-optation	Substantive Co-optation	Balancing Coalescence

adaptive pattern occurs among (1) the interaction of role stress and ambiguity that is created in the organization as a result of high environmental
turbulence and threat, (2) the individual response patterns that are evoked
under such conditions by the basic psychological factor of personal rigidity (or, conversely, flexibility), and (3) the orthodox theory of administration
that provided the context for most administrative actions and that is the
basis for most agencies' structure and processes. The complex pattern of
interaction between these three variables appeared as the field research

effort was carried out. Hence, the paradigm by which the research was designed—threat, anxiety, rigidity—turned out to be too simple for comprehending the actual situation, at least in this one agency.

The theory of administration which was employed in the agency studied contributed significantly to its response to its environment. This fact highlights another unexpected outcome of the study: the implication that if administrators are to be able to deal effectively with turbulent and threatening environments, such as the ones that are increasingly characteristic of urban areas, there must be a shift in the basic theoretical orientation of the field of public administration.

A Case Study of a Public Agency in a Turbulent Environment

Description of the Agency

The focal organization in this case was a newly established and rather small regulatory agency, consisting of about thirty-five professional personnel with a supporting clerical and office management staff. Its legal mandate had been granted only about one and one-half years before the study began out of a long-standing political controversy over the area of commercial enterprise it was to regulate—an area which had become increasingly controversial in recent years. The regulatory mandate required that the agency oversee and control a wide range of an industry's business practices. This industry, which was quite diverse in composition, operated for the most part in the ghetto areas of large cities. The regulatory task set for the agency demanded a good deal of technical expertise in the field engaged in by the industry. The agency's primary tasks at its inception were to develop general policy outlines as a basis for regulatory actions, and, at the same time, it had to make a number of specific policy decisions on a continuing basis in particular cases that occurred as it began operation. These decisions concerned whether or not to investigate or to prosecute and were made on the basis of information gathered through a regular examination process. The working structure of the agency is shown in Table II.

The head and the deputy head of the agency spent most of their time in negotiation and interaction with the environment over matters of broad policy of the agency. In this capacity they worked as a rather close team. The head himself, however, maintained a direct line of authority to the lower organization and hence, in a very real sense, was running the organization from the top. The deputy head did not engage in administrative matters to any significant extent and confined himself almost solely to problems of top policy development—interpretation of the law and negotiation with the most powerful units in the environment. In the central

TABLE II
ORGANIZATION CHART FOR REGULATORY AGENCY

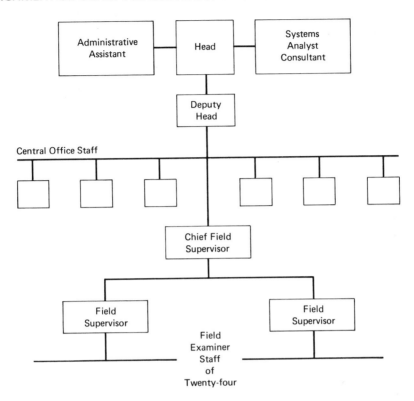

office, below the two heads, was a professional staff that performed a variety of functions, such as technical research projects necessary for the development of major policy positions and regulatory guidelines. They also acted as the main investigatory staff and participated in specific investigatory and enforcement decisions. The main line of activity in the agency was carried out by the field organization, which was supervised directly from the central office by a chief field administrator, a position that was vacant for most of the period of the study. The field organization was made up of two units, geographically divided. Each of these was headed by a field supervisor who managed a staff of about a dozen people. Also, some members of the field staff whith most experience or expertise in the job were designated as field leaders. These positions were necessary because the field staff was highly mobile and its activities were dispersed over a wide geographic area. Hence timely communication directly to the field supervisors was often impossible.

The field staff met the industry clients in each client's office. The staff's task was to identify themselves, establish rapport with the client, gain cooperation, obtain through examination a wide range of information about the business activities, execute a report of this information, and secure the client's signature on the report. The reports were passed to the field supervisor for an efficiency and substance review and then were sent on to the central office with recommendation for attention or action.

The field staff usually worked in teams of two. Wherever possible, the field supervisors arranged for the field staff to stay in the same town and in the same hotel while in the field. In addition, formal field-staff meetings were held regularly, during which the field itinerary was laid out and the field staff was kept up to date on the latest developments at the central office—especially decisions relating to the conduct of their examinations. The agency used a wide area telephone service for communication to the field staff, and each member of the field staff had a telephone credit card for communication with the central office. Movements of the staff through their geographic areas were kept secret and the examinations were not held on a regular basis. Hence, the industry clients did not know when they were to be visited by the agency.

The financing of the agency was not dependent upon a legislative budgeting. All its funds were obtained through fees assessed the clients for licenses and examinations. The examination fee constituted the bulk of the agency's budget, which, at least at the time of the study, was quite ample for its operations. The agency seemed secure financially. On the other hand, the examination fees were assessed the clients on a per hour basis. This made the clients quite sensitive to the efficiency of the examining staff; some members of the industry attempted to assess exactly how efficient the field staff was in its examining operations.

For this reason and by administrative principle, the efficiency of the field operation was from the beginning a major consideration in the agency. To maximize the effectiveness of the examination, one of the first actions of the head was to employ a system's analyst as a long-term consultant. This consultant set about to define the optimal set of procedures for the examinations. He had direct access to the head and a good deal of influence with him. But he was regarded with some disdain by the field staff, who were encountering so many contingencies in the examination process that to them his attempts to study and systematize their jobs seemed silly, if not futile.

The structure of the agency at this time was quite fluid. It was a period of growth and contingency, and the norm was that all members were to pitch in and do whatever needed doing at the moment. There was an aura of action around the agency. Its establishment had been heralded as a long-awaited solution to a serious problem, and its activities were followed closely by the press. A good deal of personal ambition was also evident because the agency appeared likely to grow and prosper, and opportunities appeared to be open for those who could take them. There was a substantial amount of motivation that could only be called a concern for protecting the public interest on the part of some of the agency personnel. They believed that the job set for the agency had great social worth.

Sources of Role Stress in the Agency

There were several sources of serious role stress evident in the agency at the time this study was carried out. Most of this stress was experienced acutely by the field personnel who encountered clients in face-to-face interviews. Perhaps the most serious source of stress was the nature of the agency's environment and its posture in regard to the environment as it began operations. Since this was a new agency, it was weak in terms of legitimacy with its clients and with a significant part of the overhead political control structure. At the same time, its mandate was clear and urgent: an important portion of the political environment and the public expected the agency to act vigorously to regulate the abuses of the industry it was to oversee.

The act establishing the agency marked a change in the normative or ideological patterns of thought on the part of the public and the political system in favor of industry regulation, but no one knew to what extent the past belief in *laissez–faire* and *caveat emptor* had changed. While a significant part of the industry had participated in and agreed to the passage of the act, the establishment of the agency signified a direct threat to other sectors of the enterprise. Furthermore, as is always the case, the uncertainty of how policy would be defined at the administrative level created considerable apprehension for those in the industry that had supported the act.

The most important source of stress, however, was the fact that the environment was to a large extent unknown. The agency did not know how many businesses were connected with the industry it was to regulate, nor where they were. One of the early tasks of the field staff was to drive up and down likely streets in urban areas and make a list of names and locations of each business that appeared to be involved with the industry. Even with such a list, however, more important information was still lacking—information as to the nature of the financial and political backing of the various businesses. Without such information, initial interviews with some of the industry affiliates were ambiguous and sometimes had severe consequences for the field staff. Further, the environment was tremendously diverse, ranging from very small to very large enterprises, and it served a wide spectrum of the public.

The agency staff perceived their precarious political position rather clearly. They knew that the environment was threatening and that a great deal depended upon their developing an initial base of good will on which the agency could develop a more stable and powerful position of authority.

A second major source of role stress in the agency was the fact that role specifications—and even the structural or authority relations—were not spelled out clearly. For the most part, this was a result of the agency's newness. It simply did not have the base of developed policy on which to write regulations, role rules, and procedures for each position. Hence, the field staff often faced rapid and unpredictable changes in policy and procedure. Some examiners told of instances in which, after completing work in one office and moving to another down the street, they found that the industry agent had learned of new policy and role changes that had taken place within the past few hours that had not yet been communicated to the examiners themselves. Communication between industry units was often easier than between the agency central office and the field staff.

While the field staff had few clear rules or policies on which to base their interaction with industry agents, their training and the messages sent from supervisors continually stressed that they should assume a posture of authority and professionalism in the field. The head of the agency wished to make it clear to the industry that it was going to be regulated. He moved in this direction by paying a higher salary with more fringe benefits than comparable positions in other agencies did, a gesture which paid off in the recruitment of an unusually young and well-educated staff for the field force. This prevented the industry from defining the examiners, according to one field man, as a "bunch of dumb asses"—which was the reputation similar forces in other agencies had gained because their low pay could not attract highly competent people. This combination of education and skill, coupled with youth and role ambiguity, however, disposed the field force to adopt a defensive posture vis-à-vis the industry. In one extreme case, an examiner was dismissed for carrying a revolver in his brief case as he visited industry offices.

This condition was exacerbated by the ambiguity of the agency structure itself. The most notable example was a conflict at the central office between two top staff people. Each felt that he had been hired as chief of enforcement operations and that the other was his subordinate. They occupied offices that were equal size and had the same furniture and the ambiguity long remained unresolved. The struggle between the two men was the subject of much talk and conjecture within the agency. Most agency personnel thought that the head left the situation ambiguous in order to see who would come out on top. The general surmise was that the head employed the Franklin Roosevelt philosophy of administration by having competition and conflict among his top staff. The top central office staff felt that the early period of the agency was one of assessment and that as soon as the head had evaluated competencies, he would promote, demote, clarify, and regularize the top structure of the agency.

A major focus of competition among the supervisory and central office staff was the office of chief field administrator, which, as noted earlier, remained vacant for most of the study. This position was considered the third ranking position of authority in the agency and hence was regarded as a significant opportunity for promotion. To the researcher, it appeared that the ambiguity of structure at the central office was not intentional, but rather the result of a slip in communication which went unresolved because none of the central office staff wished to communicate to the head how the staff felt about the situation. Since they saw the situation as a game—which they wanted to win—they did not wish to complain about the rules.

Another source of considerable role stress in the agency was this study. Because considerable role stress and anxiety were already present in the agency, it was virtually impossible for the researchers to present the study to the staff in a nonthreatening way. Rumors of the wildest sort circulated about the real motive behind the head's having the agency participate in the study. Many field staff believed that a lie detector was used in the interview, that the chief researcher was a psychiatrist, and that the objective of the study was to discover any latent homosexual tendencies in members of the field staff. It was only near the end of the study, after intensive interaction, that most of the staff believed that the study was really what the researchers claimed.

The Organizational Dynamics, Flexibility, and Rigidity under Conditions of Role Stress

As noted earlier, the variable which seemed to be most important in determining the response of the agency to conditions of environmental stress was the flexibility—rigidity of the staff members. The character traits and coping responses of flexible and rigid personalities in conditions of role ambiguity and stress are basically different and have markedly different consequences for the organization.[15]

The flexible personality is other-directed and adaptable. He is highly reality-oriented and sees reality as complex and constantly in flux. He tends to shape his behavior in accord with opinions of others and the situation he finds himself in rather than by principles. He is open-minded, easily accepts new ideas and experiences, and quickly discards old patterns that do not appear appropriate for new situations. Full perception and experience is more important to him than consistency of belief and action. The flexible person has strong needs for inclusion and participation; he is a natural team man and regards the norm of fairness highly. Consistent with this pattern, the major source of role stress for the flexible person is work overload. Because he is open to others, he constantly takes on more and more tasks as others request that he do so. He tends to be overly optimistic about possibilities for completing these tasks on time. Another major source of stress is fear of rejection by others. Often this threat is so strong that he will avoid coping responses that might be offensive and he will tend to accept influence attempts which others direct at him.

By contrast, the rigid person tends to be inner-directed, strong willed, self-confident, and guided by internal standards. He is closed-minded, persistent, dogmatic, and he has usually integrated his principles and beliefs into a highly structured and consistent ideology. In organizational relationships, he is heavily oriented to authority and status rather than to colleagues. He shifts between dependency and counterdependency in his organizational life, between being master or servant, and he is much more prone to conform to cultural and organizational standards than is the flexible person. As one might expect, given this character pattern, the major source of role stress for the rigid is any type of pressure that interferes with his ability to conform to his internalized standards of excellence. As a result, any ambiguity in his role, particularly demands aimed at him from different sources and for different behaviors, gives the rigid person much discomfort.

Flexibility and Rigidity in the Agency Staff

During the course of the field work, we attempted to assess the personal flexibility or rigidity of all of the agency staff members through various techniques. For central office personnel, the only technique which appeared feasible was personal observation, subjective interpretation, and consultation with as many of the staff as possible. All of the central office personnel who were requested to do so refused to complete a psychological scale questionnaire measuring this variable. With the field personnel, however, the assessment is based on the Gough-Sanford Personal Rigidity Scale scores.

The head of the agency was judged with certainty to be a flexible personality type. His personal bent was open and almost academic in nature. He was quite open to the idea of his agency participating in the study and was very much interested in helping the research in any way he could, though with no promise of any benefit to himself except an opportunity to read the research report. He was constantly generating new ideas and trying them out on his agency staff, and the ambiguity and lack of structure in the early days of the agency did not personally bother him at all. This personal disposition had served him well in his past career. He had held a number of advisory and research posts in government before heading the agency. He was regarded as astute politically and was often called upon by powerful figures in his political party for advice and help in writing speeches. His personal flexibility facilitated his ability to play the game of politics.

At the same time, the head brought a rigid perspective to his job in the agency. He had received an excellent education in the traditional theory of public administration and this training, as we shall see later, formed a tight filter for his perception of what was happening in the agency in its early days and what ought to be done with it. One of the head's main motives for taking his position at the agency, in addition to his expertise concerning the industry to be regulated, was a desire to practice what he had learned about "good administration" and the protection of the public interest. He told a researcher early in the study, "I wanted to get out and see how the theory I learned actually works." Hence, the principles of the traditional theory formed a rather rigid ideological overlay for his basically flexible character. He was personally flexible, professionally rigid.

The deputy head was an attorney by training, and the flexible professional style of the lawyer was matched by an equal amount of flexibility in his personality. Like the head, he was quite academic. He liked to talk about ideas—especially new ways of viewing ethical problems—with other staff members, and at one point he organized an informal theology discussion group within the agency. Also like the head, he was closely associated with the top echelons of his political party, and his political judgment was much respected. The deputy and the head formed an effective team for the political side of the agency's operations. They possessed a good deal of "clout."

The central office professional staff and the field supervisors split almost evenly into a rigid and a flexible group, and, as measured by Gough-Sanford scale scores, flexibility–rigidity followed a normal distribution among the examiners. The rigid group in the central office was made up of one field supervisor and three attorneys on the central staff. As mentioned above, two of these attorneys were in direct conflict over which was subordinate to the other, and one slowly emerged as the leader of the rigid faction in the agency. The flexible group was made up of the head's administrative assistant, a central office attorney, the investigations accountant, and one of the field supervisors. Neither of these groups was cohesive, but they were defined by the frequency and nature of their communication. This was especially true in the flexible group, where social interactions tended to be much richer and often turned to biting, witty remarks about the rigids.

Responses to Stress by Rigids and Flexibles

As the agency moved into full-scale operation and began to encounter its environment on a regular basis, conflict at the agency boundary increased markedly and a clear pattern of consequences appeared within the agency. Generally, this pattern was that the flexible agency personnel were punished for their natural coping responses to role stress, while the rigids, whose natural response appeared to be much more effective in coping with stress, were generally rewarded.

The characteristic response of the flexible person to role stress is to overload himself, seek help from others, and engage in joint problem-solving. He also manifests anxiety about his stress problem openly. The rigid, on the other hand, copes with his stress by truncating reality. He simply filters out information and pressure until his world is comfortably simplified. As part of this pattern, the rigid denies his own compromises of his principles (or impulses to compromise them) and may project these "bad" parts of himself onto others. Also, under stress, the rigid attributes little power to others and reduces his communication with them. Paradoxically, however, he may become increasingly dependent upon authority figures. Also, he often adopts compulsive work habits and totally commits himself to doggedly meeting his responsibilities.

Virtually every aspect of these patterns could be seen in the agency. Frustrated by an unknown, complex, and dissident environment, the rigids simply defined the clients as "evil" and dealt with them accordingly. They did not see the head as engaged in the process of political negotiation with industry so as to establish a power base for his agency. Rather, they viewed him as excessively compromising and equivocal. They felt he was unable to lead effectively or to give directions. They often constructed jokes around the fact that the head frequently ended instructions to his staff with the phrase, "See what I mean?" By so doing, they attempted to exclude him as a relevant authority figure.

In the field, the flexible work style differed markedly from the rigid. The rigids worked harder, or at least with more speed. Situations that seemed new and vague to the flexibles were pressed into standard categories by the rigids—hence decisions on cases came easier to the rigids. Because of the way the rigids viewed clients, it was easy for them to maintain a facade of authority and professionalism in cases that proved difficult for the flexibles. In one instance, while the researcher was on a field trip with a two-man team of one rigid and one flexible, this trait was clearly illustrated. In a city they had not previously visited, the examiners encountered an office not on the agency inventory. They stopped and entered, only to find that the company represented a group of very powerful financial and political interests. The interaction with the office manager was extremely harsh; he threatened the examiners physically and vowed he would have them fired. The flexible examiner came out visibly shaken and talking intently about how the situation should have been handled. The rigid said simply and with great intensity, "Boy, are we gonna get that son-of-a-bitch one of these days!"

Hence, the rigids appeared to be able to cope with the demands of the job well: They were more decisive, they worked harder, and they produced more. They soon emerged as leaders and "strong guys," and the other examiners often sought their advice on agency policy. In addition, they were persistently inclined to construct a functioning hierarchy within the formal structure of the agency. They soon formed an informal chain of command, leading from the rigid examiners to the rigid field supervisor, and the rigid professional staff group at the central office. This linkage further enhanced the power of the rigid group vis-à-vis the flexibles, who were more prone to maintain equalized power relations.

In addition, the rigids held the flexibles in some disdain; and though they kept this feeling private for the most part, some of the flexibles sensed it. The rigids saw the flexibles as lazy, because they could not produce, and even as weak or neurotic because they appeared indecisive and expressed anxiety about their work. The flexible field supervisor was known to be taking a Dale Carnegie self-improvement course, which was discussed as a reflection on his mental capabilities and stability. A good deal of hostility developed between the rigids and the flexibles and especially between the two field supervisors. This hostility was ultimately expressed, as shall be noted below.

As this hostility developed, relations with the environment became more difficult. At the central office delicate negotiations were being carried out between the head and the industry over key formulas that were to be used in examinations and in decisions about the information required of the industry units in their annual report to the agency. In staff meetings in the field, the rigid supervisors mainly emphasized that the examiners should present an authoritative image to the industry, but at the same time, that they be friendly and develop good will. The industry made complaints regularly about arbitrariness and inefficiency.

The head, seeing his agency through the traditional theory of administration, seemed to define the problem as stemming from personal ambition at the central office and from a lack of systematic procedure for field operations. His response to the problem as he saw it was, on the one hand, to attack personally the emerging rigid leaders at the central office in an attempt to undercut the hierarchy-within-a-hierarchy that the rigids were developing. On the other hand, he sought systematization. He often remarked: "What I need here is a good systems man to be chief field administrator."

Ultimately, he did acquire an excellent public administration systems expert for this post, a person who had taught graduate public administration courses. In addition to his professional expertise, this man had a very rigid personality. Within weeks the head and the new chief field supervisor were locked in bitter disagreement—over how far the agency could go with systematic enforcement procedures at that point in the agency's history! Soon the new supervisor left the agency, as might be expected, and the head replaced him, on an acting basis, with the rigid field supervisor. But this move failed also. One of the first actions of the rigid field supervisor in his new post was to construct a punishment experience for his former peer, the flexible field supervisor. Knowing that the flexible supervisor had departed on vacation with his wife, the rigid acting chief called him back to duty at the central office from two hundred miles away, where he had to leave his wife on the way to their vacation site. The head, upon learning of this, felt it wise to move the new chief back down to his former post as field supervisor.

As this study was ending, the agency experienced a rapid increase in turnover of personnel at all levels. It seemed clear that the role stress within the agency was taking its toll on the staff. In the privacy of the interview situation, the examiners frequently revealed a disposition to leave the agency, and some openly broached the topic of psychological stress—asking the interviewer for personal advice, to interpret fantasies and dreams, and to relay messages about their situation to the head. At this point, contact with the agency was terminated as the field research team moved on to the other organizations to be studied on a comparative basis with this agency.

Conclusions

While this case story describes a regulatory agency dealing with an industry client group, there seem to be a number of parallels between the situation it faced and the situation of public agencies in the increasingly turbulent environment of the cities. The administrator in the city no longer knows all the groups that exist in his environment. Further, the groups are diverse in the degree of power they wield and in the type of demand or threat, or both, that they might level at the agency. The legitimacy of tactics and ideology of the groups is increasingly uncertain—as it was here with the industry being regulated. The proper technology for meeting these demands and threats is often not easily discovered by the urban administrator—as was the case with this regulatory agency.

What, though, does the case illuminate about the problem of response to environmental conditions of stress? First, the case suggests a validity for the theoretical scheme presented earlier, which showed a repertoire of organizational responses that could be optimally matched to differing environmental conditions. It seems clear that if the examination staff had been structured to maintain a variable response capability, it could have dealt with the various elements in its environment more effectively. The head and deputy head did respond to the environment with such a repertoire, but lower level personnel were limited in their response pattern. It ideally would appear that optimal effectiveness in relating to the environment would be achieved if each of the field staff personally possessed such a repertoire of responses. However, a more feasible solution would have been to identify such capabilities structurally, so that a set of organizational units would be available for different environmental encounters. Given the fact that one can generally expect an approximately equal distribution of rigid and flexible types in an administrative agency, the task for the administrator does not seem to be that of selecting one type alone for his agency. Rather, it would seem more practical and productive to develop ways to employ the diversity of types one is almost certain to recruit.

The case showed vividly, however, that under the conditions of stress, where it seems most needed, there is a powerful psychological-organizational dynamic that works against the development and maintenance of this multifaceted interaction capability. This fact emphasizes the necessity of developing new forms of organizational structure and management style that will prevent such maladaptive patterns from taking hold.

The prerequisite to this type of change, in turn, seems most dependent upon a revolutionary change in the ideological base (or paradigm) of public administration theory. The major reason for the head's maladaptive emphasis on systematization as the solution to his problem was his adherence to the world view and principles of traditional public administration, which he had learned and internalized. To this view, the rigid response (described at the far left of the horizontal axis on Table I) to the stress conditions was proper, even though his experience and political judgment denied it. In order for the agency to possess the repertoire of responses it needed, it would have been necessary to base organization structure and management on a radically different view. Equalization of power, drastic decentralization of decisions, and a group method of coping with questions of responsibility and failure seem necessary. Management should be viewed as a process of support rather than control. To accomplish these and other changes that probably would be needed in management perspective and process, the role of human nature in organizations must be reconceptualized. The views of man and organizational structure that will meet these requirements have been extensively developed already in organization development literature. A major task remains, however, in building strategies of organizational development that will work under conditions of environmental turbulence.[16]

While such ideas may seem farfetched or idealistic at this point, the fact remains that, as an organizational environment, the city is evolving in a direction that allows for little, short of total, revision. The demand for citizen participation through devices such as neighborhood control of administrative agencies has already been realized. Theoretically such demands translated spell acute environmental turbulence. If our cities are to remain viable, it seems that these demands must be met and that our urban administrators much be given the new concepts and techniques of administration that are required to fill such demands.

NOTES

I conducted research project supported by the Institue of Public Affairs, now a part of the Lyndon B. Johnson School of Public Affairs at the University of Texas at Austin in 1965–1969. I wish to express thanks for this support.

1 See, for example, James A. Kalish, "Flim-Flam, Double Talk and Hustle: The Urban-Problems Industry," *Washington Monthly* (November, 1969), pp. 6–16.

2 The elitist bias of democratic pluralism is increasingly discussed. See, for example, Jack L. Walker, "Critique of the Elitist Theory of Democracy," *The American Political Science Review* (June, 1966), pp. 285–295; Henry S. Kariel, *The Promise of Politics* (Englewood Cliffs, N.J.: Prentice-Hall, Inc., 1966); Theodore J. Lowi, "American Business, Public Policy, Case Studies, and Political Theory," *World Politics*, (July, 1964), pp. 677–715; and Theodore J. Lowi, *The End of Liberalism* (New York: W. W. Norton and Co., 1969); Philip Green, "Science, Government, and the Case of Rand—A Singular Pluralism," *World Politics* (January 1968), pp. 301–326; John C. Livingston and Robert G. Thompson, *The Consent of the Governed* (New York: The Macmillan Company, 1966); and E. E. Schattschneider, *The Semi-Sovereign People* (New York: Holt, Rinehart and Winston, 1960).

3 See Eric Trist, *The Relation of Welfare and Development in the Transition to Post Industrialism,* Working Paper No. 1, Socio-Technical Systems Division, Western Management Science Institute, University of California, Los Angeles; Melvin M. Webber, "Planning in an Environment of Change," *The Town Planning Review* (October, 1968), pp. 179–195; and (January, 1969), pp. 277–295; Daniel Bell, "The Post Industrial Socity, *Technology and Social Change,* Eli Ginsberg (ed.) (New York: Columbia University Press, 1964), pp. 44–59.

4 This emphasis in the theoretical orientation of the "new public administration" was clearly spelled out and called for in Robert P. Biller, "Some Implications of Adaptation Capacity for Organizational and Political Development," in *Toward A New Public Administration* Frank Marini (ed.) (New York and London: Chandler Publishing Co., 1971.)

5 E. Pendleton Herring, *Public Administration and the Public Interest* (New York: McGraw-Hill Book Company, 1936); Paul Appleby, *Big Democracy* (New York: Alfred A. Knopf, 1945).

6 Philip Selznick, *TVA and the Grass Roots* (Berkeley: University of California Press, 1949); Leiper Freeman, *The Political Process: Executive Bureau-Legislative Committee Relations* (Garden City, New York: Doubleday and Company, Inc., 1955).

7 See the classic article, James D. Thompson and William J. McEwen, "Organizational Goals and Environment," *American Sociological Review,* (February, 1958), pp. 23–31, and James D. Thompson more recent excellent book, *Organizations in Action* (New York: McGraw Hill, 1967); also see James D. Thompson *et al.* (eds.), *Comparative Studies in Administration* (Pittsburg: University of Pittsburg Press, 1959). For an overview of the work done on organization environment relations, see Shirley Terreberry, "The Evolution of Organizational Environments," *Administrative Science Quarterly* (March, 1968), pp. 590–613.

8 F. G. Emery and G. L. Trist, "The Causal Texture of Organizational Environments," *Human Relations* (March, 1968), pp. 590–613.

9 See Michael Mont Harmon, "Administrative Policy Formation and the Public Interest," *Public Administration Review* (September-October, 1969), pp. 483–491.

10 See Orion White, Jr. and Gideon Sjoberg, "The New Politics in the United States," *Politics in the Post-Welfare State: Responses to the New Invididualism,* M. Donald Hancock and Gideon Sjoberg (eds.) (New York: Columbia University Press, date).

11 The anxiety-rigidity hypothesis, of course, forms the basis of Merton's famous paradigm of bureaucratic behavior; see, for an insightful discussion of this, James G. March and Herbert Simon, *Organizations* (New York: John Wiley, 1958), pp. 36–40. Merton originally stated the scheme in "Bureaucratic Structure and Personality," *Reader in Bureaucracy,* Robert K. Merton *et al.* (eds.) (New York: Free Press, 1952). Also see on this point Charles Hermann, "Some Consequences of Crisis Which Limit the Viability of Organizations," *Administrative Science Quarterly* (June, 1963), pp. 61–82.

12   These were a short form F-Scale of Authoritarianism, the Gough-Sanford Rigidity Scale, the Maslow *et al.* SI Scale, and the Taylor Manifest Anxiety Scale.

13   See Richard H. Hall, "Intraorganizational Structural Variation," *Administrative Science Quarterly* (December, 1962), pp. 295–308; and "The Concept of Bureaucracy: An Empirical Assessment," *American Journal of Sociology,* (July, 1963), pp. 32–40; and with Charles Title, "Bureaucracy and Its Correlates," *American Journal of Sociology* (November, 1966), pp. 267–272.

14   This scheme is fully described and related to supporting literature in Orion White, Jr., "Notes for a Model of Political Administration," a paper delivered at the Southwestern Political Science Association meeting in New Orleans, April 6–9, 1966 and "Representation in the Administrative Process," a paper delivered at the Conference on Democratic Theory, Indiana University, November 9–11, 1967.

15   The discussion of the flexibility-rigidity variable in response to role stress is based on Robert L. Kahn *et al., Organizational Stress Studies in Role Conflict and Ambiguity* (New York: John Wiley and Sons, Inc., 1964), Chap. 16. Also see Charles Neuringer, "The Relationship Between Authoritarianism, Rigidity, and Anxiety," *The Journal of General Psychology,* 71, (1964), pp. 169–175; and Charles E. Bidwell and Rececca S. Vreeland, "Authority and Control in Client Serving Organizations," *The Sociological Quarterly* (Summer, 1963), pp. 231–242.

16   The "organizational development" and planned-change field has been led primarily by Warren Bennis, Chris Argyris, Rensis Likert, MacGregor Abraham Maslow, and Robert Golembiewski. The management philosophy and structural alternatives for organization fit very well the need for change described here. See especially, Warren Bennis, *Changing Organizations* (New York: McGraw-Hill Book Co., 1966); Chris Argyris, *Intergrating the Individual and the Organization* (New York: John Wiley and Sons, Inc., 1964); Rensis Likert, *The Human Organization* (New York: McGraw-Hill Book Co., 1967); Douglas Macgregor, *The Human Side of Enterprise* (New York: McGraw-Hill Book Co., 1960); Abraham Maslow, *Eupsychian Management* (Homewood, Illinois: Irwin Dorsey Co., 1965); and Robert Golembiewski, *Men, Management, and Morality* (New York: McGraw-Hill Book Company, 1965).

Foreign Aid and Urban Aid

Jeffrey Pressman

Introduction

The parallels between American's foreign aid and domestic urban aid programs are numerous. Both are attempts by the United States government to provide financial resources to areas with an acute need for them; both seek to offer services that recipient governments cannot adequately provide on their own; both aim at stimulating self-sustaining economic growth; and both are based on the premise that economic development will further political development. Furthermore, both foreign and urban aid programs received their political impetus from a desire to stave off what were felt to be imminent dangers: the spread of communism abroad and the outbreak of urban violence at home.

Of course, the differences between these two aid programs are also significant. The independent sovereignty of foreign aid recipients limits the extent to which Washington can legitimately intervene and enforce its will in internal policy making. Also, cultural differences between donor and recipient are greater in the case of foreign aid. But an examination of both aid programs indicates that there are enough similarities between the problems faced and their attempted solutions to enable us to make fruitful comparisons between the two.

In both cases, it is clear that outside assistance has had important political—as well as economic—consequences. Writing of foreign aid, Warren Ilchman has pointed out:

> The aid-giver is squarely in the midst of the politics of the recipient country. Every choice he makes affects the distribution of authority, status, and resources in the society—either maintaining the existing distribution or bringing about another."[1]

The same could be said of the urban aid process.

One recurrent political problem is the relationship between the United States government and the government of the area to which aid is given —a foreign country or an American city. Both sets of relationships may be described as mixed-motive games, in which there is a "mixture of mutual dependence and conflict, of partnership and competition"[2] between the two governments. Although both donor and recipient have a strong interest in the success of the aid program, there is rarely complete agreement between Washington and the local regime on the appropriate level of aid and the ways in which it should be spent.

Although outside assistance can expand the resources available to a local regime, it can also cause numerous additional problems for that regime. And the dilemmas and hardships are not all on the side of the recipient government; the United States government faces tremendous organizational problems in the delivery of both foreign and domestic aid.

This essay examines the political impact of foreign and urban aid and suggests both similarities and differences between the consequences of the two programs. The experiences of foreign aid—many of which are recorded in an extensive body of literature[3]—suggest issues and problems that also characterize federal programs for cities. An explication of these problems, together with an evaluation of the organizational solutions that have been proposed to solve them, will, it is hoped, lead to some useful policy recommendations.

The essay is organized as follows: problems that outside assistance poses for the recipient regime (foreign nation or American city); organizational difficulties in the donor's delivery process; an examination of the donor's policies for political development in the recipient country or city and the effects of those policies on the recipient regime; parallels in the planning processes for foreign and urban aid; and suggestions for an urban aid policy that grows from the previous experience of aid programs.[4]

Problems for the Recipient Regime

To hard-pressed leaders of developing nations or American cities, outside financial assistance can be a vital aid for successful governance.

Physical and social projects can be initiated, political demands can be met, and governments can offer inducements to those groups with whom they wish to ally. But acceptance of outside aid may also bring a host of unforeseen administrative and political difficulties to the recipient country.

The Loss of Legitimacy

In the foreign aid experience, a major problem for a recipient regime has been the loss of legitimacy among its own people as a result of perceived dependence on United States aid. An Indonesian cabinet was forced to resign because it had accepted U. S. aid.[4] And postwar American aid to Greece, a program generally considered highly successful, required the Greek government to surrender a large portion of effective sovereignty to the United States, such as giving Americans control over the use of foreign exchange and sharing control over health policies.[5] This surrender provided opposition elements with powerful political ammunition.[6]

The loss of legitimacy that accompanies dependence on a foreign power has not been a critical problem for our cities; nonetheless, dependence on the federal government can be a distinctly unpleasant condition. To offset the tendency toward dependence, developing nations have sought to draw multilateral aid to reduce reliance on any one donor. Similarly, mayors have resisted the idea of a single federal coordinator for each city. The mayors would rather keep open numerous departmental channels of communication and funding opportunity than risk dependence on a local aid czar.

Unfulfilled Expectations

Another way in which outside aid programs can cause problems for the recipient regimes is that they create expectations that are not subsequently fulfilled. In many cases, those who are disappointed blame the recipient government. Discussing the experience of U. S. aid programs in Southeast Asia, John D. Montgomery writes that the "achievements of foreign aid may create new desires faster than the possibilities of meeting them, thus making the inevitable disappointments appear all the greater and more unjust."[7] Often, the new desires are fostered by promises that are not or cannot be fulfilled.

This same process has been repeated in urban aid programs. In 1966, the Economic Development Administration (EDA) pledged $23 million for a public works–employment program in Oakland. But because of a lack of interest and action on the part of both the federal agency and the Port of Oakland, the program is still in limbo, and funds have not been forthcoming. The result has been considerable resentment within the community and criticism of the city government, which has extremely limited power with regard to the actions of either the Port or the federal government.

Frustration and resentment result not only from expectations that are never fulfilled, but also from expectations that are fulfilled in a slow, uneven, or uncertain manner by the aid donor. It has been hard for recipient nations or cities to count on constant aid from outside sources. As Albert O. Hirschman has pointed out.

> Since political instability and strenuous competition for pathetically limited public funds are characteristic of many less developed countries, 'external' financial uncertainty has been so prominent an evil that various attempts have been made to "abolish" it.[8]

(Attempts at abolition have included the earmarking of special taxes to save favored projects.)

The unevenness and uncertainty of American aid to Greece made the position of the Greek government increasingly untenable. Because of Korean War expenditures and Washington's impatience with the slow pace of economic and political progress in Greece, American aid to that country dropped from $284.4 million in 1950–1951 to $21.3 million in 1953–1954.[9] In 1951, the American mission began to cut back all major investment projects in progress by imposing a restriction on the release of counterpart funds. From July 1, 1952, the Greek government was required to finance its own program of capital development from budget surplus over ordinary revenue. The result of American aid cutbacks was painful for the regime. An observer noted:

> Every cut in the aid program since 1952 has set up an accumulative disapproval. The restrictive credit policy that freezes heavy tractors and drilling rigs, and that checks the upward progress, becomes an American expedient to rob the honest, hard working farmer of his hopes of meat once a week. Such ground becomes fruitful to hostile propaganda. *Avghi* (the left-wing paper) announces that Russia would help. The right-wing papers grumble that Turkey (the traditional enemy) is getting x times as much as Greece.[10]

Of course, the recipient government could blame the slowdown on the aid donor, but then it would have to justify its own dependent position.

Inconstancy and uncertainty in funding has also been present in urban aid programs. Confusion over the availability and level of federal funding for the Neighborhood Centers Pilot Program (NCPP) frustrated both local Poverty Program and city officials in Oakland in 1967,[11] and the cutbacks and struggles for existence in the Poverty, Model Cities, and redevelopment programs have caused headaches for urban aid recipients. The experience of foreign aid indicates that erratic timing and uncertainty in aid giving can quickly undermine faith in externally assisted programs.

Restrictive Conditions

Even if adequate and timely aid is available, the accompanying administrative guidelines may make the aid process burdensome to the recipient government. For example, as Ilchman's study of foreign aid in India shows, numerous conditions placed on the use of aid may tie the hands of the recipient.[12] Closer to home, a Federal Executive Board (FEB) Task Force report found considerable resentment in Oakland's city government toward administrative strings attached to federal aid. A member of the city manager's staff declared:

> The strings attached to most federal programs cause all kinds of trouble. For instance, there was a big build-up last year on a new jobs program, with a lot of publicity which raised a lot of hopes. But there were so many restrictions attached that the program couldn't do what we had hoped it could. Sometimes there are so many strings that it's hard even to spend the money.[13]

Oakland's Building and Housing Department was equally critical of restrictive administrative guidelines. The Federal Task Force summarized the department's complaints:

> The City is waging a continuing and expensive battle against the spread of blight. However, none of the eleven code enforcement programs now operating in the City is assisted by federal funds, "because the federal code enforcement program has restrictions which make them inappropriate in Oakland." Underground improvements are not an eligible cost, for example, although they are usually required in a federal program. The federal program cannot be used as a "holding action" for areas in which such action could hold off deterioration for a limited time until stronger action could be taken. Oakland's citizens in several parts of the City have requested a code enforcement program in their neighborhood. HUD, however, has turned down two neighborhoods, on the grounds that one area was "too far gone," and that code enforcement in the other area would have amounted to a holding action, "which is not the intent of the program."[14]

Still, it is important to note that administrative requirements may serve as an excuse for a local political leader who wishes to put through a new and controversial policy. Thus, the mayor of Oakland was able to use EDA's insistence on equal employment policies as an argument for initiating an affirmative action minority employment program for the city.

Besides expressing frustration at restrictions attached to aid, recipients of both foreign and urban aid have resented the ways in which Washington imposes reforms without understanding their effects on the recipient. Thus, during the 1950s, the American government's attempts to stimulate a number of governmental and military reforms in South Vietnam failed because the reforms did not take into account the strength of political groups in that country or the political needs of the regime.[15] In American cities also, local officials resent programs which are imposed on their areas by the government. Discussing Concentrated Employment Program and the Neighborhood Centers Pilot Program in Oakland, the FEB Task Force report concluded that "the imposition of both CEP and NCPP, often diminishes local enthusiasm and often also runs counter to local perception of needs and priorities."[16]

Absorptive Capacity

Some of the difficulties that recipient regimes have experienced in the aid process rest on conditions that are difficult to change in a short time. Foreign aid literature abounds with discussions of absorptive capacity, the ability of a recipient nation to utilize aid in a productive manner.[17] This also deserves discussion in analyses of urban aid programs, for the lack of capable manpower in city governments restricts effective participation in federal programs. In Oakland, for example, the mayor has tried unsuccessfully to secure a greater role for the city in the area of manpower programs. One reason for his failure is the lack of administrative capacity in city hall to manage more than a token effort in this field. The lack both of staff and of willingness to expand horizons in the social program area constitutes a low absorptive capacity, preventing city government from utilizing available programs.

Communication

Another long-term problem of aid recipients appears to be shared equally with donors: the difficulty each side has in communicating with the other. Theodore Geiger and Roger D. Hansen have commented on relations between donor and recipient of foreign aid:

> This relationship has been a source of difficulty between the less developed countries and the United States. For their part, the former have increasingly resented the implication that they were not really capable of running their own development programs, which had to be prepared for them by the latter in accordance with its conception of their needs and priorities . . . Within the

aid agency itself, this practice has been responsible for the development of a self-image of the agency's role which might be called the "we complex." In their discussions with one another as well as with officials of the recipient countries, the personnel of the aid agency tended unconsciously to think of themselves as the active agents not simply in providing aid but also in managing the development process as a whole.[18]

In Oakland, an experiment in intergovernmental relations that tried to bring a federal task force (representing federal departments operating in Oakland) together with a city task force (representing city agencies) ran into difficulty, at least partially, because of mutual hostility between federal and city groups. The reasons for the hostility were similar to those encountered in the foreign aid process: city officials resented federal representatives telling them what the city's problems were, and federal officials felt that their local counterparts were not well equipped either to define or to solve problems.

Perhaps more than hostility, both foreign and urban aid programs have encountered confusion between donor and recipient with respect to the aid-giving process. Discussing foreign aid to Southeast Asia, Montgomery states: "Perhaps the most serious political obstacle to achieving objectives held in common by indigenous and American leadership was the vagueness of the decision-making locus in the administrative apparatus of both sides."[19] In the federal task force report on Oakland, federal officials complained about fragmentation among city agencies, and city officials complained about fragmentation among federal departments. In the city's view, interdepartmental fragmentation was supplemented by fragmentation within each department. Who had the controlling authority, Washington or the regional office?

Thus, as in foreign aid, a measure of hostility and confusion attends the relationships between donors and recipients of federal aid to cities. In such relationships, the problems of aid delivery are bound to be great.

The Donor's Dilemma: Problems of Organizing a Delivery System

Administrative Fragmentation and Geographic Centralization

The politics of interagency competition is, of course, a well-known phenomenon in Washington. Even among agencies charged with different administrative functions there is enough indirect competition in the search for funds, personnel, and political support to provide distraction from operational routines. But in foreign aid the principal agencies have been in direct competition for funds, for operating and policy responsibility, and even for specific projects. Here the distractions tend to overwhelm the operations.[20]

The above paragraph could have been written about urban aid as well. In foreign aid programs, successive aid agencies (ICA, AID, etc.) and the Departments of State, Defense, Agriculture, Labor, Commerce, and Health, Education, and Welfare have participated and have competed for authority. A similar fragmentation of departmental effort has characterized programs of federal aid to cities, involving the Departments of Housing and Urban Development (HUD), Health, Education and Welfare, Labor, Agriculture, and Commerce and the Department of Economic Opportunity (OEO), among others. As in foreign aid, component agencies within each department often pursue autonomous and contradictory paths. To complicate matters further, the separate agencies have stimulated their own community coordinating structures—the Community Action Agencies of OEO, Model Cities agencies of HUD, Overall Economic Development Program committees of EDA, and so on.

Besides facing a problem of departmental fragmentation, the United States government has also experienced an informational problem in both aid programs; it has been difficult to understand and respond quickly from Washington to local conditions. To meet the problems of fragmentation and distance simultaneously, both foreign and domestic aid programs have attempted to foster collaboration and coordination among departmental field representatives who could be in closer touch with the local situation. Some of the difficulties of foreign aid field coordination appear to be repeated in the urban aid experience; an analysis of past failures can indicate some of the preconditions for success in this area.

In the foreign aid experience, cooperation in the field was supposed to be carried out by a "country team"—the ambassador, the chiefs of the operations mission, the military advisory group, and the information service, in conjunction with appropriate Washington agencies. But such groups provided only general coordination,[21] with specific project decisions being made by the technical service divisions of the aid agency. Intradepartmental fragmentation did not lead to more flexibility or a desire to innovate, because each technical division was subject to strict evaluation from its home office in Washington. New or extraordinary functions could not be satisfactorily entrusted to regular divisions, because the overall performance of each division was judged by normal technical standards that did not allow for extraordinary functions.[22]

Centralization was also furthered by the aid agency's personnel system, which "attenuated local control over operations because careers were usually made in Washington, not in the field. A technician's advancement depended more upon assignments made in the technical services in Washington than on any mission director's judgment of his performance in response to local needs."[23] To the extent that aid personnel looked to Washington for guidance, approval, and promotion, the authority of the mission director in the country was weakened. Thus, the organization of aid was made up of fragments, each under strong central control from Washington. The organizational constructs of country team and aid mission were there, but career incentives were structured to encourage narrow specialization and loyalties.

For effective interdepartmental (or even intradepartmental) cooperation in the field, there must be some incentive for field representatives to work with representatives of other agencies, and there must be some authority for decision making delegated to those in the field. Failure to satisfy these conditions undercuts the effectiveness of foreign aid missions, and it appears that similar inadequacies are present in urban aid programs.

For domestic programs, the field representatives of federal agencies are located in regional offices throughout the country. Although these offices are supposed to bring the federal government closer to local governments and their problems, there are a number of obstacles to that goal.

One problem that has plagued city leaders is the uncertainty about the powers of the regional offices. The FEB Task Force in Oakland recorded the following comment from the city manager's office:

> If the City people felt that the regional people had real decision-making power, they would have more confidence in going into federal programs. As it is now, there is considerable lack of confidence, based on several experiences. In more than one instance, we've been assured by regional officials that funds would be made available, and have submitted applications on the assurance that they were mere formalities required before funds could be released. In two cases, our applications were rejected in Washington—once after we had already spent the money . . . The Mayor feels that local and regional officials, working together, could develop good programs that would have real relevance to local problems—but the regional people get overruled by Washington.[24]

In fact, the respective powers of regional and national offices vary widely from department to department. In examining Western regional officials, the FEB Task Force found that the Small Business Administration (SBA) was most decentralized (with the regional officials able to approve loans). HUD was in an intermediate position, with the region exercising day-to-day responsibility for urban renewal projects and Washington making decisions about which projects were to be funded. The Departments of Labor and Health, Education, and Welfare (HEW) were largely centralized, with most important decisions being made in Washington.[25]

The Task Force observed that federal–city communication within the region was hindered by the lack of authority of certain regional offices to commit their departments to specific actions. And where powers ranged widely from department to department, collaborative action among departments was more difficult. Furthermore, in those departments that were relatively centralized, the regional directors tended to have little control over their component regional parts. Although HUD's regional administrator and SBA's area administrator possessed direct authority over regional organizational components, the regional director of HEW could only be a broker or umpire with respect to his department's various units. Each of the major regional divisions of HEW reports directly to a regional assistant commissioner, who in turn reports both to the regional director and to a counterpart commissioner in Washington. Each of the Labor Department's thirteen bureaus and offices operating in the region are related "primarily not to each other or a regional coordinator but to their respective counterparts in Washington."[26]

With departments and agencies run from Washington and with promotions tied to performance within a particular organizational component, it is not surprising that the experience of the Oakland Task Force was similar to foreign aid attempts at interorganizational collaboration. The Federal Executive Board found that "there is little concensus among different agencies as to the major problems facing Oakland, or the priority which should be assigned to each," and that "agency officials tend to define Oakland's problems in terms of their own agency's area of responsibility."[27] The Federal Task Force concluded that interdepartmental (or even intradepartmental) coordination would continue to be extremely difficult in the light of present organizational realities.

As in foreign aid missions, which were to bring decision making to the grass roots level and encourage interorganizational cooperation, the federal regional offices have experienced grave difficulties in cooperating with each other and in responding quickly to local demands. This problem exists because the regional offices include units that are dominated and evaluated by Washington and have little ability or incentive to cooperate with each other in designing programs for a city.

But change is not impossible, and there is a current trend toward regional decentralization. The recent expansion in the number and power of HUD's field offices is a step in that direction.[28] This move does not facilitate closer relations with other departments, but it may make HUD regional personnel more accessible and useful to local leaders. Some of the organizational lessons of aid giving are apparently being learned.

Because the aid giver is "squarely in the midst of the politics of the recipient country," and because "every choice he makes affects the distribution of authority" in that country, he ought to consider the effects of his aid policies on the political life of the recipient. Particularly if those policies seek to alter the existing distribution of authority, the question of political involvement can cause irreconcilable hostility between the donor and the recipient governments. Let us turn to a discussion of the United States government's political development policies in foreign and urban aid programs.

Political Development Policies—And Some Unresolved Questions

Although an AID Program Guidance Manual has stated that a major goal of United States foreign policy is to contribute to the creation of a "community of free nations cooperating on matters of mutual concern, basing their political systems on consent and progressing in economic welfare and social justice,"[29] academic observers of foreign aid have found little interest in political development among aid administrators. After interviewing fifty-four AID officials, Robert A. Packenham concluded that declarations about democracy and social justice bore little clear relation to specific aid objectives and programs. "The approach to political development that is most often relied upon to achieve these objectives is economic; and even it is only implicit."[30] A chief planning officer in one of the AID regions told Packenham: "You know, one thing I've never been clear about is what our fundamental policy is on the question of whether we're trying to promote democracies or not."[31]

Washington AID offices did not seem to offer much guidance or show much interest in political development. For Packenham, such development would be measured by the capacity of political systems to "maintain and adapt themselves as they confront, generate, and absorb continuing transformations."[32] Political systems undergoing such development would become more responsive and more able to facilitate wide participation in political decision making.

AID has been involved from time to time in political development activities, but such efforts, according to Eugene B. Mihaly and Joan M. Nelson, "are usually semiaccidental or the result of special circumstances."[33] The semiaccidential category includes instances in which a political development project—education, public administration training, or the formation of cooperatives—is undertaken as part of an economic growth project. The special circumstances category includes instances like the following:

> A.I.D. often undertakes programs aimed at reducing clear and pressing threats to a country's political evolution. Its activities in Vietnam and Laos, and much of the program in Thailand, may be seen in this light. Sometimes the U.S. engages in concentrated rural development efforts intended to head off subversion or extremism, as in Northeast Thailand and Brazil and the Peruvian Altiplano.[34]

Mihaly and Nelson's observations seem to confirm Packenham's judgment that there is a "general stress on order and stability for their own sakes"[35] in AID political policies.

Recently, certain members of congress stimulated a movement to encourage popular participation in the foreign aid program. Hubert Humphrey, while a senator from Minnesota, together with Representatives Clement Zablocki, Donald M. Fraser, and F. Bradford Morse were leaders in this movement. The congressional initiative culminated in the passage of Title IX of the 1966 Foreign Assistance Act, which declared: "In carrying out programs authorized in this chapter, emphasis shall be placed on assuring maximum participation in the task of economic development on the part of the people of the developing countries, through the encouragement of democratic, private and local government institutions."[36] In the 1967 Foreign Assistance Act, the title was again incorporated, with provisions for civic education and political training for citizens of developing nations, and with a direction to AID to begin in-service training to carry out the purposes of the title.[37]

What has become of the popular participation of Title IX? Not much, according to John R. Schott,[38] who served as the director of AID's Title IX Division. The obstacles to effective implementation by AID have included (1) opposition to Title IX within AID itself by those who have sought to de-politicize the aid process and to rely on politically neutral macroeconomic criteria in assessing development; (2) opposition to Title IX by State Department officials, who view it as a bureaucratic encroachment on their own prerogatives; (3) lack of operational knowledge concerning the expansion of popular participation in economic development; and (4) concern among recipient countries about United States interference in their domestic affairs. These factors have combined to block the execution of the congressional mandate.

In the area of political development, the experience of urban aid has differed markedly from that of foreign aid. Federal administrators in American cities have formulated policies beyond a concern with economic development and political stability. In some cases, they have given resources to independent, indigenous institutions that have challenged city governments, and they have provided occasions for expanding participation in federal program decision making. Interventions in local authority systems have been more than "semiaccidental or the result of special circumstances"; they have been an important feature of certain major urban programs.

In contrast to the Title IX effort, in which widened participation grew out of congressional initiative and was subsequently bottled up in the Executive Branch, the "maximum feasible participation" section of the Poverty Program was never discussed by congress before the Economic Opportunity Act passed in 1964.[39] Rather, OEO staff members working in harmoney with indigenous community leaders stimulated interest in participation by the poor. Howard W. Hallman has written about the beginning of this cooperation:

> . . . the composition of the board of the local community action agency became more and more of an issue. This was the beginning of a transitional period in the civil rights movement. The Civil Rights Act of 1964 had recently been enacted, the last major national demonstrations which produced the Voting Rights Act of 1965 were just beginning, the first significant use of the phrase "black power" was a year and a half away (in the Meredith Mississippi March of June 1966), but in many places civil rights leaders were gearing up to gain a larger role in local programs. Along came the Community Action Program tailor-made for their desires. Moreover, the key OEO staff within the Community Action Program and the Office of Inspection was more than sympathetic, for they possessed deep suspicion of municipal government and other parts of local "establishments." They were talking about power for the poor.[40]

In a number of cities, Community Action Agencies (CAA) provided opportunities for organizing poor perople and for confronting already existing institutions.[41] Employment services, welfare departments, schools, health departments, and legal aid offices were challenged by Community Action Agencies to do a more effective job of reaching the poor. In many cases, CAA's entered these social fields and operated independently from established institutions. And besides providing services, some CAA's actively trained leaders and mobilized the poor as a political force.

The Model Cities Program, which was designed to concentrate and coordinate federal grants in certain demonstration neighborhoods of cities, has also provided an opportunity for community participation and control. The Model Cities legislation demanded widespread participation by citizens, but HUD offered no precise formula for nighborhood involvement. Former HUD Secretary Weaver told congress: "It will be up to the cities themselves to devise appropriate ways in which citizens will participate."[42] The federal government would act as a "mediator" or "marriage counselor" between the city government and neighborhood residents. As time went on, neighborhood residents gained an increasingly strong role in Model Cities.[43]

In Oakland, as Judith May has shown,[44] the Poverty and Model Cities Programs have provided opportunities for the creation of strong indigenous organizations. The Oakland Economic Development Council, Inc. (OEDCI) is the Poverty Program's Community Action Agency, independent from city hall; and the West Oakland Planning Committee is the spokesman for target area residents in the Model Cities Program. Through these organizations, residents or neighborhoods have increased their control over federal resources and have, in fact, created a "second government for the West Oakland community."[45]

Thus, the impact of federal urban programs on political development appears to be significant. Through the Poverty and Model Cities Programs, new institutions have been created, new leaders have been invested with resources, and the structure of authority in some communities has been challenged. In Packenham's words, a "continuing transformation" has been generated in certain urban political systems, but it is not clear how well those systems have been able to absorb or adapt to the transformations. A political development based on the expansion of participation and on the creation of new institutions to challenge existing ones raises many thorny questions. Though such an approach to development has been far from universal in federally assisted cities, those urban centers (like Oakland) in which it has been employed have had to search for answers.

The first question is one of democratic legitimacy. Who are the authentic spokesmen of the people of a given area? In *Dilemmas of Social Reform*[46] Peter Marris and Martin Rein state that the Poverty Program "faced the inherent conflict of a simultaneous commitment to two conceptions of democratic accountability. From whom were the projects to take their lead, elected government or those they served?"[47] Mayors and city councils, as elected representatives, could not be lightly shunted aside by those who valued the electoral process. "As soon as community action became national policy, it was bound to provoke local government to defend its jurisdiction. And a policy dependent upon public funds and public institutions, which called on communities to commit wholeheartedly their own resources, could not lightly disregard the duly elected representatives of democracy."[48]

In Oakland the federal government has consistently disregarded the city government by overriding the mayor's objections, lodging the Neighborhood Centers Pilot Program and Concentrated Employment Program with the increasingly independent OEDCI and by refusing to give the mayor a significant role in any employment plan (the policy area he cares about most). Federal decisions to concentrate resources in agencies outside city hall control (about one percent of total federal spending in Oakland goes to city hall)[49] have meant that elective city politics has little attraction for those desiring to participate in significant social action. Part of the reason for the virtual nonexistence of electoral politics in Oakland doubtlessly lies in the closed nature of the electoral arena itself (at-large, nonpartisan elections, and recruitment to the council by appointment), and part of the noninterest appears to stem from the fact that city hall does not control important social programs in the city.

Besides having a certain legitimacy as elected officials, mayors and councilmen are often in a position to offer resources to poverty-related programs, a fact that the federal government's political development policy for cities ought to take into account. Writing about the early goals of the Poverty Program, Marris and Rein state:

> Participation was . . . to restore dignity, redistribute power, and ensure that, wherever possible, the poor themselves were recruited for the jobs that the projects would create. But the poverty program was also convinced . . . that only the Cabinet, nationally, and the mayors locally, were powerful enough to co-ordinate the resources it needed.[50]

Even in Oakland's present government, which contains both structural and attitudinal obstacles to innovative action, the mayor—who has strong ties to business—could have played a role in job development if he had been given a chance to do so.[51] And over time, a progressive city council in Oakland could engage in appointment, purchasing, hiring, and licensing practices that might have an effect on the distribution of resources in the city. But people must be given some encouragement to start the long battle for political control and governmental redirection. For this reason, those formulating political development policy in Washington might consider ways incentives could be structured to encourage people to seek local elective office. One possibility would be to give city hall some social programs that could make elected positions seem tempting.

This is not to argue that city hall should supplant independent poverty agencies as the recipient of federal funding, for there are reasons for giving some programs to official agencies and others to militantly independent ones. Invoking the pluralist tradition of American politics, Marris and Rein point out that,

> A strategy of community-wide co-operation might well be incompatible with the uncompromising assertion of minority interests; in these circumstances, the Federal Government should be prepared to support, in the same community, both official and countervailing conceptions of a viable programme.[52]

Although this strategy might invite extensive proxy wars involving the community representatives of various federal agencies, it does appear that both city hall and indigenous groups have strengths that ought to be exploited by federal policy.

But whatever decision is made in this regard, it is clear that there will be abundant opportunities for hostility between city halls and federally funded autonomous agencies. Drawing on the experience of foreign aid, Hirschchman has outlined some of the problems attending the creation of autonomous agencies that are financed by foreign nations in developing

countries. Such agencies may become the targets of nationalistic resentment against "international interference in local affairs"; they may under-
estimate the powers of old bureaucratic units to retaliate against provocative action; and, removed from the mainstream of politics, where an
institution must maintain a certain balance in order to survive, they may
be taken over by narrow fractions.[53] In any case, autonomous bodies that
are financed from outside have been targets of considerable hostility in
developing countries, as they will probably continue to be in American
cities.

An Uncertain Reed

A final problem for the independent agencies themselves is that the
federal government may be an uncertain reed upon which to lean. Judith
V. May points out that "a small change in federal administrative or legislative policy could have an enormous effect on the viability of the West
Oakland 'government.' "[54] Federally financed community groups are not
spared the problems that beset city governments as recipients of aid
programs. Community Action Agencies have known budgetary uncertainty as they have struggled annually for existence.[55] They have also
complained of tight control from Washington, of administrative guidelines
which block innovation, and of the inability of regional officials to give
them definitive answers on policies.[56] Federal decisions made in 1969,
which both reduced funds for Model Cities and increased city hall's power
in the program, underscored some of the difficulties of community-based
organizations' reliance on federal programs.[57]

Federal urban aid programs have gone beyond the chiefly economic
and stability orientations of foreign aid programs, making conscious and
far-reaching attempts to alter the distribution of political resources in
some cities. Through the Poverty and Model Cities Programs, the federal
government has provided opportunities for poor people to organize and
to make decisions on programs that affect them. The stimulation and
maintenance of independent indigenous organizations represent a major
attempt by the federal government to influence political development in
cities. Still, difficult questions remain: What is to be the role of local,
elected officials in programs that call for wide representation of the poor?
What effect does the creation of independent agencies have on a city's
electoral process? Can the federal government simultaneously fund city
hall and anti-city hall bodies? What will be the result of hostility between
city officials and poverty area leaders? Finally, what effect does fiscal
uncertainty—or an actual cutoff of funds—have on a federally assisted
community organization? These questions, which cannot be answered at
this time, manifest some of the difficulties accompanying the political
development policies of urban programs. And those who seek to imple-

ment the participation provisions in Title IX of the Foreign Aid Act might also need them.

Parallels in Planning

In discussing similarities between the foreign and urban aid we ought to say something about the use of planning in both programs. Although a careful assessment of social problems, policy alternatives, available resources, and possibilities of implementation can be useful to any government, planning connected with foreign and urban aid programs has too often been a distinct waste of time—an isolated exercise that has served the interests of neither the recipient nor the donor.

A Bolivian delegate to a Latin American seminar on planning once remarked: "What is needed is not so much short-term plans as plans prepared in a short time."[58] Less developed countries have realized that they have a better chance of attracting foreign financial aid if they are able to produce development plans. Sometimes, in their rush to produce such plans, the technicians have not stopped to consider the preconditions necessary for the successful implementation of the blueprints. Albert Waterston notes:

> The rapid spread of planning and pressure from aid-giving countries and agencies in recent years have . . . converted some countries to planning almost solely because it is fashionable and because possession of a national development plan often makes it easier to obtain foreign grants or loans. There are countries where comprehensive plans have been prepared in a few weeks in an office in the capital without the planners having consulted with operating ministries and agencies.[59]

Brazil's *Plano Trienal* was prepared within ten weeks, and Ghana's Seven-Year Plan, prepared with minimal participation of government operating agencies, took five weeks.[60]

The same process has characterized the plans cities must formulate to gain federal grants. For example, the Economic Development Administration requires preparation of an "Overall Economic Development Program," a comprehensive picture of the local economy—resources, obstacles to economic progress, forward projections of economic health, etc. But James L. Sundquist found, on the basis of nationwide interviews, that "OEDP's were prepared because the federal government required them —not because the citizen leaders saw the comprehensive planning process as having enough intrinsic merit to justify the effort."[61] In Oakland, preparation of the OEDP was assigned to a junior member of the planning department, an organizational unit considerably detached from the day-today operation of the city. Likewise, preparation of HUD's "workable program" has been viewed by Oakland officials merely as a bothersome part of the federal application for funds.

As in many developing countries, planners in American cities often view the creation of a plan as an end in itself. With reference to the foreign experience, Waterston writes,

> Where plan formulation is viewed as an exclusive or isolated element divorced in practice if not in theory from plan implementation, as it has in fact been viewed in many countries, one finds that planners pay little attention in their plans to the choice of means to be employed to achieve plan targets. This is why most plans almost always provide detailed information only about *what* is to be achieved, but not about *how* to go about securing development objectives or targets, or about *who* in government or elsewhere should be responsible for carrying out the required tasks.[62]

In 1968, Stanford Research Institute (SRI) urged the city government of Oakland to create a unit to develop comprehensive objectives and strategies in the manpower field, identify programs and funds available from all levels of government, develop a set of priorities, and evaluate all programs in the light of those priorities.[63] The mayor, who had tried in vain for some time to gain jurisdiction and funding for city hall manpower programs, was mystified by the Stanford Research recommendations. What would the city do after carrying out all the planning? How would it gain the needed authority and money to implement desired programs? What powers would it have over existing agencies? An SRI representative tried to assuage the Mayor's doubts: "When you have a good planning unit, you can easily get control from people." This optimistic approach suggests that a satisfactory plan will automatically implement itself.

Instead of viewing planning as an isolated exercise, with implementation either forgotten or thrown in carelessly at the end, it would be more useful to consider planning as including the totality of government choice making: in budgets, in personnel decision, in the daily operation of departments. The separation of planning from implementation, which is encouraged by requirements for comprehensive and quickly drawn-up plans, means that implementation is forgotten and that the plan itself becomes the final product.

Comprehensive planning can be worse than irrelevant: it can create problems for a government by making unfulfillable promises to groups. Although plans may be used in developing countries to advertise the benefits of economic development projects in order to gain the support of certain groups,[64] a failure to achieve those benefits may make the regime a target of frustration and anger.

When the realization of the comprehensive plan depends on outside money, the potential dangers for the regime are increased. Domestic programs have experienced some uncomfortable results of comprehensive planning, as is evidenced by these remarks from an EDA program recipient:

> We spent the better part of a year putting together an overall economic development program, We involved the whole area in it. EDA requires that the OEDP set forth a listing of priorities, so we laid out our priorities. It was published, and widely distributed throughout the district. Pretty soon the word came through that EDA had approved our OEDP, and the local papers played up the good news. The whole area interpreted that to mean that the priority projects were approved as priority projects and would therefore be funded. But now they find out that isn't the case at all. They have to struggle to get acceptance of the very projects that were contained in the approved OEDP, and EDA feels free to upset the priorities that the OEDP sets.[65]

H. Ralph Taylor, who was Assistant Secretary of HUD in charge of Model Cities, said in the fall of 1968: "Many mayors have been hesitant about getting out in front politically and engaging in a comprehensive planning process with citizens because of skepticism about the federal commitment." The mayors wondered whether the federal government would respond promptly to local initiative, whether the funds would be adequate to support the plans, and whether the assistance would be coordinated. Taylor remarked: "I really don't blame the mayors."[66] Comprehensive planning may excite people by painting a glowing picture of future benefits, but governments should give some thought to the consequences of nonfulfillment. Publicized plans can be dangerous to a government with a low capacity to satisfy the demands placed upon it.

To be useful at all, planning must be related to the pattern of political power in a community; effective planning can be done only by an organization that has some capacity to enforce its will upon others. On the basis of their study of the Ford Foundation and the President's Committee on Juvenile Delinquency projects, Marris and Rein concluded:

> The crucial flaw seems to have lain, not in the financial inducement, but in the insistence on formal co-ordination as a prerequisite, rather than an outcome of changes in the power structure. Independent authorities were to commit themselves at the outset to the principles of a planning procedure which none of them could individually control.

Having witnessed the failure of these programs to achieve the goal of coordinated planning, the authors state:

> The realignment of power and policy must . . . be achieved first, and this depends as much on new men as new ideas. No formal procedure for integrated planning can persuade independently powerful executives to abandon their prerogatives.[67]

Planning cannot magically create new power relationships, the Stanford Research Institute representative's advice to the mayor of Oakland notwithstanding. (In that case, planning would be an ineffectual substitute for power.) As experience in both developing countries and American cities has shown, planning divorced from implementation and political power centers is, at best, irrelevant. At worst, it can create problems for governments by stimulating demands that may be impossible to fulfill.

This is not to argue against a careful evaluation of the needs, goals, and resources of a city, but it is to suggest that planning must be linked to the operations of government and provide for effective implementation. Foreign aid programs have encouraged rapid and overly comprehensive planning by developing countries, resulting in the preparation of plans for their own sake. Urban aid programs, some of which have stimulated a similar process in our cities, can learn something from these sad planning experiences of foreign aid.

Directions for Future Policy

Although the foreign and urban aid programs exhibit a number of interesting similarities, a comparison of the two experiences can do more than illuminate the connections between them. We should also be able to apply the lessons of past experience to future policy choices. Because this volume is most concerned with America's urban problems, this essay will conclude by suggesting some of the ways the experiences of foreign and urban aid might offer direction for future policy making in American cities.

(1) With respect to foreign and domestic recipient governments, outside aid may increase their problems as well as their resources. Some expectations that have been raised have not been fulfilled, causing recipient governments to become the targets of their citizens' frustrations. Funding has often been late, unsteady, and uncertain. Decisions have been made in Washington without adequate knowledge of local conditions, and rigid guidelines have prevented local innovation.

One solution to these problems would be the provision of bloc grants to cities, with the local governments making decisions as to the use of the funds. This idea has much to commend it: bloc grants would not only avoid the rigidity and distance of federal administration; they might also increase participation in city politics by making city governments worth fighting for.

There are, however, a number of difficulties inherent in bloc grant proposals, even if we assume that a national program along these lines is politically feasible. Among the political obstacles to bloc grants to cities are the lack of will in the administration and congress to devote financial resources to the venture, the desire on the part of states to play a role in urban programs, and the potential resistance to unrestricted bloc grants on the part of constituencies of present categorical programs. Bill Cavala and Aaron Wildavsky have pointed out that conservative cities could use bloc grants for traditional purposes, rather than for social programs or income redistribution. Also, city officials may find the pressure of how to distribute unrestricted funds too great; they may prefer restricted expenditures as a way of reducing their own discretion, thus making their lives easier.[68]

In a city like Oakland, where the Redevelopment Agency, School District, Housing Authority, and Community Action Agency are all independent of city hall, to whom would the bloc grant go? Each federal agency might suggest a different local recipient. With power in many cities fragmented, it would be difficult to find a logical receptacle for a bloc grant. Finally, if a goal of federal urban policy is to redistribute resources in cities, categorical grants could have the advantage of earmarking funds for use in certain poorer areas (like the Elementary and Secondary Education Act's Title I program for compensatory education). Bloc grants might be shared by powerful interests in a community, with weaker political actors getting short shrift.[69]

If bloc grants are not forthcoming, it still ought to be possible to minimize some of the problems of recipient governments. Expectations should be kept in line with probable fulfillment, and promises should not be made that would inflate expectations. Also, the problems of uncertainty of funding, distance of communication, and rigidity of administration might be dealt with by a change in the federal delivery system itself and by upgrading the powers of federal regional offices. If city officials could work on a continuous basis with nearby federal representatives who could explain federal policy to them and who had the authority to commit substantial federal resources, the local officials might find that their uncertainty would be reduced and that federal decisions would be more sensitive to local needs.

(2) With respect to the organizational problem of delivery, both foreign and urban aid programs have created field organizations that were supposed to bring policies closer to the recipients, to gain accurate information on recipients' needs, and to promote cooperation between agencies involved in the aid process. But both country aid missions and federal regional offices have tended to reserve important decisions for themselves —whether they involve agricultural projects in Taiwan or employment programs in Oakland. The result has been to undermine the morale of

federal field personnel and of local officials who would like to work with them but find that real power lies in Washington.

Similarly, although interorganizational cooperation has been a stated aim of field offices in both foreign and urban aid programs, little incentive has been offered for such cooperation, even within a single federal department. Evaluations and promotions have been made in Washington on the basis of performance within a particular departmental division. Foreign aid mission directors and domestic regional administrators have had uncertain authority over the component pieces of their domains.

Thus, both foreign and urban aid experiences show that field offices will not really be useful to the recipient regime unless it is given power to approve or reject projects. If federal regional offices were able to give city officials definitive answers, the feeling of confusion on the part of local leaders would be eased. Also, if cooperation among federal agencies is really desired, incentives for such cooperation must be offered; agency members cannot be asked to serve on interagency task forces in a spirit of altruism. Rather, officials must be paid and given career credit for participation in interagency projects.

In urging interorganizational cooperation, one does not need to preach comprehensive, coordinated planning by all federal departments operating in a city, nor the appointment of a federal prefect to speak with one voice for all departments and agencies. Such proposals, which are politically and organizationally unfeasible, are probably not desirable anyway. As we have seen, funding might usefully be channeled to a variety of groups in a city, each of which can perform a particular task well (a Community Action Agency in recruitment for health or job training programs, a mayor's office for job development with employers, etc.). Certain federal agencies have proven able to relate particularly well to certain local agencies, and the creation of a monolothic federal organization might cut down the opportunities for access enjoyed by local groups.

What, then, would be the goals of more limited interagency cooperation? For one thing, an interagency task force could work on a system whereby processing of applications, funding, and auditing patterns might be standardized among federal departments. As it is, wide variations in program processing and timing cause consternation among local officials. Furthermore, an interagency task force would be able to inform a mayor or community leader about how federal programs in a city relate to each other. The opportunity for federal officials to meet on a regular and frequent basis was one of the chief gains of the Oakland Task Force experiment, even though a comprehensive list of priorities and solutions was never drawn up. Such meetings give federal officials an opportunity to learn about each other's programs, besides providing a focal point for city officials who are confused by the complexity of federal programs.

(3) With respect to the planning progress, previous aid programs provide numerous examples of planning for its own sake, divorced from implementation and removed from political life. Planning has been a condition for receiving aid for both developing countries and American cities. Although the analysis of social problems, policy alternatives, available resources, and possibilities of implementation could be of great help to city governments, planning as an end in itself does not accomplish this task. At best, such planning is irrelevant; at worst, it can embarrass a government by publicizing future payoffs that cannot be realized.

If the federal government wants to stimulate better analysis of policy in cities, it might be well advised to reduce requirements for plan preparation and to provide money to mayors, city managers, and community organizations for building high quality day-to-day staffs.[70] As in developing countries, their low absorptive capacity prevents city governments from taking full advantage of available federal aid. A prime reason for low absorptive capacity is low staff capability; city halls lack people who understand and are interested in federal social programs. The provision of grants for hiring topnotch staff might help to change this situation.

Thus, the experiences of foreign and urban aid programs, similar in many respects, can provide some direction for future policy. In certain respects—such as the pitfalls of comprehensive planning or the effects on recipient governments of excessive dependence on outside aid—urban aid programs can learn a great deal from the twenty-four year experience of foreign aid. And in the case of political development, the implementation of Title IX of the Foreign Assistance Act might be informed by the observation of Community Action in the Poverty Program.

Still, successful policies cannot be brought about by organizational change and political development efforts alone; there must be a decision made in the executive branch and in congress to provide aid programs with substantial financial resources. For most of their lives, United States foreign and urban aid programs have been plagued by financial uncertainty and inadequacy. This has been the greatest common problem of both efforts, for without a national financial commitment, there are no substantial resources for an aid program to give its field offices or to foreign governments. Organizational innovation is important, but it is not a substitute for national commitment.

NOTES

The Oakland Project, under the direction of Dean Aaron Wildavsky of the Graduate School of Public Affairs at Berkeley, consists of faculty and graduate students who have worked in and studied various agencies in Oakland. I worked part-time in the Mayor's Office from 1967 to 1969.

1   Warren F. Ilchman, "A Political Economy of Foreign Aid: The Case of India" *Asian Survey* VII: 10 (Oct., 1967), p. 670.

2 Thomas F. Schelling, *The Strategy of Conflict* (New York: Oxford University Press, 1960), p. 89.

3 See, for example, John D. Montgomery, *Foreign Aid in International Politics* (Englewood Cliffs: Prentice-Hall, Inc., 1967); Montgomery, *The Politics of Foreign Aid: American Experience in Southeast Asia* (New York: Praeger Paperbacks, 1962); Eugene B. Mihaly and Joan M. Nelson, "Political Development and US Economic Assistance" Paper delivered at American Political Science Assoc. Meeting, 1966; Theodore Geiger and Roger D. Hansen, "The Role of Information in Decision Making on Foreign Aid" *The Study of Policy Formation* Raymond A. Bauer and Kenneth J. Gergen (eds.), (New York: The Free Press, 1968); Charles Wolf, Jr., *United States Policy and the Third World* (Boston: Little, Brown and Company, 1967); Robert A. Packenham, "Political Development Doctrines in the American Foreign Aid Program" *World Politics,* XVIII: 2(Jan., 1966), pp. 194–235; William Hardy McNeill, *Greece: American Aid in Action* (New York: The Twentieth Century Fund, 1957); C. A. Munkman, *American Aid to Greece: A Report on the First Ten Years* (New York: Frederick A. Praeger, 1958).

4 John D. Montgomery, *The Politics of Foreign Aid, op. cit.,* p. 6.

5 See William Hardy McNeill, *op. cit.,* p. 189.

6 See Bickham Sweet-Escott, *Greece: A Political and Economic Survey, 1939–1953* (London: Royal Institute of International Affairs, 1954), pp. 105–06.

7 John D. Montgomery, *The Politics of Foreign Aid, op. cit.,* p. 18.

8 Albert O. Hirschman, *Development Projects Observed* (Washington: The Brookings Institution, 1967), p. 58.

9 Bickham Sweet-Escott, *Greece, op. cit.,* pp. 105–06.

10 C. A. Munkman, *American Aid to Greece, op. cit.,* p. 281.

11 Oakland Task Force, San Francisco Federal Executive Board, *An Analysis of Federal Decision-Making and Impact: The Federal Government in Oakland* (1968), p. 124, (The Task Force was staffed by the consultant firm of Marshall Kaplan, Gans, and Kahn of San Francisco. Marshall Kaplan, as principal of the firm, was the Staff Director.)

12 Warren F. Ilchman, *A Political Economy & Foreign Aid, op. cit.,* p. 680.

13 Federal Executive Board, Progress Report III, p. 166.

14 *Ibid.*

15 See Montgomery, *The Politics of Foreign Aid,* pp. 62ff.

16 Oakland Task Force, Federal Executive Board, p. 129.

17 See, for example, Albert Waterston, *Development Planning: Lessons of Experience* (Baltimore: Johns Hopkins Press (1965), pp. 300ff.

18 Geiger and Hansen, in *The Study of Policy Formation, op. cit.,* p. 354.

19 Montgomery, *The Politics of Foreign Aid,* p. 103.

20 *Ibid.,* p. 153.

21 *Ibid.,* p. 160.

22 *Ibid.,* p. 166.

23 *Ibid.,* p. 167.

24 Federal Executive Board, Progress Report III, p. 167.

25 Oakland Task Force, Federal Executive Board, p. 101.

26 Federal Executive Board, Progress Report I, p. 3.

27 Oakland Task Force, Federal Executive Board, p. 23.

28 "HUD Reorganizes for Local Control" *Okaland Tribune* March 24, 1970.

29 *AID Program Guidance Manual* August, 1963. Quoted in Robert A. Packenham, *op. cit.,* p. 195.

30 *Ibid.,* p. 211.

31 *Ibid.,* pp. 211–212.

32 *Ibid.,* p. 208.

33 Mihaly and Nelson, p. 6.

34 *Ibid.,* p.

35 Packenham, pp. 222–223.

36 Foreign Assistance Act of 1966, chapter 2, Title IX, Sec. 281. Quoted in Ralph Braibanti, ed. *Political and Administrative Development* (Durham, N. C.: Duke University Press, 1969), p. 15.

37 Foreign Assistance Act of 1967, Title IX.

38 "Title IX: A New Dimension in U.S. Foreign Aid?" Paper prepared for delivery at the Annual Meeting of the International Studies Association, San Francisco, March 27–29, 1969.

39 See James L. Sundquist, *Making Federalism Work* (Washington, D. C.: The Brookings Institution, 1969), p. 35.

40 "Historical Highlights of the Poverty Program" Paper prepared for an Airlie House Conference in Warrenton, Va., sponsored by the Urban Coalition, January, 1969.

41 See Sundquist, pp. 47–78.

42 *Ibid.,* p. 85.

43 *Ibid.,* p. 90.

44 "Two Model Cities: Political Development on the Local Level" Paper prepared for delivery at the annual meeting of the American Political Science Association, New York City, Sept. 2–6, 1969.

45 *Ibid.,* p. 1.

46 Peter Marris and Martin Rein, Dilemmas of Social Reform (New York: Atherton Press, 1969)

47 *Ibid.,* p. 215.

48 *Ibid.,* p. 218.

49 *Digest of Current Federal Programs in the City of Oakland* Prepared by Jeffrey L. Pressman for Mayor John H. Reading, 1968.

50 Marris and Rein, p. 215.

51 Sundquist, pp. 52–53.

52 Marris and Rein, p. 220.

53 Hirschman, pp. 156ff.

54 May, p. 2.

55 Sundquist, p. 68.

56 *Ibid.,* p. 73.

57 See *New York Times,* April 29, 1969, for increase in mayor's powers. See AP story on October 10, 1969, for funding cuts in Model Cities.

58 Quoted in Waterston, p. 103.

59 *Ibid.,* p. 104.

60 *Ibid.*

61 Sundquist, p. 193.

62 Waterston, p. 337.

63 *Human Resources Development for Oakland: Problems and Policies.*

64 See Warren F. Ilchman and Norman Thomas Uphoff, *The Political Economy of Change* (Berkeley: University of California Press, 1969), p. 242.

65 Sundquist, p. 248.

66 *Ibid.*

67 Marris and Rein, p. 159.

68 Bill Cavala and Aaron Wildavsky, "The Political Feasibility of Income by Right" in *Public Policy,* Vol. *XVIII,* No. 3 (Spring 1970), pp. 346–349.

69 Professor Frank Levy, having observed urban education administration in Oakland, suggests the possibility that bloc grants could go into teachers' salary raises, while ghetto schools—which are now the recipients of compensatory education programs—might be left out.

70 In an article entitled "Leave City Budgeting Alone!" (in J. P. Crecine and L. H. Masotti, eds., *Financing the Metropolis,* Vol. 4., Los Angeles: Sage Publications, 1970), Arnold J. Meltsner and Aaron Wildavsky suggest that a group of policy analysts, separate from budget staff, should be established to work directly for the mayor or manager of a city. With such a group, top city officials would be able to undertake short-term studies of major policies.

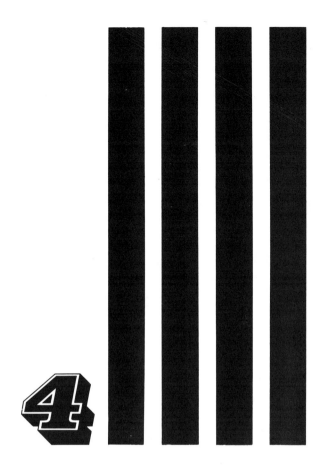

New Politics,
the Neighborhood,
and the Citizen

Local Strategies for Attaining Neighborhood Control

John H. Strange

This essay is not a research report. It does not make arguments in support of decentralization of decision making within existing cities, neighborhood control, or community development. It does not attempt to consider whether these objectives are desirable or not—either as ends or as means to other goals. It does not compare neighborhood control as a means to equality and human dignity with other means designed to attain these objectives. These questions are being dealt with in other essays herein.

Nor is this essay a guidebook to alternative structural arrangements for neighborhood control. The essay also provides consideration of such questions as: is a community based on natural geographic boundaries or cultural associations? can a community exceed 50,000 persons? can it be that large?

Rather, this essay is a consideration of an entirely different problem. Given the desirability of decentralized decision making and neighborhood or community control, what actions, strategies, plans, or tactics might result in that political arrangement? The purpose, then, is not to provide a handbook for achieving community control. Rather, it is intended to array some alternative possible stretegies (local rather than national) for accomplishing neighborhood control.

Having already made more disclaimers than are contained in any cleverly worded contract, let me add a few more. First, all strategies aimed at attaining neighborhood control must be tailored to local situations. They must take into account the different traditions, political situations, and personalities. Second, change often results as much from inaction or passivity on the part of some as from action on the part of others. Consideration is given in this essay only to actions that would be made directly on the local environment and that were not means to incapacitate or deactivate opponents. Third, accidents, unique events, unforeseen mistakes, personalities, and individual perceptions play a large part in any process of social change. Would, for example, Judge Carswell have been confirmed without the surprising and politically costly plea by Senator Hruska for representation of mediocrity on the Supreme Court? We can certainly hope for advantageous events. We may even assist in their occurring. We cannot however manipulate all actors and events.

Alan Altshuler concludes his excellent book on community control with the observation that if community control becomes a reality it will not be a result of white altruism, but rather "a product of protest and pragmatic compromise."[1] Protest and pragmatic compromise will be essential. But also necessary will be the successful use and manipulation of symbols.[2] Just as labeling a judge mediocre, a racist, or a judicial activist can enhance or detract from his political support, so can the identification of neighborhood control with symbols ease or hinder its acceptance.

In addition to discussing the possibilities for protest, compromise, and positive symbol manipulation, this essay considers what actions might alter the costs and benefits to present decision makers. Harry C. Bredemeier has analyzed the attempts to abolish poverty on the assumption that having some people poor is a function of the rewards it brings, the rewards doing away with it would bring, the costs of having it, and the costs of doing away with it.[3] These four factors will be discussed in relation to attempts to achieve neighborhood control.

Protest as a Strategy

Some observers of the American political scene have recently argued that protest, as a useful political tool, has been severely weakened. Sit-ins, peaceful demonstrations, letter writing campaigns, boycotts, and threats of violence are no longer as effective as they once were. They are becoming commonplace and accepted as normal events. They have become increasingly expensive to undertake, can be easily ignored, and can be quickly and inexpensively undercut or co-opted. It is argued that to be effective, protest must now be violent or semiviolent. This often results in repression, rather than change, and is counterproductive. Protest then, the argument goes, is no longer useful to achieve social change.

This is not necessarily the case. Certainly, protest, as a means for achieving neighborhood control, appears to be a viable technique. Protest can still incapacitate a neighborhood facility, such as a school, a precinct station, a business community, or a branch welfare office. In these situations strikes, boycotts, even occasional violent outbursts are still possible as political tools. Leaving aside the very important question of whether neighborhood support for protest action can be attained, it is on the neighborhood level, rather than the city, state, or national level, that protest remains a viable political tool.

Protest to achieve neighborhood control must take different forms. If Altshuler is correct in arguing that inefficient and disinterested bureaucracies are the real targets of those seeking community control, many new possibilities for protest are present. Legal challenges, long a favorite and often an effective form of protest, can be brought against local bureaucracies. These attacks can be used to weaken the bureaucracies or to gain specific ends. Bureaucracies are especially vulnerable to legal attacks on discrimination by sex and new but vigorous allies could be acquired in attacks on these grounds. Legal challenges might also be brought against school systems that do not allocate funds equally among neighborhoods. Recall and referendum procedures might also give neighborhood control advocates a weapon to use, or provide opportunities for a compromise, such as withdrawing a referendum effort in exchange for specific steps toward neighborhood control. The tactic of overloading bureaucratic systems, such as maximizing use of welfare programs, is still a useful tactic. Boycotts, if support for them can be attained, of the schools in a specific neighborhood still make sense.

Other possibilities for protest include the support of protests by potential opponents to neighborhood control when those protests might provide possibilities for compromise or weakening public support for opponents of neighborhood control. For example, widespread support of continued, prolonged, intransigent strikes by public school teachers could possibly result in the weakening of teachers' unions, often major opponents to neighborhood control. Such strikes might also result in increased support for establishing new governmental units to bargain with teachers. Other protests, such as those against the war in Vietnam or those by college or high-school students, should be carefully considered as vehicles for furthering neighborhood control.

Protest then is a useful tool which should be used as much as possible. Where carried out by others, the possibilities for furthering neighborhood control should be carefully considered. The potential for protest as a technique for demanding neighborhood control and decentralization is still present.

Pragmatic Compromise as a Strategy

Several existing situations might allow for compromises that would result in increased community control. Perhaps the most widely known compromise is the suggestion that proponents of neighborhood control agree to metropolitan consolidation in return for community control on a neighborhood basis. The resulting governmental system would be a two-layered, federated metropolitan government. The metropolitan structure, composed of representatives from neighborhoods, would handle regional problems. Neighborhood governments would handle other matters. (Specific details would have to be negotiated.) Taxes could be collected on a metropolitan basis, but distributed on a per capita, or other formula, basis to the neighborhoods. The existing city structure would, in effect, be eliminated. Most likely some compromise would have to be made to involve existing city officials in the new two-layered government. Existing suburban governments would be the equivalent of the newly formed neighborhood units. The Chamber of Commerce's Committee on Economic Development has recently endorsed such a plan.[4] Altshuler also notes his preference for this type of arrangement.[5]

A second compromise that has been suggested is the elimination of busing or school district realignments to achieve school integration in return for real neighborhood control of schools. Another possibility would be to support several definitions of "community." For example, community could be defined as members of a religious group. In such a situation an alliance might be made with Catholics who, if community control were adopted, would receive support for their schools while communities defined by other criteria would govern their own schools. Other definitions of community could include business areas and ethnic neighborhoods, each of which would have jurisdiction over police forces or other services.

There are other situations that might be acceptable interim arrangements, although they may not insure community control. Ward or precinct, rather than at-large, elections is one example. Ward elections would not guarantee community control, but they would increase minority-group representation in city government. Another interim device might be a rotating mayor, who was the representative of wards on a rotating basis. The mayor could either be elected or could be the ward councilman.

It was suggested earlier that recall and referendum procedures might be useful in furthering protest activities. Such devices might also give neighborhoods a veto procedure not now available, or they might provide neighborhoods with bargaining, if not governing, power.

Certainly proponents of neighborhood control would be well-advised to support the principle that federal grants be available to entities other than state and local governments. Many observers have argued that the most important provision of the Economic Opportunity Act was the requirement that there be "maximum feasible participation" of the poor. The way in which community action agencies were defined was just as important if not more so. The critical factor was that local, private, non-profit agencies were made eligible to receive funds. This allowed federal grants to be made to other than state and local governments. The availability of federal funds to neighborhood organizations is an essential ingredient of neighborhood control. Such funding authority should be supported and expanded.

Another institutional development important to proponents of neighborhood control is the growing number of organizations such as leagues of black patrolmen and black teacher federations. These organizations can provide essential support for the objectives of neighborhood control.

Positive Symbol Manipulation for Achieving Neighborhood Control

Proponents of community control have many opportunities to use symbols and values that have been popular and respected in American political history. They should take full advantage of these opportunities. Certainly it has long been an article of faith, if not scientific accuracy, that government should be close to the people. Neighborhood control certainly supports that value. Neighborhood control also facilitates democracy which, except for those who contend that "This is a republic—let's keep it that way," is a widely supported value. Other positive values furthered by decentralized decision making include local involvement, relevance, citizen participation, and limited central power. These values cannot be overemphasized and they should be continually utilized by supporters of neighborhood control.

Perhaps the most important argument to be made is that inner city residents should have the same political options that are available to suburban dwellers. Suburban governments are an accepted part of the American political system. A suggestion that large cities be divided into a multitude of suburban type neighborhood governments could possibly generate widespread and enthusiastic support.

Cost and Benefit Analysis of Neighborhood Control

Thus far it has been argued that protest is still a useful political tool, that there are many possibilities for practical compromise, and that many traditional values support the concept of community control. It is also useful to consider how community control might alter the costs and benefits accruing from the present governmental arrangement.

Benefits of Obtaining Neighborhood Control

If neighborhood control is desired, it is essential to maximize the benefits that adoption would bring to those who would decide whether or not to implement neighborhood control. Several tradeoffs have already been outlined earlier. In exchange for neighborhood control, demands for busing school children could be dropped; demands for integration through changing school boundaries or other devices could be ended; competition for public jobs could be restricted to neighborhood residents; metropolitan government could be agreed to; and protests could be eliminated, reduced in number, or shifted to other objectives.

A second benefit has also been mentioned. Community control, defined by criteria by than geography, could provide benefits to religious groups, tenants or homeowners associations, business groups, or associations of users of facilities.

A third possible benefit would be the division of administrative responsibilities to guarantee incumbents continued employment. For example, police functions could be divided with neighborhood groups controlling traffic supervision, patrol beat operations, crowd control and service functions. Central control might be retained over investigative activities, robbery details, record keeping, and purchasing equipment. Neighborhood groups might waive claims for controlling central functions for a specified number of years in return for comparable agreements from the central organization. Or neighborhood groups might provide services on a renewable contract basis with other neighborhoods.

In lieu of neighborhood control and operation, neighborhoods might be given authority to contract for police, education, health, and other governmental services with public or private organizations offering such services on a competitive basis. This approach might gain support from private groups capable of offering services or from government bodies eager to market their educational or police techniques and personnel.

The availability of federal grants to private organizations should be energetically supported. Moreover, current definitions of governmental or geographic units eligible for federal programs or grants should be altered to include neighborhood organizations. Where possible, neighborhoods should be given preferential treatment. For example, neighborhoods, even those with large populations, cannot, under the present system, be designated labor–market surplus areas. Such a designation gives preferential treatment to contractors seeking government business. Neighborhoods should be designated as units eligible to receive federal grants or as areas that qualify for special programs.

Altshuler notes that between 1965 and 1969 the number of metropolitan councils of government increased from 8 to 142 as a result of federal authorization of grants to support these organizations.[6] Similar assistance should be sought for the establishment of neighborhood units or, perhaps, metropolitan councils of neighborhood organizations.

The psychological benefits emanating from community control should not be overlooked. To the extent that reference is successfully made to positive symbols, and to the extent that the establishment of decision making is linked to these desired values, psychological benefits of no mean importance will result.

One final benefit that can be maximized if community control is attained is the reduction of violent attacks upon the existing political system and the curbing of demands for revolutionary action and radical change. In part this could be a planned reduction. If neighborhood control is attained, an agreement could be made to end demonstrations, boycotts, and other protests. More importantly, demonstrations and protests would be more likely to diminish automatically in number and intensity. Large numbers of those who presently have no stake in the existing system will acquire status and power and their accoutrements. This will result in support for the newly established reward structure with a consequent lessening of vigorous, violent complaints. As Altshuler points out "the possession of property and the exercise of responsibility are both 'conservatizing' experiences. Power is a form of property; it gives its holders a great psychic stake in the system." He goes on to add "home and business ownership would probably be even more effective moderating influences on ghetto politics; it should be recalled that they are important parts of the full community control package."[8]

Costs of Obtaining Decentralization

Proponents of neighborhood control should make every effort to minimize the costs of attaining it. A first way would be to implement neighborhood control in stages. Different governmental functions could be taken over by the community over a period of time. Schools might be first, then day-care centers, health programs, and finally police activities. Included in this, the takeover of the schools, and other services as well, could proceed in stages. First control over the design of curriculum might be obtained, then veto power over personnel selection, and finally complete authority for operating the schools.

A second way to minimize the costs of attaining community control is to institute community government power in new programs where there are no established bureaucracies and traditions. Community action programs, and, to an extent, Model Cities programs have provided this type of opportunity. Neighborhood control is much easier to attain, and far less costly to existing decision makers, if it is introduced at the start of a federally funded program.

A third possibility would be to establish a single-purpose special district, operated by appointed officials, that had conterminous boundaries with neighborhood. Neighborhood residents would be appointed to the special district governing board. This procedure could be followed where it was not desired to announce publicly the implementation of neighborhood control procedures. The special purpose district has a long and distinguished history in American government. It is highly flexible in its arrangement, and often politically inexpensive to establish. It could be used to serve the interests of the neighborhood at little psychological expense to the broader political community.

Another inexpensive way to pursue neighborhood control is to maximize citizen employment, and employment of the poor, in community action programs. This concept, which has drawn much opposition, has now acquired a degree of legitimacy that could enable it to be applied, more or less effectively, to other private and public programs. Every effort should be made to extend the concept of employment of the poor in every possible service program.

One concluding point is to be made concerning the reduction of costs in obtaining community control. The previous suggested strategies have not compared costs of acquiring neighborhood control with other alternatives. Altshuler argues persuasively that of all the demands being made by black Americans, community control is the least expensive demand for the general community to absorb. If community control is not the single end most desired by black Americans, the attainment of it without the attainment of other more substantive goals would be unfortunate. Such attainment might be possible, however. And it might indeed be, as Altshuler says, "the most feasible major demand that blacks are now making. White resistance to massive desegregation and redistribution is overwhelming, and it comes from all segments of white society. The resistance to community control, by contrast, is centered in the big city public bureaucracies. Many other whites are hostile . . . but they really have no stake in who governs the ghettos."[8]

Costs of Not Implementing Community Control

Supporters of decentralized decision making should seek to maximize the costs of not attaining community control. First, it seems logical that it would be necessary to maximize protests that are costly to the existing decision makers. Various possible forms of protest have been discussed previously.

Second, legal action should be taken to contest the legality of suburban governments and the benefits they receive from state and federal governments. Attacks could be made on the distribution of school aid, highway construction grants, federal housing grants, and all other programs in which suburbs receive more benefits than do other areas. Although it would be useful to succeed with these actions, their real value lies in the time and expense that a defense would cost to suburban areas. It would be understood that these complaints would end upon the attainment of neighborhood control. Legal attacks might also be made on racial discrimination, on land-use restrictions, and on lack of public housing in suburban areas. Where possible, state officials should be induced to bring these actions. Efforts could also be instituted to block or delay the provision of water or sewer services to suburban areas by the central city.

A concentrated effort should be made to foster busing of school children to attain integration in suburban schools. Efforts should also be made to require reverse busing of suburban students into ghetto areas. Although desegregation might be one real objective of such efforts, the major goal should be to encourage a compromise agreement preventing busing and providing for neighborhood control.

Efforts should also be undertaken to institute community review procedures for all service functions of the city. Official sanction should be sought for these neighborhood panels where possible. Where this is not feasible, they should act informally. Evaluation teams should carefully scrutinize all actions of school, health, sanitation, police, and other officials working in the neighborhood.

Richard Cloward and Frances Fox Piven suggested that one way to induce reform in the welfare system would be to maximize its clientele—to overload the system. This is an example of a strategy of maximizing the costs of not changing the system. Not only should the welfare system be overloaded, but all possible techniques should be used to overload the school, health, police, street, transportation, water, and sanitation facilities that the neighborhood wishes to control.

One final technique is to appeal every possible decision made by the local bureaucracy. This is an overload strategy applied not to the provision of services but rather to the internal operation of the bureaucracy. The objective would be to disorient the system so much that change would be necessary. Neighborhood control could then be put forward as an alternative to an obviously failing system.

Benefits of Not Obtaining Community Control

Many people would benefit from a retention of the system in which neighborhoods have little influence in policy development, program planning, and provision of services. To the extent possible, proponents of neighborhood control should work to minimize those benefits. One major group benefiting from the present arrangement are employees of city government who are afraid they will lose their jobs with the advent of neighborhood government. Many of these employees are protected by civil service rules and traditions, strong unions, and an apathetic and unaffected white majority. The benefits of the current situation can be minimized in several ways. First, existing bureaucratic organizations, and the unions that protect them, should be weakened. Two techniques are available. One would be to organize select groups of workers, such as minority group teachers or policemen. These groups would provide a check on the unions. Strikes could be prolonged and made financially costly for the strikers. At the same time they could create opposition in the broader community. A sufficiently long strike would seriously weaken existing bureaucratic arrangements. It is therefore logical to support continuing strikes of present city employees.

Second, thought should be given to the creation of competitive service systems. Schools, day-care centers, breakfast programs, and community protection services should be started where possible. Organizations, such as churches, which currently provide competitive services should be encouraged. Experimental programs operated by church, private and nonprofit, or commercial organizations that compete directly with programs operated by bureaucratic systems should be supported.

Third, vigorous opposition to city employee pay increases, unless and until neighborhood control is a reality, could also be pursued. This might also assist in prolonging or causing strikes. Opposition could also be voiced against current merit system programs. Legal action could be brought charging discrimination by race and sex. Appeals could be made for a revision of testing and examining procedures. Demands could be presented for the establishment of new criteria for hiring and promotion. One suggestions, which Altshuler has made, would be to define good job performance to include the ability to get along with specific racial, ethnic, or economic class clientele.[10] As Altshuler notes, this is already done by survey research organizations and political parties that select representatives who will avoid automatic unfavorable responses.

Fourth, demands could also be made for quotas or target compliance rates for opening up the bureaucracies to minority group members. Seniority requirements could be dispensed with and special training in examination procedures could be given to those potentially eligible for promotion according to existing bureaucratic procedures.

Conclusion

Some general strategies that might be pursued by those who wish to achieve some measure of neighborhood control have been outlined. Certainly there is no guarantee that these strategies will work. Nor can it be claimed that the activities described are desirable. In fact, some might even result in more difficulty in achieving goals that are equally or more important than neighborhood control. Thus, the presentation of these strategies does not constitute a recommendation that they be followed. They are offered in the hope that they will stimulate intelligent concern with the question—given the desire for neighborhood control, what can be done to attain it?

Early efforts toward neighborhood control should be undertaken in an experimental spirit. We should not expect dramatic results from these experiments, but we can expect to acquire some practical knowledge about how neighborhood control might work; we could certainly get a few instances of neighborhood control through the experiments conducted. Success could be claimed for the experiments (as is always done: Head Start was declared a success the day it began), which would assist in the expansion of the idea.

Second, maximum attention should be called to arguments and evidence supportive of neighborhood control. This is a commonly understood, but often neglected, tactic. Special attention should be given to statements of opponents that nominally support neighborhood control.

Third, plans should be developed, and a willingness should be fostered, to enter into compromise and trade-off agreements. Several possible compromises have been suggested earlier in this essay.

Fourth, for the use of positive symbols to support community control should be maximized. Community control will not be adopted as a result of the normal workings of a rational decision making process. It will be the result of political action, and the manipulation of symbols is an essential political activity.

Fifth, opponents to neighborhood control should be kept as confused and uninformed as possible.

Sixth, proponents of community control should take advantage of unusual opportunities to further neighborhood control—personality clashes, demands for metropolitan reorganizaiton, annexation efforts, or other peripherally associated events.

Seventh, all attempts to achieve neighborhood control will have to be fiexible in their implementation. I cannot, nor can those reading this essay, guide efforts to achieve neighborhood control according to some set formula. There can be no master strategist, just as there can be no single director of action pursued. Flexibility is an absolute necessity. Of course it would be useful if there were a small but vocal group that inflexibly demanded faster and more complete decentralization and community control to stimulate action by those engaging in the difficult political activities. Neighborhood control will never be achieved, however, without political action, which will of necessity be persistent, flexible, disorganized, and filled with compromise.

NOTES

1 See Alan Altshuler's excellent and provocative book, *Community Control: The Black Demand for Participation in Large American Cities* (New York: Pegasus, 1970), p. 216.

2 Murray Edelman, *The Symbolic Uses of Politics*, (Carbondale: University of Illinois Press, 1967).

3 Harry C. Bredemeier, "The Politics of the Poverty Cold War," *Urban Affairs Quarterly*, 10(1968), pp. 3–35.

4 Committee for Economic Development, *Reshaping Government in Metropolitan Areas*, (Washington, D.C.: U. S. Government Printing Office, 1970).

5 Altshuler, p. 203.

6 Altshuler, p. 183.

7 Altshuler, p. 205.

8 Altshuler, p. 197.

9 Altshuler, p. 163.

National Strategies for Neighborhood Control and Citizen Participation

Ronald J. James

Introduction

> This country, with its institutions, belongs to the people who inhabit it ... Why should there not be a patient confidence in the ultimate justice of the people? Is there any better or equal hope in this world?

Abraham Lincoln

This essay is a look at the future of neighborhood control and administration, seen from the medieval forest of Washington politics. The research apparatus—only the author's eyes and ears—is not formidable.

It seems that all groups turn at some point to the legal, financial, and messianic authority of the federal government to help them meet their needs. The modern city does not have the means to adequately meet its problems. And ofttimes, it lacks the desire or will. Local governments are often too small to deal with problems that extend beyond their legal limits; problems and jurisdictional boundaries seldom match. Some local governments are too big and their bureaucracies too impersonal to deal empathetically with people at the neighborhood level. But cities, large and small, are asking the federal government for help. One aspect of the federal response has been an interest in neighborhood control. In light of past experiences and present realities, this essay will examine aspects of neighborhood control and prospects for winning congressional support.

I define neighborhood control as the placing of power of governance, to the maximum extent possible, in the hands of those who are most directly affected by public institutions or programs. The essential purpose of neighborhood control is to increase the power of people who live in neighborhoods or, alternatively, to decrease the dependence of those people on the administrative or political elite of the city.

The Urban Problem

The question for our society is not whether we are better than we used to be. The question is whether we are good enough.

John W. Gardner

Our country has long been considered the "Land of Efficiency." Public administration has been characterized by such slogans as "Only the best shall serve." In reality, government administration is unresponsive and often insensitive. Furthermore, it does not seem to be especially efficient or economical. Our most populous cities have little citizen participation or effective local democracy, and the individual has little, if any, self-determination. So cumbersome is the administrative system that jobs are created daily for lawyers solely assist rich clients in finding their way through the maze of bureaucracy to secure the right service, grant, or favor. Despite the various apparatuses on which to vent one's opinion—boards, commissions, committees, "an evening with the Mayor," and political parties—inner city residents do not have much influence on the day-to-day planning and delivery of services.

There is a stalemate in the House of Representatives on most social issues, particularly when it comes to new appropriations to benefit our inner cities. Some southern congressmen possess enormous blocking or vetoing power thanks to the seniority system through which they have become the chairmen of some of the most important committees, especially appropriations. The so-called conservative coalition of southern Democrats and conservative Republicans was strengthened in the 1968 congressional election. Therefore, the legislative branch has been in an excellent position, implementing the mood of the Nixon administration, to curtail spending in order to fight inflation. The future does not seem bright for a so-called liberal majority in the House of Representatives to be capable of enacting laws or appropriating significant sums of money for inner city problems, or both.

In light of the exodus from the inner city, reapportionment will shift power from rural areas to suburbs rather than to the inner cities. Even among the so-called liberals there is a fundamental question as to whether or not elected officials representing the suburbs might vote sums to substantially increase the taxes of their constituents. The poor, the black, the Chicano, the Appalachian white, and often the not-so-poor inner city resident[1] lack not only resources but power to elect representatives. In the bargaining arena of city politics, they often have little to trade. The real political power brokers are bankers and captains of industry who usually reside in the suburbs.

Neighborhood Control: Facade or Substance?

At a time when there is a mounting pyramid of governmental structures at the local level and a move toward metropolism, should not concerned academicians be discussing the urgent question of how to reshift our national priorities to provide more resources for local government?

Local government, in short, has few possibilities without resources. For example, the government designed a Philadelphia Plan to insure that minority workers would receive a "range" of jobs in certain unions participating in government construction. The plan was, and is, a significant breakthrough in job opportunities for minorities. At the same time, however, government construction was cut seventy-five percent; thus, more people were competing for fewer jobs. It is estimated that only ten percent of the eligible population is served by such manpower programs.[2]

Why give blacks the power to design their own school system and then provide no money with which to operate it? The only result will be to create more despair, so that blacks will turn on their own brothers and say, "Well, things have gotten worse since you, my black brother, took over."

On the few occasions when the Indians won a battle, they found the conquered land plundered, devoid of game, and unfit to support their people. So too will blacks, who finally are beginning to capture some of our large cities, find that the city is no longer a livable habitat nor a viable institution. Having a black mayor, sometimes viewed as a move toward more local control, will not automatically lead to the solution of ghetto problems. To effect change there remains the critical matter of resources, the shortage of which may produce even greater frustrations when a black man is in charge and fails to deliver.

Mayor Hatcher recently pointed out:

> Perhaps one of the most tragic consequences of the fiscal crisis facing our cities is the ethnic division and polarization created by the competition among the poor for the inadequate funds which are available. This competition among what might be described figuratively (and sometimes literally) as the starving for the crumbs of an affluent society is a dastardly trick to play on our citizens. It has caused blacks to fight blacks, and browns to fight browns and poor whites to fight poor whites. And, it now has the struggling lower-middle class ethnic whites fighting the poor blacks, browns and Appalachian whites for the fiscal crumbs which are being offered to meet the combined needs of them all.[3]

Real dignity and a decent place in American society depend, however, on the position minorities hold in the economic and social orders. Major emphasis should be placed on ways of bringing inner city residents into the mainstream of society to involve them more effectively in those institutions that govern, educate, employ, and service their needs as well as provide a social order. Real and meaningful citizen participation is the only guarantee, frail as it may be, that inner city residents will honor and that will endure the terms of the social contract. Such participation is the only alternative to civil disorder, for participation alone will generate among inner city residents sufficient faith to work within the order of the system. Especially in our large urban centers, citizens need fulcrum points—mini-city halls—where they can apply pressures and make their desires known. New York and Atlanta, among others, have begun efforts to establish neighborhood city halls but have encountered financial problems.

It is, therefore, particularly important to realize that the question of neighborhood control cannot be separated from the question of the available resources, both fiscal and human. However, we should not wait until sufficient resources to attack our inner city problems are available before addressing ourselves to the question of neighborhood control. We must work simultaneously on both, making sure that whatever we are doing with one is not contradictory with what we are doing with the other because each, in fact, can contribute to the attainment of the other.

Neighborhood control is not a short cut method of solving our urban problems. It is in the nature of social debts that they must always be paid in full. On the other hand, adequate resources alone do not insure a responsive and sensitive government. Community control may not be the answer, but it cannot be worse than the present system, and at least it forces us to think about new approaches to old, unmet problems.

A Short History of Neighborhood Control in Congress

The So-Called War on Poverty

To have the symbols of freedom and no power is to be denied the substance of freedom.

Rev. Jesse Jackson, Director of
Operation Breadbasket

The least understood and most controversial section of the Economic Opportunity Act of 1964 reads: "A Community Action Program means a program . . . which is developed, conducted and administered with the maximum feasible participation of residents of the areas and members of the groups to be served." In the period since the poverty law was signed, the Office of Economic Opportunity's (OEO) administration of it has been the subject of bitter contention, wild hope, and political intrigue. Aside from some references to grass roots democracy, there was little debate on the language of this section when the bill was passed.

The section evidently was designed to provide the poor with a voice in what is envisioned to be a new community dialogue. As a result of this section, the consensus of opinion in any community was to be established by taking the poor into account. The philosophical under-pinning of the section seems to be based on a belief that the poor, although they have much to complain of, have traditionally been cut off from the power sources of cities and denied a voice in government: poor housing, inferior education, rats, and racial discrimination.

In the early days (1965) of OEO, Sargent Shriver quickly made clear that participation of the poor was a condition for local receipt of federal funds. Initially, some courageous stands were taken but politics took its toll, mainly because local tax-paying constituents and politicians became alarmed at the increasing demands of the poor.

Two things happened. First, Vice-President Hubert H. Humphrey, responding to pleas from mayors across the country, began to pressure Mr. Shriver to be cautious about the inclusion of the poor on local policy-making boards. The League of Cities and the Conference of Mayors sought to limit the involvement of the poor.

Second, Representative Adam C. Powell of New York no longer spoke out strongly for the participation of the poor. Earlier, Mr. Powell had said he would hold a series of public hearings around the country to examine the poverty program. Several of Powell's key staff members in the House Education and Labor Committee were vocal advocates of "maximum feasible participation." Congress authorized $200,000 for the investigation, but the hearings were never held. Congress "replaced" —fired—the staff members who had initiated the idea of investigating the poverty program.

Since that occasion, the degree of participation at different levels has varied. Michael Harrington, whose book *The Other America* helped popularize the poverty program, said in the February 9, 1966 *Christian Science Monitor*, "Shriver can ask the impoverished in, but he doesn't have the authority to force the local powers to honor the invitation at the door."

Since then, congress has restricted the operation of Community Action Programs (CAP), primarily because of their intrusion in local decision-making and the subsequent rising noise level of participants concerning decisions affecting their share of the pie. The Green Amendment of 1967, designed to provide local governments with the option of running CAP, was passed by the House. Such a vote was clearly against local control by community groups.

There are, however, a few political prophets around Washington who view the House's rejection, in December, 1969, of the Quie-Green Bill— designed to fund Community Action Agencies through state governments —as a blow for the neighborhood control program. Such a view is politically naïve.

On the Friday evening shortly after the House vote took place, a Washington-based labor lobbyist approached a southern Democratic congressman, chairman of one of the most powerful House committees, to express thanks for voting right—to reject the state-oriented OEO proposal. The congressman swept past the lobbyist saying: "Do you think I'd vote to turn any program over to that governor." The governor of the state in question was a Republican. The issue of who should run local poverty programs did not rise or fall on its substance or merit but, largely, at least for this key vote, because of politics. But the politics were not necessarily partisan, for some mayors and governors within the same party were urging that control be vested in their sphere of government.

A survey of the past debates on anti-poverty legislation shows few vocal advocates at the congressional level for community action programs or citizen participation, or both. Elusive success in the form of cohesiveness one day and scandal the next has encouraged muted praise in the political area. As a result of its short but stormy political past,[4] CAP may be dead or at least toned down, but, as will be shown below, the idea and the impact of letting the poor assist in the management of their own affairs is spiritually, if not politically, much alive.

Model Cities

The Congress hereby finds and declares that improving the quality of urban life is the most critical domestic problem facing the United States.

TITLE I, DEMONSTRATION CITIES ACT

Congress really did not know what it was getting when it passed the Community Action Program in 1964. However, by the time of the Model Cities legislation, it was much more aware of the political overtones of citizen participation. Model Cities had another forerunner of decentralization, urban renewal, which saw citizens—recipients of services—exercising some influence in an advisory role on the planning of such services. Introduced in 1966, the Model Cities Program was "designed to concentrate on public and private resources in a comprehensive five-year attack on the social, economic and physical problems of slums and blighted neighborhoods."[5] "Residents of the inner city were to have a role to play in planning and carrying out the program; however, community responsibility for the Model Cities Program [was] vested in the principal local executive officer and elected governing body. The role of inner-city residents in planning has thus far been limited and the program has not been funded at the level originally planned. The original budget request in 1968 of $750 million was subsequently cut to $500 million. One wonders whether the funds appropriated for some seventy-five cities are sufficient to make the promise of Model Cities possible and to foster the active involvement of neighborhood residents."[6]

The Community Self-Determination Act

We had full employment on the plantation.

OLD HARLEM PROVERB

With the push of Roy Innis of CORE, the Community Self-Determination Act was introduced in the 90th Congress with broad bipartisan support and reintroduced in the 91st Congress with less fanfare. The announced purpose of the act was to give ghetto residents control over their destiny by "securing gainful employment, achieving the ownership and control of the resources of their community, expanding opportunity, stability and self-determination, thus giving them power to shape their communities and lives."

The proposed act provides for: (1) establishment of locally owned community corporations; (2) creation of locally owned community development banks, serviced by a central bank; (3) funding to enable community corporations to hire management assistance and training of their choice; (4) use of profits generated by community corporation subsidiary businesses to finance improvement and service programs desired by the people of the community; and (5) use of tax credits to induce established corporations to engage in contracts with fledgling community development companies or subsidiaries.

The act has come under considerable opposition—partisan, political, and substantive. One economist has described the bill's economics as awful. The bill's purpose was laudable, and many bills are in "awful" shape when first introduced. There is no reason to believe that technical drafting assistance cannot cure many of the bill's alleged and actual substantive flaws.

The immediate impact of the proposed Community Self-Determination Act produced adverse reactions from various elements of the politically active community. Established financial institutions, such as the banks and savings and loan associations, saw the development of Community Development Banks as direct competitors. In 1968, at hearings before the Senate Banking and Currency Committee's Subcommittee on Financial Institutions, reaction was, to wit, that the present financial community could handle the problems of ghetto economic rejuvenation if certain changes were made in the laws and sufficient government backing was given for further private involvement. In addition, the Community Self-Determination Act proposed certain tax advantages for Community Development Corporations and related businesses. This caused consternation among established competitive businesses, both within and without the inner city.

Most, if not all, of the people who would be given jobs and training in these newly financed businesses would be nonunion. This fact creates problems with organized labor, which often resists any new groups that it fears may take jobs away from union members now employed in established, organized concerns. An AFL-CIO statement denounced minority entrepreneurship strongly. "Attempts to build separate economic enclaves, with substantial tax subsidies, within specific geographically limited ghetto areas, is apartheid, anti-democratic nonsense."[7]

Local government officials discourage the development of independent power bases as potential competitors of the established political order.

The act was not attractive to the traditional civil rights groups, such as the NAACP, for it allegedly smacked of separatism.

The concept of tax credits ran into considerable opposition. First of all, organized labor opposes this method of redeveloping impoverished areas. Secondly, the Senate Finance Committee and the House Ways and Means Committee both have several members who dislike the tax-credit method of financing programs of this nature. All this opposition clouds the possibility of attracting the number of established corporations needed and desired.

With political opposition from so many quarters it should not be surprising that the Community Self-Determination Act is dead, at least in its present form.

Radical Decentralization as an Alternative

There is nothing more difficult to carry out, nor more dangerous to handle than to initiate a new order of things.

Machiavelli

He who will not apply new remedies must expect new evils; for time is the greatest innovation.

Francis Bacon

The most critical task of our nation is to assist those persons whose social mobility, education, skill, and experience are not equal to those of most people in the United States. It is imperative that any model of government provide for their relief from their present mode of dependence and powerlessness.

It is interesting to observe that our government was based on the concept, implicit in the Bill of Rights, that a federal government is best that governs least. In fact, most of the founders of this country believed that a strong, centralized government was the greatest threat to individual freedom. Incredibly, it has been the national government that we have looked to as the chief institution to guarantee individual rights—the very reverse of our historical concept of government. More recently, we have begun to look to government to provide intervention mechanisms so that the powerless might receive some standing in the administrative state. In its efforts to solve social problems, the federal government has used the traditional funding pipeline of the institutionalized state.

The direct beneficiaries of the federal government's social programs have not been the people that it wanted to help. Instead, state governments, city governments or local districts, foundations, and protest prostitutes—the social agencies that suddenly appear after the riot—have received the monies for federal government social rehabilitation programs, e.g., job training, such as Aid to Dependent Children, as distinguished from social welfare programs.

States, cities, and local governments (districts) secure funds according to certain guidelines and criteria. However, local and state governments do not put that money into the hands of needy victims and poor people and, instead, create jobs for others—professional poverty warriors, probation officers, visiting teachers, school nurses, and employment counselors. Our social programs create an entire group of publicly paid persons, whose members surround and determine the fate of those that government said it wanted to help. The "colonized" citizens of our ghettos and barrios, who are supposed to be assisted, have no determination over their own fate and have no say about the kind of program they want. The effect is, with few exceptions, dismal, for, as the distance from citizen to governing body widens, an even larger army of technicians is interposed. Freedom in the political context should be viewed as the ability to determine one's own fate, and power as the ability to determine real choices. It is important to understand that the pipeline system of monetary flow allows little power of freedom to the man in the inner city.

A few years ago, a group of somewhat restless, somewhat ill-trained men were brooding in our country, as they too had been left out of the mainstream of society for a period of time. These men were the returning World War II GIs. It is interesting to note what the government does for people it really cares about. The government did not establish massive housing programs, massive education programs, or job training programs. Instead, it gave freedom of choice to all veterans. Among the best options was the VA home ownership program that allowed them to choose a house of the kind and in the neighborhood they desired. The existing social institutions are proof of the success of that program: these programs intruded so little that, in 1970, World War II veterans, now fifty years old, believe that they did it all by themselves, that they pulled themselves up by their bootstraps.

The inner-city resident is confronted with a monopoly, be it the local school system or the entire administration of local government. A monopoly need not genuinely concern itself with the individual, who has no option but to use the services available regardless of their quality. The distributor of the services, rather than the consumer, determines the nature of the service and the terms and conditions of delivery. As long as a social-services department can be assured of state aid and increasing federal aid without the accountability and responsiveness that inevitably come with a competitive system, it is saying prayers to the wind to anticipate any significant sensitivity in our public agencies.

An example of responsible and responsive competition is OEO's involvement in the employment field, which has challenged and often forced state employment services to extend their recruitment outreach and become more sensitive to the community served. This responsiveness is not due to a great desire for change on the part of employment services, but to a large extent to the threat of, and actual competition in, areas of previous monopoly.

Such an approach could find application in the health service fields, particularly in those rural and urban areas where the only service available, especially for the poor is the county hospital. We need a health system that provides decentralized health centers, including mental centers, that would not only be accessible, but would provide a choice.

Our young nation is overly muscle-bound with tradition, but I hope and believe that the realistic approach to saving our public administration delivery system lies in finding the formula to demonstrate to the public at large that the present level of inefficiency has reached an intolerable level —a level courting public disaster. Alternatives in the form of viable competition can and must be found. American industrial and material wealth was made possible through industrial competition. Politics thrives on it. Why not provide the ultimate in decentralization by giving the individual the choice and the power to determine his fate, by providing a GI Bill of Rights form of delivery for those services which could be individually or neighborhood directed, or both? The competitive model could provide a reform mechanism.

The Jacksonian democracy of the 1820s and 1830s was a genuine reform. It helped to restore the common man's faith in government, to destroy the control of government by the aristocrat, and to narrow the gap between the people and the leaders of government. The right of the common man (a definition limited, unfortunately, only to whites), to participate in the administration of government was recognized. It seems that we in the 1970s, some one hundred fifty years later, would not be moving precipitately if we extended the concept to include those poor blacks, whites, and browns who are residents of our inner cities.[8]

The Politics of Achieving Neighborhood Control

Politics is not something to avoid or abolish or destroy. It is a condition like the atmosphere we breathe. It is something to live with, to influence if we wish and to control if we can. We must master its ways or we shall be mastered by those who do.

Raymond Moley

In its 1968 annual report, the Advisory Committee on Intergovernmental Relations notes that the drive to decentralize the city government has been met with "varying degrees of cynicism, alarm and vigorous opposition by political leaders and municipal administration. A number fear these developments might further clutter the already fragmented local government landscape." The report also found that "civil rights militants, poverty workers and other advocates of closer, more personal government" feel that steps such as neighborhood city halls do not go far enough.[9] At the same time those on the outside are clamoring to get in, and administrators are faced with increasing demands for a say by those already within. Public employee strikes, unheard of in the past, are becoming an almost daily occurrence. The question for us is how to initiate, out of this morass, a political movement toward neighborhood Control.

Our system's record in responding to the needs of the people casts considerable doubt on politicians' argument that the political system provides for pacific methods to effect change. The system operates on the concept that the squeaking wheel is the one that gets the grease. Thus, dams and dikes are built after the flood; hair pin curves on highways are reconstructed after a number of auto accidents; stop lights are placed at school crossings after pedestrians die. Like most organizations, congress operates on a fire-fighting basis, dealing almost exclusively with those problems that are immediately before it. Protest or some form of attention getting is an essential part, but not a panacea, for the initiation of political action.

It is a political job to get congress to back federally funded programs for citizen participation. After all the demonstrations, speeches, and threats, it is still the federal government that controls appropriations. Not a single city in this nation has the money to put the poor back to work, or to rebuild housing, or to improve schools.

To engage in political action it is necessary to have a sufficient power base to build a community of interest around a given issue. This requires coalition and alliance.[10] Political alliances are not built on love and affection, but on mutual interests at the moment.[11] Political maturity is a must, for it enables one to perceive whether or not, despite their ulterior motives, others want what advocates of neighborhood control want.

The harsh reality is that most whites want to manage their own environment without participation on any level by blacks. The President, in his "definitive" message on civil rights, spoke of desegregation rather than integration. The shift from integration by blacks is, in part, a failure of white society to offer any real hope for large-scale, meaningful integration and, in part, from a growing lack of results from current public policies. Blacks are saying, "Why not turn to our own communities to improve conditions there and secure a much stronger voice in controlling things?" The present political climate warrants the conclusion that there is no logical chain extending from states' righters at one end to black militants on the other. Whites want to "save our schools," while some blacks see integration as a route that has been tried and found impassable.

The obstacle that one encounters is whether or not the strain of racism in America is so great that it prevents groups from coalescing on matters of mutual benefit. Even bigots have a price, at some point, when the salient issue involves their own self-interest. Not all the whites have left the city—some can not afford to—and services for them are also deteriorating, especially essential services like health. Neighborhood health centers should then be an issue on which agreement between whites and blacks could be reached, without seriously affecting the other's interest. Neighborhood control of schools is another issue that provides the groundwork for alliances in other areas.

Such a coalition would not be possible for neighborhood control of the police because of the actual or alleged fear of whites that black militant and Black Panther influence would control the police. But this is the outer limit of a black–white coalition on the issue of neighborhood control. Most of the poor and powerless in this country are whites who need intervention mechanisms to secure some social standing in the mainstream for delivery of services. Therefore, some whites, along with Chicanos and Indians, are likely recruits for such an alliance.

Black power, local power, and neighborhood control are patterns fully consistent with those of other immigrants—the Irish, for instance. Such recent arrivals had bargaining power with the system via the local political machine. The machine did not exist in spite of society but, first, because it filled real needs in providing services not recognized by a callous society and, second, because it was a product of universal suffrage—citizen participation—as services were offered for a vote.

Legislative funding of neighborhood corporations could meet the objections of the representatives of rural areas by encouraging undertakings in rural (especially low income) as well as urban areas.

A few basic principles hold some hope for a broader-based political support. In the political arena, new institutions always have a certain amount of appeal. The very existence of need is ipso facto evidence of a failure on the part of the old institution. The present system has not delivered the good life to people in the inner city. John Lindsay, Liberal Party Mayor of New York City, Senator John Tower of Texas (R), Senator Birch Bayh of Indiana (D), and former Governor George Wallace of Alabama have all endorsed neighborhood control in one form or another. The reason for such diverse political support lies in a hope for a more responsive government, although the supporters expect different responses.

The 1968 Democratic platform pledged to "support . . . the principle of meaningful participation of the poor in policy making and administration of community action and related programs." The Republican platform of 1968 also pledged, "In programs for the socially and economically disadvantaged . . . participation by representatives of those to be served. The failure to encourage creative and responsible participation from among the poor has been the greatest among a host of failures of the War on Poverty."

In some ways, being against citizen participation and neighborhood control is like being against apple pie. For it is, especially to conservatives, in the finest tradition of the accepted belief in a direct democracy, whereby other minority groups and immigrants have lifted themselves up by their bootstraps through ethnic cohesiveness and growth at the neighborhood level.

The Quid Pro Quo

> Power concedes nothing without a demand. It never has and never will. . . . Men may not get all they pay for in the world, but they must certainly pay for what they get.

Frederick Douglass

The question that all participants in potential coalitions must ask is, "What is it going to cost?" I do not see these costs as prohibitive, but as problems which must be weighed against desired goals.

Neighborhood control would be attractive to the Nixon administration in that it deflects pressure for racial integration. It also focuses on process rather than on substantive problems. Any move toward decentralization would be helpful to the administration, which is pushing for redistributing authority into governmental units below the federal level. The administration's Manpower Bill (S.2838), which would provide for a major role for governors and state employment services is a good example. However, the danger of a coalition with the administration is that its view of decentralization is conservative and would push authority only one or two levels below the federal, e.g., to the states or standard metropolitan statistical areas. If the administration was successful in decentralizing to a limited extent, it would have no need of supporting decentralization, desired by inner-city residents, on the neighborhood level.

Power given to some is power taken away from others. Veto groups, as David Riesman calls them in *The Lonely Crowd,* will have to be neutralized, which usually means sharing or further dividing the potential golden egg. In the case of decentralization of schools, one must reckon with teachers; in the case of new housing, it is the union; and with health services, it is the entire medical profession. All of these groups have inputs of professional regulations, advisory boards, and committees. Even at the neighborhood level, they will fight to get in a program or seek to kill it if they cannot secure some entry. The realities of politics are that a federally funded neighborhood corporation is by its nature not totally independent of governmental requirements. When decentralization is built upon someone else's money, it is exceptionally difficult to keep all the veto groups at the level of noninterference desired.

Inevitably, any legislation will be presented as the new way to approach the ghetto, undercutting all the existing ways of doing things. In 1964, Community Action was the way to handle our social problems, through "maximum feasible participation." Two years later, other politicians came along and said problems would be solved through Model Cities, the effect being to make Model Cities the coordinator of social services and to undercut Community Action to a certain extent. Everything was to be pulled together and sponsored under Model Cities. Then the Nixon Administration came along with its solution. The President first flirted with the Community Self-Determination Act. Now the issue of the day is the funded neighborhood corporation. One of the consequences of these new programs is that the political support we have for extant programs will be badly undercut. Now everybody on Capitol Hill who is against OEO and Model Cities will have an easy way to dispense with those programs. The programs will not be cancelled yet, but they will be phased down. It will be argued there is no need to continue to put money into Model Cities or OEO. But do the administration's newer and better schemes allow the community to organize and fight for its own social services? Maybe CAP and Model Cities should go, but that is a question deserving a hard look, particularly until the new programs are evaluated. The ultimate test for any poverty program should rest on ability of the people to control their own destiny. It is particularly an important test for blacks at this time in our country, for only if we have some control of our destiny does the choice between integration and separation become real.

NOTES

I owe a debt of thanks for having the opportunity over the past nine years to listen and discuss the matter of how government can effect change with John McKnight, Assistant Director at the Center for Urban Affairs, Northwestern University.

1   Here, the inner city is viewed as a residential area restricted by social and physical barriers and often, but not necessarily, economic barriers, as portions of the inner cities of Atlanta and Washington are predominantly black but contain many wealthy and middle class residents.

2   Testimony by Charles Killingsworth, economist, University of Michigan, before the Senate Subcommittee on Employment, Manpower and Poverty, March 25, 1970.

3   Address by Richard G.Hatcher, mayor, Gary, Indiana at the steering committee of the National Urban Coalition, Washington, D. C. December 10, 1969.

4   "The controversy was inevitable; what is being attempted is a fundamental change in the way government responds to the needs of the poor." President Lyndon B. Johnson, Message on Urban and Rural Poverty, March 15, 1967, p. 3 (90th Congress 1st Session, House of Representatives, Document No. 88).

5   "Model Cities," U. S. Department of Housing and Urban Development, Washington, D. C. , GPO D/IP-99 (December 1968)W.

6   For a definitive analysis, see Larry F. Parachini's "Model Cities—More Drops of Trickle-Down," unpublished paper, Urban Coalition, December 29, 1969.

7   Statement by the AFL-CIO Executive Council on "Economic Progress of Minorities," Bal Harbour, Florida, February 21, 1969.

8   Arthur M. Schlesinger, *The Age of Jackson*, (its: publisher, 1945), Ch 5.

9   ACIR, Tenth Annual Report, Washington, D. C., January 31, 1969.

10   Viable coalitions stem from four preconditions:
   (1)   the recognition by the parties involved of their respective self-interests;
   (2)   the mutual belief that each party stands to benefit in terms of others;
   (3)   the acceptance of the fact that each party has its own independent base of power and does not depend for ultimate decision making on a force outside itself;
   (4)   the realization that the coalition deals with specific and identifiable—as opposed to general and vague—goals.

See Stokely Carmichael and Charles Hamilton, *Black Power* (New York: Vintage Books, 1967), p. 74.

11   Political relations are based on self-interest, benefits to be gained, and losses to be avoided. For the most part, man's politics are detetermined by his evaluation of material good and evil. Politics results from a conflict of interest, not of conscience. *ibid.*, p. 74.

THE POLITICAL EVALUATION OF EDUCATIONAL POLICIES

Norman I. Fainstein and Susan S. Fainstein

The Prevailing Ideology of Educational Expertise

One of the legacies of the progressive movement in education has been the belief that education should be isolated from politics. Early educational reformers, like their political counterparts who were seeking to make general municipal administration more efficient and more responsive to the public interest, saw rational policy formulation as antithetical to political decision making. As Roscoe Martin acerbically comments:

> Any contact between urban politics and the schools is held to be destructive of sound educational practice; and since the city is widely conceived to be dominated by politics, it is natural and easy to bring it within the interdiction. Distrust of the city, its political system, and its government long since completed the journey from tentative formulation through habit of thought to state of mind, and may be said not to permeate all professional school thinking from the highest rationalizer of public school doctrine to the lowliest classroom teacher.[1]

The canons of professionalism have been institutionalized in education through the requirement of credentials for teachers, tenure for teaching and administrative personnel, the dominance of the superintendent in the formulation of school policy, and the use of scientific testing as the principal measure of school performance.

While there have been critics of the separation between politics and pedagogy in the past, the doctrine of professional expertise in education is only now receiving its first sustained assault. The main thrust of the attack comes from the movement for community control of urban schools. Opponents of community control unhesitatingly defend the ideology of professionalism and contend that lay participation in the running of schools is inimical to the educational welfare of children. But, as will be shown later, even members of the community control movement are ambivalent about the extent to which political interests should intrude on educational issues. The concept of professionalism, then, is deeply imbedded in educational institutions and widely accepted by the general public.

Our use of the term ideology in connection with professionalism derives from the conclusion that the claims of expertise are used by professional educators to justify their ruling position within the educational realm.[2] We will show that, while school personnel make some educational decisions that are truly nonpolitical, they also make many that are unavoidably political, whether or not political groups are explicitly involved in the decision process. The refusal of educators to admit the political implications of their policies represents a self-serving evasion of reality and thereby constitutes an ideology.

The new critics of American education have gradually come to question the ideology of professionalism and to assert the right of the school's clients to hold teachers and administrators directly accountable for what happens in the schools. Disillusionment with the claims of educators grows out of three major accusations: (1) the experts have failed to deliver according to their own standard: they have failed to educate the children; (2) schools have institutionalized racism: educators both discriminate against minority group children and inculcate in them feelings of inferiority; and (3) educators have failed to treat children and parents with respect and are unable, because of excessive bureaucratization, to respond to parental demands for change within the schools. Each of these claims leads to a fundamental questioning of the legitimacy of the educational system as now organized.

Educational Failure

The most obvious evidence of educational failure is the poor performance of black children on standard measures of academic achievement.

The basic story of academic achievement in Harlem is one of inefficiency, inferiority, and massive deterioration. The further these students progress in school, the larger the proportion who are retarded and the greater is the discrepancy between their achievement and the achievement of other children in the city. This is also true for their intelligence test score.[3]

In a society where the possibility of obtaining a decent livelihood depends on academic attainment, the educational failure of black children reinforces the disadvantages already present because of class and race.

Black parents and their spokesman have become increasingly aware of the discrepancies in achievement between black and white children, and they are making forceful demands for remedial measures and school integration. In addition, they are questioning the adequacy of teachers to educate black children.

It became increasingly clear that the attitude of the teachers toward their students was emerging as a most important factor in attempting to understand the massive retardation of these children.[4]

If teachers, selected according to prescribed impartial methods, can not function when called upon to teach black students, then the whole system of teacher training and licensing is challenged, and the claims of special knowledge made by teachers are undermined.

Whereas blacks attack the competence of pedagogues on the basis of educational results, another group of critics examines the actual process of teaching within the classroom and argues that it discourages children from learning. These critics are the direct descendants of the original formulators of progressive education, who also wanted to eliminate formalism in the classroom and exhorted the teacher to treat the child as an individual. John Holt's book *How Children Fail* has been perhaps the most influential of the attacks on prevailing pedagogical methods. Holt makes his points through the recapitulation of his own experiences as a teacher.

There was a lot of room for improvement in the rather loose classes I was running last fall, but the children were doing some real thinking and learning, and were gaining confidence in their own powers. From a blind *producer* Ben was on his way to being a very solid and imaginative *thinker;* now he has fallen back into recipe-following production strategy of the worst kind. What is this test nonsense, anyway? Do people go through life taking math tests, with other people telling them to hurry? Are we trying to turn out intelligent people, or test-takers?

There must be a way to educate young children so that the great human qualities that we know are in them be developed. But we'll never do it as long as we are obsessed with tests.[5]

He has long since quit expecting school to make sense. They tell you these facts and rules, and your job is to put them down on paper the way they tell you. Never mind whether they mean anything or not.[6]

Although a number of the advocates of more open classrooms argue on the basis of their experiences as teachers within ghetto schools, they do not have much of a following among black parents. Their audiences are largely white. Black and Puerto Rican parents demand for their children more rigor and discipline rather than the greater freedom and creativity called for by this group of new progressives. For example, one activist Puerto Rican mother, when asked to evaluate an experimental open classroom program in a local school, commented:

It's a middle class thing! It rewards very verbal children. I watched one of these classrooms. It's the verbal white kids who get the teacher's attention. The other kids hang back. Besides, we want more discipline for our children. We're strict at home, and we want the school to use the same kind of methods. And we're not interested in the school's teaching our kids to be creative. We want them to learn the fundamentals, cause if they don't, they're not going to get anywhere.[7]

Thus, the new progressives start from a very different point of view than those who criticize the schools for failing to make black students measure up on standard tests. Their arguments have also been significant, however, in the challenge to professional legitimacy. First, they have their roots in a philosophy of education to which most American educators pay at least lip service. Second, their doctrines have great appeal to a very important element in the white population that previously supported professional integrity and the insulation of schools from uninformed public debate. The new progessives now would like to see the schools encourage greater freedom in the classroom. Their demands, however, are incompatible with the status quo. Thus, they are forced to challenge the ideology that prevents lay citizens from imposing their pedagogical ideas on those entrusted to run the schools.

In their efforts to compel a spirit of innovation in the classroom while advancing different, and sometimes antagonistic, programs, the new progressives and the blacks have confronted similar obstacles that have, to some extent, made their cause a common one. Both groups have come to blame the deficiencies of the educational process on the way in which school systems are organized. In particular, they point to bureaucratic rigidity and ritualism that inhibit a constructive response to criticism and cause defensive reactions and strategies rather than flexible adaptations to changed conditions.

> But so far, the [Boston] system's long list of changes . . . has had almost no effect on educational substance for most of the children most of the time. Many of the innovations affect only a handful of pupils—a school here, a few classes there—and there has been little carryover to regular practices, either in program or in attitude. The innovations tend to remain well encapsulated, like droplets of oil on still water. . . . Individual administrators complain that everything is moving too fast, that they do not have time to plan, or even to think. At bottom, most of them simply don't know how to run the system their way *and* to make changes at the same time. . . . Their defensiveness is neither malicious nor cynical. It is the defensiveness of decent, honest men caught in a revolution they did not make, don't understand, and in which they want no part.[8]

Both the new progressives and the black groups share a similar goal: undermining the professional ideology sufficiently to allow the introduction of new classroom methods and new personnel. This means that both groups must attack procedures, such as teacher tenure and the requirement of credentials, that maintain the inviolate status of professional educators. When the political battle is between educators and a disaffected clientele, there is a natural alliance of interests among different groups within the clientele; it is only after the status quo disintegrates that the differences within the opposition coalition assert themselves.

Racism in the Schools

In justifying their attacks on the competence of school personnel and in defending themselves from the charge that the source of educational failure lies in their children rather than in the schools, blacks criticize the schools for fostering racism. They accuse teachers of discriminating openly against black children. More significantly for the argument being developed here, they maintain that educators exhibit subtle prejudices through expectations and reactions that cause black children to lose self-esteem and become psychologically unable to learn.

Black critics argue that in essence, the recruitment of teachers and adminstrators by ostensibly universal criteria of merit effects particularistic outcomes. They note the prevalence of prejudice among teachers and the low representation of blacks in teaching and administrative cadres. They point out that certain supposedly impartial practices, such as intelligence testing and ability grouping, while neutral in their procedures, are discriminatory in their effects. Thus tracking, for example, leads to effective segregation in the school and to a self-fulfilling prophecy of failure for the children in the bottom track. They remark on the absence of topics in the curriculum that are meaningful to black children. As Charles Hamilton puts it, "We simply cannot assume a common secular political culture."[9]

The attack on supposedly neutral, or technical, procedures constitutes a basic assault on the concept of universal, rational norms underlying the professional ideology.

> Insofar as the educational system promotes the secular ideal, it conforms to the liberal perspective. . . .
>
> From this broad perspective, a number of specific theorems derive: The schools should embrace heterogenenous populations; schools are to be ethically neutral, except for their endorsement of the scientific ethic; the curriculum is to be secular, and is to emphasize the shared culture; school personnel should be selected and advanced according to their merits, the best approximation being the civil service laws; children fail for idiosyncratic (individual) reasons, or because of insufficient funds or wisdom, not because they occupy a special stratum in society.
>
> These several beliefs . . . conform quite closely, in fact, to the views of the present educational establishment in most cities.[10]

Hence, while the first assault on the professional ideology directly attacks the competence of the public schools to educate children, the second argues that the universalistic ethos underlying the concept of expert decision making is invalid. The attack becomes explicity directed at the political values underlying the public education system.

> What I am stating (in as kind a way as possible) is that setting criteria for measuring equal educational opportunity can no longer be the province of the established "Experts." The policy-makers must now listen to those for whom they say they are operating; which means of course that they must be willing to share the powers of policy-making. The experts must understand that what is high on the liberal social scientist's agenda does not coincide with the agenda of many black people. The experts are still focusing on the effectiveness of existing educational institutions. Many black people have moved to the evaluation of the legitimacy of these institutions.[11]

In sum, according to contemporary reformers the public educational system is illegitimate because of both the incompetence of educators and the unacceptable value substructure of education. Its flaws are best revealed not through a direct examination of pedagogical theory and values but rather through direct examination of the the effects or outcomes of the educational process.

Lack of Responsiveness

The third major accusation against the educational system, and the one which is most overtly political, is that those responsible for running the schools are not responsive to the needs and requests of the parents and students. This is essentially an attack on procedures. In its most general form, the attack opposes central bureaucratic control, as in the following illustration:

Scarsdale has one of the finest school systems in the United States.

It has 5,122 students. And a school board consisting of seven members. Which makes one board member for every 732 students.

New York City has much the same system.

It has 1,100,000 students. And a Board of Education consisting of 13 members. Which makes one board member for every 84,615 boys and girls.

The arithmetic alone shows you why our school system is in trouble.

The job is simply too big for one Board of Education. And who pays for our mistakes?

Our children.[12]

More specificially, critics of large school systems accuse these organizations or perpetrating injustices on individual parents and children. Parents, in particular, consider themselves abused in cases of suspension and other disciplinary actions against their children. A long case study of a suspension proceeding, composed by a New York parent activist, has the following preface:

Current student rebellion against arbitrary and oppressive actions by professional educators made it pertinent to record a minor victory in the struggle of one mother to protect her son. Perhaps it will clarify issues for the many parents, of all races and backgrounds, who fail to recognize the importance of obtaining justice for children.[13]

Parents not only challenge the control over general school policy vested in school bureaucracies and central school boards, but they also contest the right of school personnel to make unilateral administrative decisions that affect the general welfare of their children. In the suspension case mentioned above, sympathetic parents joined with the mother of the suspended child in sitting in on the district superintendent's office, and they were subsequently arrested and jailed. They were implicitly arguing that alleged injustices to individual parents and students did not result from occasional miscarriages of justice, but rather from procedures biased against their interests.

> Parents and other members of the community had met regularly with Mrs. H (mother of the suspended child) and had become increasingly outraged by the violation of Douglas H's rights. Early that morning, they met at the District Office and advised that they would remain until the District Superintendent carried out his own decision to reinstate Douglas. He refused to do so and instead ordered the police to arrest anyone who would not leave the office. Twelve men and women were arrested. Six of the eight women were public school parents, including Mrs. H. One mother has children enrolled at P.S. 145 and another formerly had children enrolled at 145. They had been harassed out of the school under similar circumstances.[14]

Several of those arrested, whom we interviewed later, stated that they were in no position to judge the merits of the individual case. Rather, they contended that the whole policy of suspensions was unjust and discriminated against blacks.

Parents, demanding an increased voice in school policy making, claim that the procedural norms governing the relationship between the schools and their clients are weighted against the interests of clients. They argue that in large urban systems they are unable to hold their representatives accountable and cannot participate in the making of school decisions that have a profound impact on themselves and their children. They contend, moreover, that administrative procedures, ranging from restrictions on parents visiting the schools to judgments in disciplinary cases, are biased in favor of school personnel over children and their parents.

The Symbolic Importance of Political versus Educational

In American educational debate, the term political is usually one of opprobrium. It implies venality and narrow partisanship. The intrusion of political interests into educational decision making is interpreted to mean that decisions will be made according to some criterion other than the general good. In a certain sense, all participants in the debate accept this notion. Many of the most ardent spokesmen for community control feel that the need to weigh political considerations is deleterious to the interests of children in the schools and should not have to occupy the time of educational policy makers.

> I would be happy if we could be free from political struggle, if we could deal only with the education of children. But I don't think in terms of enjoyment. I don't have a choice.[15]

Both sides in the community-control controversy regret the prominence of politics, and each side resents the other for forcing it to devise strategies for gaining or maintaining power. Although much school decision making is political, even if it is not being challenged, participants in the controversy tend to see their own decisions, but not those of their opponents, as nonpolitical in instances where there is no overt resistance and controversy.

As outsiders, reformist groups argue that, at least now, all school decisions are political. They deny the claims of expertise and employ extreme rhetoric tending toward vilification of teachers and school administrators. The reformers look forward to a situation in which they are in control and school issues are once again nonpolitical. But meanwhile, they must expose the present supporters of the status quo as undemocratically selected exponents of particular interests rather than qualified individuals who achieve their place in the hierarchy on their own merit. For example, in an article advocating community control, Preston Wilcox states:

> The civil rightists have campaigned to get Negro history onto the agenda of the school; the black power theorists have pushed to get Afro-American history into the schools. The civil rightists want all students—black and white —to understand Negro history; the black power theorists emphasize Afro-American history as an identity building tool for blacks. Both fail to note that *our public education system is bankrupt because it is being controlled by a group of conservative thinkers. White and black students alike are not being taught citizenship and social responsibility.* The emphasis is on "scholarship," despite its lack of social relevance in today's world.[16]
>
> (emphasis added)

As well as accusing the present educational policy makers of being defenders of particular interests—that is, of being a group of conservative thinkers—Wilcox claims that he represents the general interest. When he says "white and black students alike" are being mistreated, he is claiming universality for his cause.

Within the symbolic debate over who deserves power, no group can afford to state that its claims are opposed to those of the general public. The demands of a disadvantaged group are always placed in a context to show that their realization will, ultimately, result in greater benefits for all. In any particular instance this may well be the case, if only in the long run; but the rise of disadvantaged groups often exacts from the remainder of the public real costs, which the public may regard as intolerable.[17]

Those seeking power in the schools attempt to show that the educational system is run for the particular advantage of certain social groups and assert that when they, themselves, gain power, the governance of schools will be democratic and not partisan. Like the reformers at the beginning of this century, they wish to make government more responsive and also less political. Members of the demonstration governing boards in New York City just like members of established nonpartisan school boards (themselves a product of the earlier reform movement), deny particularistic motivations in joining school boards and see themselves serving the entire community.

In response, defenders of the system argue that schools should be judged solely according to their success in educating children. The New York City Board of Education, when it established the demonstration districts, assumed that their continuation would depend on the direct effects on the children in the schools. An incident recounted by the Niemeyer Committee, which was entrusted by the Central Board with the task of evaluating the districts after their first year, illustrates this point.

> The issue of obtaining outside funds also came up at this meeting (between representatives of the Ocean Hill–Brownsville Governing Board and the New York City Board of Education). The representative of the Board of Education stated emphatically the Board's commitment to experimenting with the ways and means of increasing parental participation. Thus, if the Demonstration Project gains substantial sums from other sources, *then the possibility of showing the effectiveness of local control will be uncertain.* The Board contends that *experimental variables must be limited in order to pinpoint the cause-and-effect relationship* so that the experience can be replicated in other areas. To significantly increase the amounts of monies spent in the Demonstration Project would not prove the value of community involvement. *The Board prefers to test whether community involvement will affect student achievement levels.* However, former Board President Alfred Giardino stated that the Board would welcome any new funds, although such monies must be channeled through and approved by the central agency.[18]
>
> (emphasis added)

Although the last sentence suggests that the Board was being at least somewhat disingenuous, the quotation does clarify the extent to which educational policy makers choose to limit policy evaluation to technical measurements of their own devising. The question of who controls the money that goes into Ocean Hill–Brownsville clearly has implications beyond its influence on the parameters of a scientific experiment in assessing the effects of local control. It is, however, against the interests of those who hold power, due to their special qualifications, to admit that political as well as educational benefits should be taken into account. Thus, the Niemeyer Committee also notes,

> Many principals (in the regular New York districts) professed a belief that the principal should be involved in certain community issues but felt that the clerical work and meetings created by decentralization and community involvement drew them away from the classrooms and *their roles as educational leaders*.[19]

(emphasis added)

People who occupy positions by virtue of their expert qualifications can justify their decision-making power only by defining their role narrowly. If principals consider their participation in parents meetings a significant part of their office, they would then (as, of course, some principals do) need to accept such additional bases for their authority as parental approval and a more common requisite of administrative office degrees and examination scores. The apparent modesty of principals in seeking to limit their roles serves to insure their position. And, in so limiting themselves, they rely on the symbolic meaning of their self-denial. For, by contending that they act as educational leaders rather than as political decision makers, they place as partisans those who attempt to force them into more public contact, while they themselves remain simply educators.

The very nature of the educators' defense against the reformers—arguing that the reformers are injecting politics into matters that should be decided impartially—compels the reformers to accuse educators themselves of being fundamentally political and, thus, hypocritical. The importance both to oneself and to one's audience of seeming free from particuarlism structures the nature of the debate. The reformers attack members of the establishment as being self-interested protectors of the status quo; the educators claim that the reformers are seeking political power rather than the education of children. Both sides defend themselves as concerned with the general welfare and therefore, in the highest sense, nonpolitical.

The following analysis presented of the relationship between educational policies and political benefits indicates that both sides are closer to the truth in their accusations than in their defenses. Most important educational decisions, at least at this point in history, differentiate beween significant political interests. Many decisions are intractably political, and the goal of both sides to escape politicization is unattainable. Participants in educational controversies are, accordingly, forced by the situation to look for power, whether they wish to maintain the status quo or to alter radically the present distribution of benefits.

A Theoretical Framework for Analyzing Educational Policies

In a despotism it makes no real difference to most of the population whether a particular governmental decision is defined as technical or as political, for in neither instance are governmental decision makers subject to popular control. From the perspective of a powerless citizenry, it is a moot point whether the wielders of arbitrary power base a policy choice upon political or nonpolitical criteria or how the citizenry itself classifies a decision by its rulers. Where the citizen has no say over any governmental policies, he is little interested in alternative rationales for the policy process.

Central to democratic thought and to American political culture is the premise that political decisions should be made only by publicly accountable individuals. Within our tradition of representative government, it is difficult to justify political decisions made by individuals free from popular control, for the citizenry is sovereign and is the ultimate judge among alternative governmental policies. But all governmental offices are not political offices whose occupants play political roles. Indeed, only a very small part of the government is defined as politicized. The important point is that political policies must be legitimized in a way that technical decisions are not. It is therefore significant how a policy choice is defined, because from that definition we infer who has the right to make the policy decision. It is on this basis that we judge whether the decision maker need be bound by the constraints of democratic representation or may operate free from popular control.

Our national belief in popular sovereignty over political matters makes it symbolically important whether a policy is defined as political or nonpolitical. This would suggest to us, as analysts studying urban education, that we pay careful attention to how the terms political and educational are employed as symbols within the political arena. But it would not lead us to create our own definition of political. We are concerned with the intrinsic meaning of this term as opposed to its operational use because we ourselves stand within the democratic tradition; we attach normative significance to whether or not political decisions are made by a democratic, representative process. In judging for ourselves, as democrats, the legitimacy of a particular administrative arrangement, we need to decide upon a means by which to distinguish between political and nonpolitical policy decisions. For democratic theory, although explicit about how political policies should be made, fails to define which policies are political. The analysis of educational policies in terms of democratic theory thus necessitates a theoretical framework with which to differentiate between political and nonpolitical policies.

Students of public administration have often tried to separate administrative from political decisions on the basis of the decision maker's position in a formal, organized hierarchy or by an examination of the substance of the decision maker's tasks. Our approach is different. We begin by accepting Harold D. Lasswell's definition of politics as the process that determines "who gets what, when, how,"[20] and David Easton's statement that a political interaction is one which is "predominantly oriented toward the authoriatative allocation of values.[21] Lasswell's "who" refers to groups that may be distinguished by their position within the social structure, by common economic interests, or by shared consciousness. By synthesizing Lasswell's and Easton's conceptions we conclude that a political decision authoritatively determines how benefits are to be distributed among such groups.

Our analysis will show that, in fact, this is the same as saying that a political decision is one which, for a given benefit criterion, creates benefit groups which may be identified with structural groups, economic groups, or consciousness groups. A political decision is therefore one in which the winners and losers by some explicit criterion of benefit are also groups which may be distingushed in social terms. Accordingly, a given policy choice may or may not be political depending upon how benefits are measured and who receive them.

The Theoretical Framework Explicated: Policies, Decisions, Benefits

The theoretical framework for identifying political decisions is built upon three basic elements—the definitions of political policies, of political decisions, and of benefits. We recognize first of all that public schools are governmental institutions. They are created by the state legislatures and either constitute functional agencies within general purpose local governments or are themselves special purpose local governments. They have authoritative power and make authoritative decisions within the scope of their legislative mandates. As governmental institutions, they are formally a part of the political process. But only some of the policies made within schools determine how benefits are to be distributed among important structural, economic, or consciousness groups and only those policies are political. All other policies are nonpolitical. They may be based upon technical criteria or rationalized in any number of other ways; but so long as they do not actually determine the distribution of benefits among important social groups, they remain nonpolitical, regardless of how they are labeled. Thus, a political policy is defined functionally in terms of its effect on social groups.

By first asking "who gets what" from an institutional or procedural arrangement and then stating that a political policy has been made if benefit groups may be identified with social groups, we have in effect also created a functional definition of a decision. Until now we have distinguished between political and nonpolitical policies without explicitly considering the nature of a decision itself. We may, however, infer from the previous argument that a political decision is a choice—explicit or implicit—among policy alternatives so as to affect the distribution of benefits among important social groups. It then follows that a political decision is a choice—explicit or implicit—among alternative political policies.

This definition of a political decision—the second point to be noted about the theoretical framework—is broader than the common meaning of the term. It includes both the decisions about which men think and consciously, if not publicly, decide, and those which men make by adopting a particular policy, even though they fail to recognize that they have made a choice among alternative logical possibilities. The use of the term decision does not imply anything about the behavior or motivation of a policy maker as such; all we need is a policy and one or more logical alternatives to it. Our decisions include what Peter Bachrach and Morton S. Baratz have called non-decisions or policy choices unrecognized as such in public discourse and even in private thought, but which produce in their effect a bias in favor of some social group or groups.[22]

Thus, for example, the law that compels children to attend school until they reach a certain age comprises a decision which in a sense is still being made daily. To a child who sees the policy choice of compulsory attendance as limiting his freedom, the alternative possibility of voluntary attendance is indeed real, even though no policy maker has made a conscious choice to institute compulsory attendance in many years.

There are very few decisions which were not once made explicitly. A decision made long ago is, in its effect on the distribution of benefits, precisely the same as if it were made every day. It is, however, much more likely to be recognized as a decision by individuals who are both dissatisfied with its effect on them and accept it as a natural fact. Indeed, only by demonstrating that a policy decision has in effect been made can a dissatisfied group make demands for a different policy; for it a particular distribution of benefits is inevitable, then there is no way to press for policy change. This, then, is the reason for our particular conceptualization of decision.

The final aspect of the theoretical framework demanding particular attention is the concept of benefit and its corollary, benefit group. We use benefit here in a neutral sense, so that one must differentiate between positive benefits and negative benefits. Benefits may then be interpreted as identical with values in Easton's definition of political. In order to differentiate between positive and negative benefits, one must adopt a criterion of benefit. The difference between positive and negative benefits is relative and is determined only by an ordinal relationship along a dimension defined by a criterion of benefit. There may be any number of benefit criteria employed in analyzing the effects of a particular policy. Examples of such criteria include money, prestige, power, liberty, security, reading achievement, and job appointment. The choice of a benefit criterion is logically independent of the choice of policy to be examined. However, it must be demonstrated empirically that there exists a causal relationship between a given policy and the distribution of benefits measured in terms of a given criterion.

Social Groups and Benefit Groups

So far we have developed a way of showing that a policy can be traced to the point where its benefit groups may be defined by its differential impact on individuals. Within the terms of the discussion, it should be clear that only policies which create such groups can be political. But, in fact, most educational policies do fall into this category. The crucial step in distinguishing between political and nonpolitical policies rests upon the empirical relationship between benefit groups and social groups. When there is an identity between the two, a policy may be said to be political. In other words, a governmental policy is political when it differentially benefits social groups.

Three different criteria may be used to define social groups. The first is structural. A structural group encompasses all the occupants of the same status or position within a social structure. Thus, we may sometimes speak about the social structures of particular institutions, like hospitals or schools or government bureaus. At other times we may think of status defined by a national or even a universal social structure, such as positions determined by age, sex, or marriage. The important structural groups likely to be considered in their relation to education include, for example, teachers, students, boys, girls, parents, administrators, middle class people, and blacks.

Economic groups are also structural groups. We single out economic criteria as a second category, not because they are logically distinct, but rather because they are empirically important in affecting political behavior. Economic groups may be defined either in terms of the relationship of individuals to the process of production or in terms of their share in the distribution of material benefits. Economic groups of the first kind include mechanics, drill press operators, share-croppers, landlords, and professors, while those of the second encompass the rich, the poor, and individuals with below median income.

The third way of defining a social group is by the shared or collective consciousness of its members. The basis for shared consciousness may be psychological or ideological or both. The important thing is that the groups' members identify with one another, share common ideas, and label themselves in similar ways. Consciousness groups include Jews, Italians, advocates of community control, socialists, Mormons, Catholics. The basis for self-identification or shared consciousness may be, but not necessarily, derived from the common structural or economic characteristics of a group's members. Under certain historical conditions such a group may cut across structural or economic lines, as was the case, for example, during the short-lived coalition of businessmen and the poor supporting urban renewal or during the long-lived history of Catholicism.

For the purpose of the present analysis it matters little whether we classify a particular social group as structural, economic, or consciousness. Thus, we can avoid issues that arise when we try to demarcate clearly a typology of such groups. It is, however, necessary for us to recognize that not all social groups are of interest in discussing the distribution of benefits from a specfic policy. Some groups that would be defined as social groups by at least one of our three criteria are simply insignificant. Only those policies that distribute benefits among significant or important social groups should be called political.

The test of whether a relationship exists between benefit groups and important social groups can be specified quite easily. How do the winners differ from the losers under alternative policies? If the difference can be expressed in terms of an attribute associated with a significant social group, then the governmental policy determines the distribution of benefits among such groups and is thereby political. Operationally, we examine the composition of pairs of benefit groups, i.e., of the winners and losers, to see whether a particular social group is overrepresented among the winners and underrepresented among the losers. Thus, for example, we would find that public school suspension policies result in an overrepresentation of black children (the social group) among those who are suspended (the losing or negative benefit group). Such policies are therefore defined as political.

An entirely equivalent test, and one for which we have available standard notation, involves our asking whether identifying the social group of an individual tells us anything about the probability of his being among the winners as opposed to the losers. Are we more likely to specify correctly the individual's benefit position when we know he carries some social group attribute than when we do not? If, in fact, we are, a relationship exists between benefit groups and social groups. For example, if a man is identified in social group terms, is the conditional probability of his being in a positive or negative benefit group different from the probability of an unidentified individual being there? If so, then the policy under scrutiny is political. Thus, in the case of the suspension policy, knowing a child is black does increase the probability of determining correctly whether or not he will be suspended. The conditional probability of being suspended is different from—specifically, greater than—the probability of being suspended in general.

The choice of alternative procedures for the election of elementary school principals in Manhattan provides a clear example of a political decision. Manhattan has a student population that is about eighty percent nonwhite and all but two or three of its regularly appointed principals are white. Under the present arrangement, principals are chosen administratively from a list of qualified candidates. To be on this list an individual must have served as an assistant principal for several years and have passed written and oral examinations specially created by the Board of Examiners of the Board of Education. State certification for the position of elementary school principal, itself requiring the passing of an examination, the completion of specified college courses, and years of experience, is not sufficient for a permanent appointment within New York City. Black and Puerto Rican critics of the New York City appointment procedure have suggested an alternative policy under which parents in elementary schools would choose their own principal from a list of candidates with New York State certification. In effect, they are suggesting a policy that would shift the distribution of benefits in Manhattan to the advantage of nonwhites. Both the extant policy of the Board of Education and the suggested alternatives determine the distribution of benefits to important social groups and are thereby political. The choice between the two policies is therefore a political decision.

Education policies need not be political. Consider the choice between two policies for teaching reading: (a) phonics and (b) look–say. If a benefit criterion is defined by children's reading achievement, each policy creates related benefit groups. But there is no reason to believe that better or worse readers under either policy may be identified in social-group terms. Because benefit groups are not under present circumstances related to social groups, "a" and "b" are nonpolitical, as is the decision to implement one or the other.

During the days of Sputnik, when Rudolph Flesch wrote *Why Johnny Can't Read,* the shortcomings of American schools were associated by many political conservatives with the introduction of look–say and other progressive methods. At that time, the choice of method was political. So, to make the point once again, there is no way to tell whether a policy is or is not intrinsically political. The distinction must be made in terms of what a policy does, rather than what it is. At some historical moment a policy may determine the distribution of benefits among social groups; a decade later the same policy may no longer do so, and thereby become depoliticized.

We are led to conclude, in sum, that political policies should be identified by the effects they produce rather than by any attributes of policy makers or of the policy process. The argument rests upon two premises: first, that all policies embody procedures that define the distribution of specific benefits among a set of individuals; second, and more fundamental, that politics is the process by which benefits are authoritatively allocated among significant social groups. By relating the premises through the necessary intermediating concepts and notation, the theoretical framework provides a logically consistent set of terms for a functional definition of political. Such a definition tells us to look always first—but not solely—at the outcomes of an institutional arrangement when we wish to analyze the nature of institutional policy and to judge the legitimacy of the process by which it is made.

The analysis provides a functional definition of a political decision. Our approach contrasts with that usually taken by political scientists, who see such decisions as explicit and more or less rational choices made by individuals who are usually but not always the occupants of public offices. Much of the debate during the last decade over the methodology to be employed in studying community power has centered on how the analyst knows a decision has been made, whether significant decisions always involve public discussion or conflict, and whether non-decisions are, in effect, also decisions.[23] We begin with an essentially sociological orientation and define decisions as existing whenever logical alternatives to an extant policy can be identified. This position, which is very similar to that taken by Bachrach and Baratz,[24] implies that so-called nondecisions are, indeed, decisions, just as the nondecisions to retain rather than repeal the compulsory school attendance laws, though never publicly discussed and probably not even privately considered, is in its effect a decision.

A political decision defined to include the *de facto* choice among two or more alternative political policies need involve no open conflict at all. Social groups that benefit negatively from such a decision may not rise in public clamor. They may not even recognize that alternative policies could shift the distribution of institutional benefits to their advantage. Our analysis of the political aspects of educational institutions involves "conflicts among contending values and participants . . . conflicts among values and groups [which] will only be resolved through the techniques of the political process: influence, bargaining, persuasion, accomodation, compromise."[25]

By framing the concept of political decision broadly, we permit the analyst of educational policies to identify policies and decisions as political, even though he may have little access to a policy process hidden by bureaucratic obscurantism. Moreover, we permit the critics of governmental outputs, particularly the members of negative benefit groups, to claim that political decisions have been made to their benefit. For those who benefit by the policies and procedures embedded in the status quo typically claim the inevitability or naturalness of existing arrangements. Deprived groups, on the other hand, must always show that different policies could have been or can be followed, that the status quo is itself a product of human choice, i.e., decision, and can be changed by different political policies resulting from different decisions.

The Political Control of Educational Policies

The theoretical framework shows us that many educational policies are inevitably political. This conclusion legitimizes the argument of the proponents of community control that school decisions should be made according to democratic procedures rather than through techniques designed to preserve the inviolability of professional judgments. Democratic values require that political decision makers be placed under controls different from administrative decision makers.

However, it is not obvious that the only way to make educational organizations democratically accountable is through the participation of neighborhood representatives in the formulation of educational policy. Different ways of defining constituencies cause policy makers to be accountable to different social groups. If democracy alone were the value we were seeking to maximize, then we might choose a centralized system of control as the most feasible way of insuring majority rule over the schools. We wish, however, to increase the benefits received by disadvantaged social groups, and while we value democratic procedures, we would like to combine them with devices that improve the social position of the poor. Community control provides representation to minority interests that lack power in a system of centralized majoritarian representation. Specifically, it increases the power of blacks in the school policy making process.

The judgment that community control of education promises to make the educational system more responsive to the disadvantaged contrasts with the argument in favor of centralized political control presented by Robert Salisbury in a well-known article on schools and politics. Salisbury argues:

> Direct political-system control of the schools (historically anathema to educators) might have significant virtues in making the schools more effective instruments of social change and development. . . . Autonomous schools may be unresponsive to important groups in the community whose interests are not effectively served by the dominant values of professional schoolmen.[26]

He suggests that mayors should be given direct control over the schools on the grounds that mayors are more inclined than educators to favor the interests of racial minorities.

> Mayor Daley might have achieved more effective (racial) integration than Superintendent Willis seemed disposed to provide had the mayor chosen to violate the educators' code of independence and exert more direct control of the situation.[27]

Salisbury offers no evidence to support his faith in Mayor Daley. An analysis of the multiple pressures on big-city mayors reveals few forces that would motivate them to compel educational changes which whites or entrenched educational bureaucracies regard as inimical to their interests. Decentralization, by creating more homogeneous districts, when combined with local political representation, could force the administrators of some districts to respond to black pressures.

A functional approach to the political evaluation of educational policies shows that the first place to look when judging an educational decision is at its consequences, at its effect on the distribution of benefits across social groups. The analysis also shows why, when evaluating various modes of representation, one should examine how the benefit groups they create correspond to significant social groups. Formal analysis of decentralization and community representation leads to an arid and often incorrect weighing of results. It is simple enough to say abstractly that centralized control leads to efficiencies of scale and accountability to the entire public: but it is equally easy to argue that decentralization creates efficiency through improved communications and direct accountability. Likewise, it is possible, albeit difficult, to compare the effects of centralized and decentralized districts on pupil performance. The political significance of community control, however, lies in how it redistributes benefits to social groups, and one benefit criterion is plainly power. In power terms, community control increases the benefits to citizens in ghetto districts both vis á vis whites who previously received more benefits from the school system and in relation to those professionals who previously headed the system.[34] Ironically, although community control is itself a political policy, its implementation, while making citywide educational decisions overtly political, might partially depoliticize intradistrict decisions. Decentralization to neighborhoods results in the creation of local districts relatively homogeneous as to class and race. Decisions such as ability grouping are political on a citywide basis because they benefit different social groups unequally. In a homogeneous district they might cease to be political because they would affect all groups uniformly, unless what we have called a consciousness group formed around a policy choice.

The community-control movement provoked strident opposition from the teachers' union precisely because that group recognized the political nature of the proposed reform. Those who argued that the New York legislature should have left the experimental districts alone until they proved themselves completely failed to recognize the political nature of the controversy. The supporters of community control were right in arguing that the schools had always been political, although they tended naïvely to believe, or at least hope, that the future of community control in New York could be determined by nonpolitical criteria.

Educational reformers must realize that almost any reform upsets the current distribution of benefits and will thereby encounter resistance. Only the naïve reformer hopes to be judged simply on the merits of his proposal. Once the political nature of educational reform is recognized, it becomes possible to devise political strategies and mobilize political support around reform measures. Failure to see the inevitable need for political strategies leads either to an unfounded optimism or a self-defeating pessimism—either the optimism of thinking that the best method will be adopted, or the pessimism of feeling that the status quo is unchangeable because vested interests refuse to yield their positions when shown a superior policy choice.

NOTES

1   Roscoe Martin, *Government and the Suburban School* (Syracuse: Syracuse University Press, 1963), p. 58.

2   Karl Mannheim, *Ideology and Utopia* (New York, Harvest, 1936). I am using ideology here strictly in Mannheim's sense. He says, "The concept of 'ideology' reflects the one discovery which emerged from political conflict, namely, that ruling groups can in their thinking become so intensively interestbound to a situation that they are simply no longer able to see certain facts which would undermine their sense of domination." (p. 40) "The use of the term 'ideology' in the sociology of knowledge has no moral or denunciatory intent." (p. 266).

3   Kenneth Clark, *Dark Ghetto* (New York, Harper and Row, 1965), pp. 119–20.

4   Ibid., pp. 133.

5   John Holt, *How Children Fail* (New York: Delta Books, 1964), pp. 140–1.

6   Ibid., pp. 144.

7   Susan S. Fainstein, notes taken at a public meeting, November 16, 1969.

8   Peter Schrag, *Village School Downtown* (Boston: Beacon Press, 1967), pp. 71–72.

9   Charles V. Hamilton, "Race and Education: A Search for Legitimacy," *Harvard Educational Review*, 38 (1968) p. 679.

10   Leonard J. Fein, "Community Schools and Social Theory: The Limits of Universalism," in Henry M. Levin (ed.), *Community Control of Schools* (Washington, D. C., Brookings Institution, 1970), p. 90.

11   Hamilton, *op. cit*, p. 674.

12   Urban Coalition Advertisement, *Amsterdam News*, November 30, 1968.

13   Rosalie Stutz, "With Justice and Equality for All - Including Children," July 10, 1969, mimeograph.

14   Ibid.

15   Interview with I.S. 201 Governing Board member, February 10, 1970.

16   Preston Wilcox, "School and Community," *The Record*, LXIX (November 1967), p. 135.

17   Ralf Dahrendorf, *Class and Class Conflict in Industrial Society* (Stanford, Stanford University Press, 1959), see for discussion of the intractable bases of conflict.

18   "An Evaluative Study of the Process of School Decentralization in New York City" ("Niemeyer Report"). Final report by the Advisory and Evaluation Committee on Decentralization to the Board of Education of the City of New York for the period: July 1, 1967 to June 30, 1968, (July 30, 1968), pp. 92–3.

19   Ibid., p. 55.

20 Harold D. Lasswell, *Politics: Who Gets What, When, How* (New York: McGraw Hill, 1936),

21 David Easton, *A Framework for Political Analysis,* (Englewood Cliffs: Prentice-Hall, 1965), p. 50.

22 Peter Bachrach and Morton S. Baratz, "Two Faces of Power," *American Political Science Review,* LVI (December, 1962) pp. 947–52. For a highly sophisticated discussion of the important theoretical issues underlying the conceptualization of decision, see Ralf Dahrendorf, "Homo Sociologicus: On the History, Significance, and Limits of the Category of Social Role," *Essays in the Theory of Society* (Stanford: Stanford University Press, 1968); and Robert E. Agger, Daniel Goldrich, and Bert E. Swanson, *The Rulers and the Ruled* (New York, John Wiley, 1964). They define decision as a six-stage process that may become arrested at the first stage of policy formulation. In other words, an alternative policy may be conceived but never debated or seriously considered; thus a decision has been made, in a sense, to sustain the status quo.

23 Todd Gitlin, "Local Pluralism as Theory and Ideology," *Recent Sociology* Hans Peter Dreitzel (ed.), (New York, The MacMillan Company, 1969), vol. I, pp. 61–87. See for a brilliant discussion of the theoretical and political issues involved in the community power debate.

24 Bachrach and Baratz, *op. cit.*

25 Michael Decker and Louis H. Masotti, "Determining the Quality of Education: A Political Process," *The Quality of Urban Life; III: Urban Affairs Review* Henry J. Schmandt and Warner Bloomberg Jr. (eds.), (Beverly Hills, Sage Publications, 1969), p. 369.

26 Robert H. Salisbury, "Schools and Politics in the Big City," *Harvard Educational Review,* XXXVII (Summer 1967), p. 409.

27 *Ibid.,* p. 424.

Two Model Cities: Negotiations in Oakland

Judith V. May

As colleague confronts colleague, so also do the constituent orders of the Roman Republic: the sovereignty *(imperium)* of the magistracy confronts the sovereignty *(majestas)* of the people not on a line of vertical subordination but horizontally coordinate. The Roman body politic is not one, but two. The two principles cannot operate except as they cooperate; so that, as Mommsen says, "law was not primarily, as we conceive it, a command addressed by the sovereign to the community as a whole, but primarily a contract concluded between the constitutive powers of the state by address and counter-address." The schism in the body politics known as the secession (not rebellion) of the plebs is only an aggravation of the inherent separation of the constituent orders. The extraordinary institution to which that secession gave rise, the tribunate of the people, with its veto over the acts of the magistracy, amounted to legalized, and institutionalized, civil war.

Norman O. Brown, *Love's Body*

In Oakland, California, under the auspices of the Model Cities Program, the federal government precipitated a conflict between the "sovereignty of the magistracy" and the "sovereignty of the people," and the immediate consequence was the creation of a second government for the

West Oakland community. West Oakland residents, in effect, declared their independence from the authority of the local government and established new institutions, which they vested with legitimacy. Led by newly sanctioned leaders in their battle over Model Cities planning, they fought for the right to govern their own community in concert with city officials —to share authority on a large number of important matters. Their negotiated victory may prove short-lived; a small change in federal administrative or legislative policy could have an enormous effect on the viability of the West Oakland government. Even should the Model Cities structure fail to survive, however, the contest will continue. At stake are alternative visions of the model city, one compatible with existing institutions and policies and the other premised upon major changes in them.

During the course of the negotiations, West Oakland leaders articulated with increasing clarity an alternative to the economic growth ideology held by city officials and embodied in the city's political institutions. In so doing, they tackled some of the most politically repressive features of the institutional and intellectual changes that have occurred in this country since the advent of the welfare and warfare states: political legitimacy based upon conformance to procedures rather than performance; political authority delegated to experts; and governmental policy directed toward economic growth at the expense of economic redistribution—features found in many American governments, not only in the city of Oakland.[1] Social scientists are becoming increasingly sensitive to these developments and are beginning to see the inadequacies of the paradigms that have guided their research in recent decades. If, as I contend, we are witnessing the exhaustion of another generation of ideas, then perhaps at this point in time, when the search for a new paradigm is under way, social scientists should examine the reactions of those who are struggling with the overripe fruits of old ideas.

City officials and West Oakland residents evaluated the possible benefits of the Model Cities Program in terms of different conceptions of the proper relationship between government and economic life. In general, city officials and their supporters believe that Oakland's economic future depends upon the city's ability to attract and retain private capital investors. Economic growth will not only expand the city's tax base, creating resources that can be reinvested in the city's advancement, but will also create employment opportunities and, thereby, productive citizens rather than public liabilities. Recent changes in Oakland's population and economic base have increased the burdens upon the city. During World War II, its population increased rapidly as the demand rose for workers in the Oakland shipyards and war-related activities. A large minority population remained after the war, and the white population began to move to the suburbs over newly completed freeways. Simultaneously, manufacturing decreased while transportation, distribution, communications, and service industries expanded. Thus, while the skill level of the city's population decreased, the skill demands of its economic institutions increased. Nevertheless, Oakland's economic future is promising. Despite the many enterprises that have moved out, those that remain are attracted in large part by Oakland's location in a nexus of transportation facilities. These firms have a stake in Oakland and are potential supporters of long-range economic development strategies.

A relatively coherent strategy for achieving economic development has emerged. A private investor's willingness to invest in Oakland is affected by his confidence in Oakland's economic future. Public policy must be directed toward creating this confidence. Two means to this end have been identified: maintaining racial peace and programming public investment. In the short run, racial peace is achieved through a combination of coercion and co-optation; in the long run, through individual upward mobility.

Sources of public investment funds have changed in recent years. Bond elections have repeatedly failed and numerous structural innovations have been necessary to capture new sources of investment capital. As a result, government on the local level has become increasingly fragmented. Increasingly, capital resources within Oakland are provided by other governments, which attach conditions to the use of these funds, conditions that dissipate the city's authority still further. A recent study[2] initiated by the Mayor found that the federal government spent a total of $487,356,372 in Oakland in 1968, $95,459,372 of which was for nondefense purposes. The Port of Oakland, whose commission members are appointed by the Mayor with the concurrence of the City Council, received $8,275,780. The relatively autonomous Oakland Redevelopment Agency and the Oakland Housing Authority received $8,158,110. The City of Oakland itself received $1,009,323. Under the circumstances, it is not surprising that city officials welcomed the Model Cities Program and its promise that the city government would play a major role in coordinating federal programs within the city.

Despite its handicaps, the city government has used the capital investment resources it controls to increase the city's attractiveness to investors. Major bond issues have financed a museum, an airport, and a police and municipal court building. Several urban renewal projects are under way, and the present Mayor, John Reading, hopes to revive the downtown area with a major hotel and convention center assisted with urban renewal funds. Despite these investments in Oakland's future productivity, the city has one of the highest unemployment rates among urban areas of its size in the nation.[3]

Recently, city leaders have begun to realize that there is no necessary correlaton between economic growth and the alleviation of Oakland's social problems and have increased their support for programs that invest in human as well as in capital development projects. Mayor Reading, in particular, believes that reducing unemployment will solve all other social problems and that the key to increasing employment lies in raising the skill level of the population. Much of the money available for this purpose is administered by the Oakland Economic Development Council (OEDC), the community action agency in Oakland. Reading is convinced that the OEDC has spent its money unwisely and is unsuited (by virtue of its composition) to administer employment programs, and he has attempted to wrest control over the program from the agency's board. Embittered by the federal government's willingness to bypass the city government, he also tried to force the agency, then functioning somewhat autonomously although attached to the city government, to observe normal administrative procedures, i.e., to funnel all communications through the city manager's office. These conflicts and their culmination in a break between the agency and the city overlapped the period of the preparation and revision of the Model Cities application.

When West Oakland residents viewed the results of the city's social and economic policies—as they experienced their effects on their daily lives—their general conclusion was that the objective of economic productivity was a long-run strategy that, in the short run, visited harsh consequences upon the low income and minority communities, and that city officials were more concerned with promoting economic growth than with increasing political and economic equality. As a result of capital improvement projects—freeway and rapid transit constructions and urban renewal programs—West Oakland sustained a net loss of 5100 housing units between 1960 and 1966. A clearance project lay dormant for six years; when it was finally carried out, housing was constructed for moderate rather than low income tenants. A rehabilitation project in West Oakland advanced the interests of home-owners at the expense of renters; the coliseum and arena, museum, and police administration building were given priority, although many streets in West Oakland lack curbs and gutters. Nor did West Oakland residents benefit indirectly from public improvements: millions of local and federal dollars have been invested in the Port, but Port commissioners have resisted employment clauses that would increase job openings for ghetto residents. The city made little effort to enforce employment clauses, agreed to by industries moving into the Acorn clearance area, for fear the industries would move away. Employment training programs have become an acknowledged hustle, since few jobs are available at the end of the training period.

Furthermore, West Oakland residents had little hope of altering these policies through normal political processes. In Oakland, councilmen reside in districts but are elected at-large in nonpartisan elections. They pride themselves on representing "the community as a whole" rather than special interests, and are notably conservative in ideology. Since 1937, when the council-manager form of government was installed, one-third of the council members achieved office through appointment to vacancies caused by death (8) or resignation (11) between election periods. Of the mayoral and councilmanic incumbents who ran for reelection between 1953 and 1969, eighty-five percent retained their seats. Two of the three minority representatives now on the council, one black and one Japanese, were originally appointed to office; the third, who is Chinese, defeated an eighty year old incumbent from West Oakland in his third campaign effort. The two Orientals share the conservative views of their colleagues; the black councilman was largely isolated from the rest of the black community until recently. Needless to say, the low income and minority communities do not regard the city council as responsive to their interests. In Oakland, blacks comprise approximately forty percent of the population and Mexican-Americans another ten percent; but lower registration and a high proportion of young people have so far reduced the electoral strength of the minority population.

Whereas city officials wanted to make everyone better off while retaining the existing relative shares, West Oakland residents wanted political and economic advantages distributed more evenly over all sections and classes in the city. Whereas city officials located the source of Oakland's problems in its changed economy and the low skills of a large part of its population, West Oakland residents pointed to the failure of the American government to assure political and economic equality to all of its citizens. Given these differences, it is not surprising that city officials and West Oakland residents also differed on the way in which decision making for the Model Cities Program should be structured.

Oakland has a weak-mayor–council-manager form of government. Members of the city council are accustomed to delegating responsibilities to the city manager and relying upon his advice. In October 1966, a month before the Demonstration Cities Act was passed, the city council directed its city manager, Jerome Keithley, to prepare an application. He assigned the task of preparing the application to Marshall Kaplan, a planning consultant, and assembled a task force of city and county agency heads to assist him. Since Kaplan had previously been hired by the Redevelopment Agency to appraise the existing urban renewal program within the city, he was able to draw heavily uopn that report[4] and completed the application within a relatively short time. The city manager restricted participation in what he called "the preplanning processes" to members of the task force on the grounds of an imminent deadline (April 15, 1967) for submission of the application. When the application was nearly completed, two target area residents were added to the Task Force and endorsements by various citizens boards, including the poverty board, were sought.[5]

The structure that Oakland officials projected for citizen participation in the Model Cities planning process relied upon the advocacy principle. In summary its premises were: (1) although community residents in the past had been unable to insert their views into the policy-making process, they are able to do so if they are supervised by an established organization (the Oakland Economic Development Council, the community action agency) and assisted by professional advocates; (2) planning itself is a job for professionals who possess both technical skill and political sensitivity; plans for the Model Cities Program are to be hammered out in negotiations between the city's planners and the community's advocates; (3) responsibility for the plan's preparation is properly delegated to the City Manager, who is the city's superintendent of administrative matters; (4) the Model Cities Program concentrates resources within a particular area, but the interests of the whole community are to be given weight in the planning process; and (5) final policy determinations are properly made by the city council after all interested parties have had a chance to be heard.[6]

On November 16, 1967, federal officials announced that Oakland's application had been conditionally accepted. Among the five or six conditions attached to the contract one was that the city would have to clarify the role of community residents in the planning process before final approval would be granted. Federal officials held a meeting in Oakland on November 28, 1967 to explain their reservations. Immediately thereafter, the West Oakland Planning Committee proposed a structure that eliminated all intermediaries between the spokesmen they selected and the political leaders of the city. In effect, they proposed the creation of a subgovernment for the West Oakland community that would author Model Cities plans subject to the concurrence of only the city council. In the city's original application, planners dominated the planning process; in West Oakland's proposal, community residents. Oakland's experience suggests that both planners and community residents view the new federal interest in urban problems as an opportunity to reduce their past ineffectiveness in influencing urban policies; each has invented an ideology justifying this new route to communal upward mobility: "advocacy" in the case of planners, and "community control" in the case of community residents.

West Oakland residents wanted to control the Model Cities planning process because they thought city officials were neither willing nor able to plan and implement programs that met their needs as they defined them. As a result of their experience with the poverty program, they were strengthened in their conviction that if only they controlled the program would they obtain results that satisfied them. West Oakland leaders were among the indigenous target area representatives who fought for majority control over the poverty board—the Oakland Economic Development Council. Many of the attitudes and strategies they brought to the Model Cities fight were formed in the evolving relationships between the twenty indigenous representatives, four from each of the five target areas and the nineteen at-large members of the Oakland Economic Development Council and between the Oakland Economic Development Council and the city. For that reason, the principal stages in the evolution of these relationships will be summarized here.

During the first stage, beginning in 1965, black professionals among the at-large members of the OEDC played a dominant role in defining the strategy followed by that body. They assumed a tutelary role in relation to the poor and continued the strategy of responsible opposition to the city they had developed as leaders of civil rights organizations. Through control over poverty funds, they hoped to enhance their effectiveness in negotiations with established agencies to improve the quality of services delivered to poor people. Their effectiveness depended upon their ability to maximize the amount of funds controlled by the OEDC (thereby increasing their bargaining leverage), to negotiate skillfully with federal and city officials, and to maintain an aura of responsibility about the poverty program, that is, to reduce visible conflicts both within the OEDC and between the OEDC and the city.

The second stage began when, at an OEDC program review meeting on March 12, 1966, target area representatives walked out after demanding that the OEDC give them fifty-one percent control over the board and allocate more of its money to poor people rather than to agency professionals.[8] They argued that poor people could better define their own needs than professionals. While at-large members continued to focus on changing the ways in which professional programs were run, the target area representatives wanted to run their own program. During this period, the at-large representatives retained effective control over the OEDC and their commitment to the negotiating strategy. However, since that strategy depended upon maintaining a low level of conflict within the OEDC, they acceded to some of the demands made by the indigenous representatives. A change in the guidelines permitted the OEDC to use the Ford Foundation's grey area funds for financing indigenous projects, while continuing to use Office of Economic Opportunity (OEO) funds to create negotiating leverage with established agencies. Thus, for a time, both the black professionals and the indigenous representatives were satisfied.

However, a number of changes occurred that upset the equilibrium and initiated the third stage. A new city manager (Jerome Keithley) took office, who was less interested in social problems and less amenable to behind-the-scenes negotiations. At the same time, spurred by the indigenous representatives, the OEDC began demanding greater changes in city policy than city officials were willing to make (e.g., creation of a police review board). Through skillful negotiations by its at-large members, the OEDC gained control over a new federal employment program funded by the U.S. Labor Department; this thoroughly alienated the new mayor

(Reading) who had vigorously opposed OEDC's expansion into this area. Each of these factors strained the relationship between the city and the poverty program and undermined the efficacy of the negotiating strategy. The OEDC decided to sever its attachment to the city and become a nonprofit corporation. The executive director of the OEDC—Norvel Smith, a staunch and skillful advocate of the negotiating policy—resigned. The appointment of his successor, Percy Moore, marked the beginning of more open conflict between the OEDC and the city and within the OEDC itself.

Moore rejected the negotiating strategy. Using it, the OEDC could win no more than agencies were willing to concede. He urged the OEDC to use its funds to create an independent political base from which it could extract concessions that agencies were unwilling to make. Moore chafed at taking directions from those who had participated in the negotiating strategy and characterized them as brokers. Because he sometimes made aggressive public statements in the name of the OEDC without consulting them, he periodically alienated their support. He also antagonized some of the indigenous representatives when, in an effort to strengthen the OEDC, he attempted to consolidate some activities which had been decentralized in the target areas. (And he angered the Mexican-Americans and some blacks, callling the former black, instead of black and brown or, the less divisive term, poor.) Relations between the OEDC and the city were strained, and conflicts within the OEDC were unresolved at the time West Oakland mobilized to revise the Model Cities application in negotiations with city officials.

The advocacy planning structure in Oakland's original Model Cities application was compatible with the negotiating strategy, since it preserved for black professionals a tutelary role in relation to West Oakland residents and a bargaining role in relation to the city. With the support of Percy Moore, West Oakland leaders rapidly demonstrated that they would not allow OEDC members to mediate between community residents and city officials. The OEDC's at-large members at first resisted West Oakland's declaration of independence from the OEDC on Model Cities matters because they feared that West Oakland leaders lacked sufficient skill and resources to carry on successful negotiations with the city. However, they soon acquiesced in the *fait accompli* and confined their activities to providing political support and advice upon request.

For the first time, lower-class community residents and their chosen representatives carried on direct negotiations with city officials over the form and objectives of a social program. The strategy they prepared for this confrontation reflected their response to the conflicts then occurring within the OEDC. They endorsed the strategy of negotiations, but insisted upon participating directly rather than through the mediators who had carried responsibility for past negotiations and they elected to build an independent political base, but rejected the centralization of authority that Moore had urged. By their actions, West Oakland residents explicitly rejected definitions of themselves as deficient. Acting on their conviction that the City of Oakland was unresponsive to their wants, wishes, and desires, they created a parallel government for West Oakland. At first this government was largely symbolic. Ralph Williams (who had been chairman of a district council under the grey areas program and of a target area advisory committee under the poverty program) was referred to as the Mayor of West Oakland, and West Oakland leaders cultivated other analogies with the city government. As a result of the Model Cities negotiations, however, West Oakland residents actually won the right to share authority with the city council on matters of importance to their community. The Model Cities structure itself was founded upon a contract concluded between the two sovereigns.

The first task confronting West Oakland leaders was to create an organization that could legitimately claim recognition both from community residents and city officials as the spokesman for the West Oakland community. Given the divisions within that community, this task was not easy. Next, West Oakland leaders had to choose between controlling the planning administration and governing a community. They chose to try to govern a community. Having made this choice, they first established their relation to experts within and outside the West Oakland community and then they set out to determine the extent of their authority. They operated on the premise that control over Model Cities planning without control over the implementation of those plans would severely limit their ability to ameliorate or eliminate the coercive side effects of social change. They hoped that authority over the use of resources that others needed to accomplish their objectives would create opportunities to negotiate mutually beneficial policies. By means of this authority they hoped to bring about policies that were genuinely redistributive in their outcomes, rather than policies that sought to adjust West Oakland residents to the existing distribution of advantages and disadvantages.

Reclamation of Sovereignty

In striving to build an organization and gain recognition as the legitimate spokesman of the West Oakland community, West Oakland leaders had (1) to create a structure that permitted the mobilization of a broad base of support while preventing old antagonisms from disrupting the new organizations's unity, (2) to create trust among their constituents in their responsiveness and ability, (3) to gather political support in various forms from outside the organization, and (4) to establish their equality with city officials in negotiating a Model Cities partnership. With support from a unified organization that had the confidence of the diverse factions and groups in the community, West Oakland's leaders could drive a hard bargain, capitalizing on the city's reluctance to lose promised federal funds.[9] Disunity would give city officials the opportunity to confer recognition on the most congenial faction, and thereby continue the practice of co-optation which they had used so effectively in the past.

Divisions within the West Oakland Community

The pattern of conflicts within the West Oakland community threatened to prevent the mobilization of a broad base of support. Organizations ranging from fundamentalist churches to revolutionary parties operated in West Oakland, but three identifiable leadership factions, sustained by the citizen participation provisions of federal legislation and reflecting the class divisions within the community, have emerged in recent years. Each has experienced successes in its area of special competence.

The faction dominating the West Oakland Advisory Committee (WOAC)—who were to form the leadership core of the new Model Cities organization—had shared with other indigenous leaders the triumph of securing fifty-one percent control over the citywide poverty board and of redirecting funds from established agencies to indigenous organizations. Most members of this faction had migrated to Oakland from the South during World War II. Many of them were veteran participants in community affairs (district councils, church and school groups, and fraternal organizations). Upwardly mobile in spite of their low educational attainment and working-class occupations, a large number took advantage of the poverty program's new careerists employment opportunities.

The second faction had initially formed around the Peter Maurin Neighborhood House, a Catholic social service agency. They went on to form the Western-End Model Cities Organization (WEMCO) and were also active in various block clubs. Members of this faction live in the most dilapidated section of West Oakland, separated from the rest of the community by a freeway, and are generally less mobile, less well-off, and less sophisticated politically than members of the other two factions. Nevertheless, with the assistance of Dorothy Kauffman, and other volunteers from outside the community, they achieved a high degree of community organization, accomplishing such goals as the construction of a community nursery school that uses the Montessori teaching method, the conversion of several vacant lots into small recreation areas, and extensive painting and repair work. They are more concerned with improving local social services and living conditions than with local autonomy and they antagonized the West Oakland Advisory Committee faction by using outside assistance as well as by having access to private resources. Moreover, their accomplishments undercut the WOAC's attempt to monopolize access to such scarce resources in their area as membership on boards, money for indigenous programs, jobs in programs financed with poverty funds, enjoyment of social status or esteem, accesses to formal and informal information flows, opportunities for publicity, and interaction with city officials and civic leaders.[10] Bitter controversies frequently occurred between the two groups, which WEMCO appealed to the Oakland Economic Development Council.

The third faction, organized around the Oak Center Neighborhood Association, consisted primarily of middle-income homeowners, many of whom had lived in Oakland prior to World War II and who had long participated in community affairs (including social activities). The Oak Center Neighborhood Association, though preventing clearance of the Oak Center area and winning the right to be consulted by the Redevelopment Agency, has little concern with the problems of tenants within the rehabilitation area; it generally shares the Redevelopment Agency's goal for the area, namely, to recreate a middle class integrated community in the central city. The poverty program has strengthened the ability of the upwardly mobile working class, represented by the West Oakland Advisory Committee, to challenge both the class-related views and the leadership dominance of this longer established, higher income group.

The Structure of the West Oakland Planning Committee

In a remarkably short time, a group of West Oakland leaders achieved their goal of creating the West Oakland Planning Committee (WOPC), a single organization which would bridge the divisions within the community and become the spokesman for the target area residents in negotiating with city officials a revised application for Model Cities. The West Oakland Planning Committee was established as a delegate assembly. (The leadership could complete its work very quickly because they had previously experimented with this form.)[11] Any organization of at least ten members operating totally or partially within West Oakland could become a member by submitting the names of two representatives. Political, religious, social, economic, and professional organizations joined. At the organizational meeting on December 8, 1967, representatives from sixty-five organizations were present; by August 1968, one hundred sixty-five organizations belonged.

The West Oakland Planning Committee's structure, based upon group rather than individual membership, reduced the possibility that more than one organization would seek recognition as spokesman for the community. The fact that each member organization, regardless of its size, has two delegates, quieted fears that the Planning Committee could be dominated by a single faction or by large church congregations. The group membership policy of the Planning Committee encourages political entrepreneurship and rewards the politically active. Those who belong to more organizations have more opportunities to become delegates. An enterprising individual can create an organization which he can represent. Highly organized neighborhoods have a greater number of representatives than an electoral system provides, whether it bases representation on territory or population. Because membership on the WOPC is easily accessible to groups and leaders, any struggle over leadership is more likely to take place within the Planning Committee than between rival organizations. Because the selection and removal of delegates is left entirely to its member organizations, the WOPC is not subject to conflicts in filling vacancies. The policy of inviting all groups to join—bowling clubs as well as block clubs—eliminates contests over eligibility. This delegate assembly structure enabled the West Oakland Planning Committee to organize quickly and with a minimum of conflicts.

The Leadership of the West Oakland Planning Committee

The West Oakland Planning Committee had not only to unite jealous factions, but also to create support for its executive committee, elected by the delegate assembly at the December 8th meeting. The executive committee consisted of nine regular and four alternate members.[12] At least one member was affiliated with each major division within the community, but nine of the thirteen were closely associated with a single faction, the West Oakland Advisory Committee. These leaders consequently had to overcome the distrust generated by their past political activities. In the West Oakland Advisory Committee, they had controlled the scarce resources (money, personnel, status, authority, and information) available through OEO legislation and had not wanted to share them; therefore, they had used an assortment of techniques to control admission to membership. Now, as leaders of the West Oakland Planning Committee, they were seeking access to the much greater supply of resources made available under the Model Cities legislation and, to gain this access, they needed a broad base of community support. For this reason, they fully endorsed the open membership policy of WOPC. In fact, they ritualized the inclusiveness of the organization with lengthy roll calls and elaborate solicitations of new memberships, called frequent mass meetings where the assembled delegates reviewed the actions and voted on subsequent steps of the executive committee and stressed repeatedly that their power to act was limited to steps authorized by the delegate assembly.[13]

The ideology of community control united West Oakland leaders and their followers. A parenthetical explanation is necessary here. Although West Oakland is a predominantly black community, community control is not a specifically "black" response. Most West Oakland residents appear to be motivated by righteous indignation, built up over long years of experience with an unresponsive government; only a few feel comfortable articulating this experience in the language of black ideology. The others do not lack racial pride; rather, they are rejecting an ideology that implies separation of West Oakland from the rest of the city. The apparent paradox dissolves on closer inspection: the goal West Oakland Planning Committee leaders call community control (and some observers term it black control of a black community) is premised upon a strong identification with the fate of the city as a whole. In the model city they hope to achieve, all races, all classes, and all communities share a common fate. To quote Ralph Williams, "The piano player has to play the black keys and the white keys together for the most harmonious, melody-ous music"—an observation he makes almost every time the issue of race arises. He and other leaders encourage pride in and a strong identification with West Oakland, but visualize its future as inseparable from the whole city's. As an ideology, community control was intended to unite the community across class lines and to reduce opportunities for established leaders to selectively co-opt individuals—a process that divides the community. Community control holds that the only lasting social mobility is communal and that communal mobility requires a political base from which redistributive policies can be either negotiated or coerced.

An organizational ideology called "functional unity," articulated by Paul Cobb, significantly increased the effectiveness of the Planning Committee leaders in negotiations with city officials. This ideology allowed the highly heterogeneous WOPC and its executive committee not only to survive despite its diversity but also to utilize that diversity to its own advantage. It was intended to reduce the envy and jealousy that flourish in all settings and particularly where opportunities for power and status are relatively scarce. Functional unity acknowledges a division of labor and specialization within the political world, and promises support rather than negative sanctions to the exercise of political initiative. It encourages a permissive attitude toward conflict within the organization and unity when confronting the opposition. However, it teaches that this unity is compatible with many different political styles. It calls, not for conformity to norms deemed appropriate by city officials—a complex of political virtues revolving about a rather sedate conception of responsible behavior —but for each member of the executive committee to participate in the negotiations in the manner best suited to his talents and skills. Any single meeting or negotiating session activated a wide range of political modes: invocation of religious norms, recitation of bombastic analogies, deferential behavior, *ad hominem* attacks, demagoguery, and pleas for unity, plus the standard political maneuvers. When city officials responded inflexibly, the West Oaklanders won a bargaining advantage.

Mobilizing Political Resources

The West Oakland Planning Committee's most powerful resource was its ability to speak for a wide range of groups in West Oakland, to communicate with these groups through their representatives, and to mobilize large numbers of community residents at crucial points in the negotiations. In addition, the WOPC needed to mobilize political resources outside their immediate organization in order to enhance its effectiveness in negotiations with city officials. West Oakland leaders systematically cultivated the support of city councilmen, newspaper reporters, a newly formed coalition of white liberal and church organizations, and black public officials and political leaders.

The staff of the poverty board, the Oakland Economic Development Council, gave invaluable support. Percy Moore, the OEDC executive director, outspokenly endorsed the goal of community control for West Oakland residents and the separation of the West Oakland Planning Committee from the OEDC. Paul Cobb, Planning Director of the OEO-funded West Oakland Planning Center, headed a small staff based in West Oakland to assist residents with planning a model multi-service center, and he made his staff's services available to the West Oakland Planning Committee to prepare meeting notices, informational packets, organization charts, letters, and counterproposals. Cobb had been a member of the West Oakland Advisory Committee until appointed to the planning position and he participated in every phase of negotiations as political advisor and staff man to the West Oakland Planning Committee. His willingness to work behind the scenes, rather than to insist on public recognition of his leadership role, won the confidence of indigenous leaders although, in West Oakland's turbulent political environment, that confidence has to be continually rewon.

The administrative guidelines for the Model Cities Program did not prescribe a citizen participation structure. The regional Model Cities administrators repeatedly reiterated that, within broad limits, they would accept whatever agreement was reached between Oakland public officials and West Oakland residents. but would not intervene to dictate a settlement in the event of a stalemate. However, they did play a facilitative role. For example, when city officials and West Oakland residents reached an impasse in their negotiations, they arranged a meeting on neutral territory in a federal post office building. They also rendered opinions on the acceptability to the U.S. Department of Housing and Urban Development (HUD) of certain initiatives. By getting federal officials to legitimate their counterproposals, the executive committee used this noninterventionist posture to bolster their position.[14]

Winning Recognition from City Officials

West Oakland leaders insisted upon public acknowledgement of their peer status with city officials. To them, the rhetoric of partnership (marriage, divorce, and more ribald analogies abounded) that surrounded the Model Cities Program meant that they were to be treated with dignity and respect and not as supplicants. They reasoned that they did not have to feel grateful for a program whose real objective was to buy racial peace, especially since the money came to Oakland because of deprivations they were suffering. They used visits of public officials to West Oakland as occasions for securing recognition of the various facets of their euality. They sought recognition of the legitimacy of their initial bargaining position, of their leaders, and, finally, of the West Oakland Planning Committee itself as the policy-making body for West Oakland.

The first such visit occurred on December 9, 1967, before the negotiations had actually begun. A tour group of federal officials and invited local guests crowded into the room where West Oakland leaders were conducting a large planning meeting. Business was interrupted briefly for an exchange of remarks between Walter Farr, federal Model Cities administrator and Ralph Williams, Planning Committee chairman. Farr lent support to the Planning Committee's initial bargaining position by referring to Model Cities as a partnership between the city and the community to which both parties had to agree, and a friendly reporter from the *Oakland Tribune* recorded his remarks in a three column banner and story.

A second visit took place the following month, January 4, 1968. This time the visitors were an assistant to the city manager and a city department head, and the Planning Committee meeting was held in a church basement in the heart of West Oakland. The WOPC officers purposely did not acknowledge the visitors' presence in the front row until the end of the meeting. In the interim the visitors sat through a long drawnout roll call of member organizations, solicitation of new members, an emotion-charged review of the action of the executive committee in removing a member who could not reconcile himself to group rather than individual representation, and a detailed recounting of West Oakland Planning Committee history to date. What they witnessed supported West Oakland leaders' allegation that they were the duly selected spokesmen of a properly constituted and representative body to which they were accountable.

At the time of the third visit, the Planning Committee executives were insisting upon a "dual green light" approach to Model Cities planning under which both the West Oakland Planning Committee and the city council would have to agree before a policy became binding. They wanted symbolic recognition that the entire Planning Committee—the delegate assembly as a whole—was West Oakland's policy-making body; thus, the executive committee had been calling for public negotiating sessions to be held in West Oakland in the presence of the delegate assembly. The city manager, speaking for the task force, refused an invitation to the February 7th meeting of the West Oakland Planning Committee on the grounds that it had been issued on too short notice. The West Oakland residents who attended the meeting expected to see a public negotiating session but, instead, heard supportive statements from miscellaneous public officials and black leaders there to help executive committee members save face with their followers. Near the end of the meeting, leaders of rival factions (the Western-End Model Cities Organization and the Oak Center Redevelopment Council) asked questions challenging the legitimacy of the executive committee and the delegate assembly. Their questions did little more than cause a stir in the audience, but their actions illustrated that the ability of the leadership to maintain its position depended on its effectiveness in dealing with the city.

By virtue of the fourth visit on February 21st, the executive committee won the recognition they sought from the city: the entire task force, including the city manager and the mayor, presented themselves for public negotiations before more than three hundred spectators at a meeting of the West Oakland Planning Committee in West Oakland. Executive committee members were jubilant. Their success in doing what had never been done before eliminated the possibility of serious challenge to their leadership from other factions within the community, at least for the period of the negotiations.

Subordination of the Technocrats

Examination of the issues raised during the actual negotiations can procede somewhat chronologically. In a letter to City Manager Jerome Keithley in December of 1967, Ralph Williams described the West Oakland Planning Committee's initial proposal for a Model Cities planning structure. He proposed that planning begin in open-ended study committees, receiving inputs from a miscellany of public officials and private citizens; that the WOPC executive committee (analogous to the city manager) supervise the staff, receive the products of the study committees, and prepare them for WOPC review; and that the West Oakland Planning Committee (analogous to a city council for the West Oakland community) be given the responsibility of approving the plans prior to direct submission to the city council for final approval. The city manager sent his formal response to the WOPC on January 15, 1968. In an attempt to circumvent normal administrative procedure he ignored the WOPC's effort to deal directly with the city council and proposed instead a merger of his task force with the WOPC executive committee, to be designated the steering committee. He proposed (1) that the steering committee direct the Model Cities planning staff, receive proposals from the study committees, and prepare Model Cities plans for review first by the City Manager and then by the city council; (2) that West Oakland residents be assured of majority control on the steering committee; (3) that the WOPC select West Oakland members on the steering and study committees. He further proposed that (4) the city manager select the project director from a list of three names submitted by a five-man screening committee acceptable to both sides; (5) that the project director act under his supervision; and (6) that the city council have final review authority, including the right to veto actions adopted by the steering committee.

Members of the executive committee were initially gratified by the concession of fifty-one percent control of the steering committee and pleased with the prominent role they would play. But further reflection led to divisions within the executive committee based on different aspirations for the future role of the West Oakland Planning Committee—whether it would be as the governor of an agency or the governor of a community, that is, whether the WOPC would confine its activities to selecting representatives to the steering and study committees in the manner outlined in the city manager's response or whether the WOPC as a body would retain ultimate authority for the West Oakland community over decisions in the Model Cities planning process, in the manner described in the West Oakland Planning Committee's original proposal.

Percy Moore and Paul Cobb[15] had been united in preparing the West Oakland Planning Committee's initial proposal; both had urged the WOPC to seek veto power over Model Cities planning, subject to the final authority of the city council. However, they now differed over the appropriate rebuttal to the city manager's response. Both sought community control, but they disagreed over timing and over locus of control. Surprised that city officials had conceded as much as they had, Moore was willing to settle for the city manager's response with some modifications; Cobb disliked key features of that response and hoped that prolonging the negotiations might win larger concessions. In responding to the city manager's proposal, Moore's primary concern was efficiency, whereas Cobb's was responsiveness. Relying upon the administrative strategy of controlling the alternatives, Moore sought control over the Model Cities planning agency in order to control the actual plans submitted to the city council for final consideration. Favoring a more political approach, Cobb sought not only to control the alternatives but also to create a political organization in West Oakland that would be strong enough to influence the choices the city council would make.

Ironically, this issue—the one that most severely divided the West Oakland Planning Committee—had little importance for the city's negotiators. Having made the decision to give community residents a veto at some stage in the planning process, they cared little whether that veto was exercised by WOPC's representatives on the steering committee or by the West Oakland Planning Committee as a whole, so long as the city council retained ultimate review authority. The conflict over the WOPC's future role occurred in the context of a struggle between the executive committee and the task force over how much authority the city manager would be able to exercise over Model Cities planning; however, West Oakland's negotiators could make little progress on that issue until the role of the West Oakland Planning Committee was decided.

Moore applauded the opportunity that the city manager's proposal gave WOPC executive committee members to interact as peers with agency administrators on the steering committee. He contended that, at the local level, administrators are more powerful than elected officials and he regarded the steering committee as the proper focal point for West Oakland initiatives. He, too, believed that the Planning Committee as a whole should confine its activities to selecting leaders rather than to reviewing substantive policy: it should permit its leaders discretion in representing West Oakland's interests on the steering committee, subject to review in periodic elections. Since Moore opposed a more active role for the WOPC, he also opposed allocating funds to the organization for an independent staff. He felt that through majority control of the steering committee, West Oakland representatives would have adequate control over the Model Cities planning staff and that an independent staff for the WOPC would raise the possibility of and confrontation on every issue a gravely interfere with the efficiency of the planning process. In short, Moore assumed that the normal processes of local government were less in need of change than the decision makers, and with the assignment of a dominant role to West Oakland representatives, the planning process would be responsive to the needs of the West Oakland community.

Cobb felt that majority control of the steering committee was necessary but not sufficient in itself to increase the city's responsiveness to West Oakland's needs. He conceded that administrators might be more powerful than politicians in local government, but insisted that this need not be so. To him, a model partnership required recognition of the West Oakland Planning Committee as the peer of the city council, not merely recognition of the Planning Committee's representatives as peers of administrative officers. Parity between the city council and WOPC demanded that both groups review the work of the steering committee. Thus, he expanded the role of the West Oakland Planning Committee from that of an electorate to that of an active policy maker and required that the Planning Committee hold executive committee members accountable not only at election time for their overall performance but on a continuing basis for substantive issues. Cobb felt that administrative efficiency in planning was desirable, but that it was more important to alleviate residents' fears of the Model Cities Program and spread support for change beyond a small circle of leaders and planners—goals he hoped giving the WOPC an independent role would achieve. Cobb advocated a separate staff for the West Oakland Planning Committee. An independent staff would reduce the autonomy of the steering committee and the Model Cities planning staff; it would be an additional resource available to the executive committee, thus increasing their independence in interaction with other steering committee members and with the Model Cities staff and public officials. All West Oakland leaders have the ultimate objective of erasing inequality between the West Oakland community and other Oakland communities, and many of them share two interim goals: securing authority over federal funds in order to allocate resources in line with West Oakland priorities and building a political base in order to gain access to larger amounts of resources. Moore advocated an administrative route to these ends; Cobb, a political route.[16] Cobb argued that the time was right not only to change decision makers but also to alter the institutions that had consistently put West Oakland residents at a disadvantage.

Victory of the "Dual Green Light" Definition of the Model Cities Partnership

The relative merits of the positions defended by Percy Moore and Paul Cobb were not readily apparent to members of the executive committee and the WOPC, because they were premised on relatively subtle political and empirical judgments. The conflict between these proposals took place in an atmosphere of great uncertainty over the prospects for mobilizing community support behind the WOPC leadership, the ability of indigenous working class leaders to successfully negotiate with the city's spokesmen, and the options available under the provisions of the Model Cities legislation. Not surprisingly, during this period, the WOPC membership suffered bitter internal clashes and mounting anxiety. Disputes revolved, nevertheless, around the underlying problems of the proper relationship between professional and political decision makers and whether the WOPC would control an agency or govern a community.

With the assistance of Percy Moore, the WOPC executive committee prepared a counterproposal limiting the city manager's veto power and right to prevent the project director from carrying out the steering committee's instructions while accepting the major part of the city manager's proposal. This counterproposal was passed out at the January 27th meeting of the West Oakland Planning Committee, but was never discussed. In subsequent actions, the WOPC progressively modified its counterproposal in the direction of incorporating additional features of its original proposal. Gradually the WOPC moved from virtual endorsement of Percy Moore's position to adoption of that championed by Paul Cobb. This movement occurred as the WOPC resolved particular aspects of the relationship between experts and community laymen.

As the conflict between Moore and Cobb emerged, so did a feeling of anxiety about the ability of executive committee members to hold their own in negotiations with professional administrators on the projected steering committee. In order to augment their bargaining skills, West Oakland leaders invited the Oakland Economic Development Council to participate as a partner of the West Oakland Planning Committee in negotiations with the city on January 24, 1968. When the OEDC accepted this invitation West Oakland leaders gained the assistance of more experienced negotiators and reestablished ties between indigenous community leaders and black professionals. Subsequent revisions of the organizational chart for Model Cities planning included one representative from the OEDC on the steering committee. Significantly, WOPC leaders invited the OEDC representative to participate as their peer rather than an intermediary between them and city officials, the relationship that had precipitated the initial alienation of the WOPC from the OEDC.

However, addition of one OEDC representative to the negotiating team was not sufficient to quell mounting anxieties about the competence of WOPC representatives to negotiate with city officials. In the February 1, 1968 meeting of the WOPC, Donald McCullum, chairman of the Oakland Branch of the NAACP and vice-chairman of the OEDC, strongly urged that lay members of boards and commissions, rather than professional administrators, represent agencies on the steering committee.[17] A vote in the February 5th meeting endorsed this policy; another placed the WOPC on record as supporting an independent staff to provide technical assistance to the WOPC. It was but a short step from this proposal to that outlined by Paul Cobb on February 7th: that there be a "dual green light" —both must say "go." The requirement that products of the steering committee be submitted to both the West Oakland Planning Committee and the city council would maintain the supremacy of political decision makers over administrators. This arrangement relieved the fears of executive committee members that they would be taken advantage of by the more knowledgeable agency heads on the steering committee. Under Cobb's proposal, they would have a second chance and their own technical assistance to correct any oversights in their effort to protect and advance the interests of West Oakland.

In endorsing this structure, the West Oakland Planning Committee resolved an important aspect of the debate over the relationship between experts and citizen policy makers. Community residents trusted their own ability to engage in politics, where conflicts are resolved through negotiated agreement, more than their ability to compete with knowledgeable administrators on technical matters. Resolution of the conflict within the West Oakland community coincided with recognition of the West Oakland Planning Committee as the legitimate spokesman for the West Oakland community by city officials—the fourth visit described earlier. In the public negotiating session before the assembled West Oakland Planning Committee, the city manager agreed with no demurrer that both the West Oakland Planning Committee and the city council would have a veto over Model Cities plans. Having resolved its internal split over role and won its point with the city, the West Oakland Planning Committee was at last ready to negotiate its differences about the City Manager's authority.

The Role of the City Manager: Definition of Administration

A persistent theme in the negotiations between the WOPC and the city concerned the role of the city manager. Recalling bitter experiences under the poverty program, when the city manager refused for months to attend an OEDC meeting in spite of repeated invitations from that body and failed to respond to community demands to be involved in Model Cities planning "from the day one," West Oakland leaders were determined to reduce the city manager's role in Model Cities planning to the minimum necessary under the law. Three specific aspects of this issue caused Model Cities negotiators to miss two deadlines set by federal officials for submission of a revised application. The first concerned the manner in which the project director (an assistant city manager) would be selected; the second, the manner in which his work would be supervised; and the third, the right of the city manager to interpose himself as an independent review authority between the WOPC and the city council.

After several unsuccessful attempts to negotiate the three points of difference extending over two and one-half months, the city manager announced that he was unable to reach agreement with the WOPC and turned the matter over to the city council. The WOPC had requested meetings with the city council from the beginning and were pleased when they came to pass. In their first meeting on April 2nd, the two groups of political representatives rapidly disposed of administrative matters. The composition of the screening committee for selecting the project director, which up to that point had variously combined city and community representatives on a five-member committee, was set at three representatives from the city and three from the community, with one member of the city's three being determined in advance by the WOPC; five votes were required for action, and final selection was to be made by the city manager from a list of three names submitted in order of preference. The project director was to be held responsible by the city manager for the day-to-day adminstration of planning and by the steering committee for policy. Products of the steering committee were to be submitted to the WOPC for review and then to the city manager, who was specifically enjoined from altering policy matters. Thus, the role of the city manager was limited, but not eliminated; however, the distrust expressed throughout the negotiations undoubtedly alerted city officials that community residents had a much narrower definition of administration than did the city manager and that the assumption of more than technical responsibilities would provoke out cries in the future. The city council and the WOPC took longer to dispose of political matters.

The Struggle for Authority

The WOPC sought authority over the Model Cities Program in order to be able to control the coercive side-effects of progressive policies. Having won the right to exercise authority in concert with the city council, the WOPC turned to the next problem: authority over what? Two subjects occupied negotiators during th next four and one-half months: defining WOPC's veto powers and drawing the boundaries of the Model Cities area. Little doubt remained that, to the extent they were able, the WOPC leaders intended to establish the WOPC as the governing body over a given territory rather than merely to instert the views of the West Oakland community in the planning process.

Broad Veto

Immediately after securing recognition for the WOPC as the legitimate spokesman for the West Oakland community, WOPC leaders initiated the next phase of the negotiations: clarifying the extent of their veto. In a press release issued February 29th, WOPC leaders remarked: "They say that the City Council and the West Oakland Committee shall have mutual veto power but we do not know at what points this can be exercised if indeed it must." A negotiating session with the city manager's task force on March 15th clarified the matter somewhat; the WOPC was granted a veto over block grant proposals initiated by the city. The WOPC also had the right to initiate proposals for the use of these funds. Thus the WOPC secured access to decision making on the expenditure of approximately $5 million the amount estimated that Model Cities would bring to Oakland annually. But the original intention of the Model Cities program was to coordinate the use of federal funds within a particular area. In fact the size of the block grant varied with the size of present federal commitments to projects in the Model Cities area: the city would receive up to eighty percent of the local contribution of these projects. Additional federal programs were anticipated as a result of the effort to concentrate social and physical programming in a specified area. Allocating this small amount of money was less important to WOPC leaders than overseeing the expenditure of all federal funds within the West Oakland community. They feared that local agencies, when thwarted by Model Cities planning decisions, would use other funds to pursue their objectives anyway. Having been recognized as the governing body for West Oakland in respect to planning for the future of West Oakland, the WOPC leaders sought authority to assure that those plans would be respected.

The WOPC followed two courses of negotiations in seeking to broaden their veto powers: (1) with federal officials to secure veto power directly and to win recognition of the validity of an agreement between a local agency and the WOPC granting such authority; and (2) with local agencies to secure the right to review federally financed programs slated for the West Oakland area. On March 27th Ralph Williams sent a letter to Mel Mogulof, Regional Model Cities Administrator, asking that a meeting of federal officials be convened in West Oakland on April 10th to clarify the extent of West Oakland's veto. In the interim the WOPC executive committee met with the city council on April 2nd and resolved the administrative matters which had divided the city and the community for so long. But the mayor and the city council reacted testily to West Oakland's desire for a broad veto. The matter was postponed pending the outcome of the April 10th meeting.

At the April 10th meeting, federal officials representing the Departments of Health, Education and Welfare; Labor; Housing and Urban Development; the Community Relations Service; Economic Development Administration; and the Office of Economic Opportunity, were asked:

> Is your agency willing to grant a veto by the WOPC over all of its funding for West Oakland, whether or not it is part of the Model Cities program?; or,.
> . . . Is your agency willing to respect agreement between WOPC and your local counterpart agencies (such as the Public Housing Authority, the School District, etc.) granting veto authority to WOPC over the use of all federal funds for West Oakland through that agency?[18]

Significantly, the questions posed by WOPC leaders had not been dealt with in the federal guidelines. In their replies, federal officials indicated that they were more willing to respect local grants of authority than to grant such authority directly.[19] Although their replies were ambiguous and relied in two instances on confusing the West Oakland Planning Committee and the West Oakland Advisory Committee (the poverty board in the West Oakland community), the WOPC succeeded in having its questions taken seriously and, consequently, established the legitimacy of future efforts to secure review authority over federal programs in the West Oakland area.

In a tumultuous meeting of the city council and the WOPC leaders on April 15th, the deadline for concluding one phase of the negotiations, the issue of the broad veto was again discussed. The mayor and the city council maintained that they did not have the authority to grant West Oakland a veto over programs administered by other jurisdictions. WOPC leaders denied that they expected city officials to grant veto powers over nonmunicipal activities. In the end, they concluded their agreement with the city and announced their intention to negotiate with the other public agencies individually.

Boundaries

West Oakland is bounded on the south by the downtown business district and on the west by the Port of Oakland. City officials and their supporters assign important roles to both of these locations in formulating their strategies for the future economic development of Oakland. Both areas are projected to receive large amounts of federal funds. West Oakland leaders, working out their own strategy of economic development, perceived the value of reviewing how these funds would be spent. On April 23rd, the West Oakland Planning Committee received a copy of the city's proposed revisions of the Model Cities area and discovered that this draft, unlike previous ones, excluded both the site of a future downtown center redevelopment project and the Port. City officials had learned that inclusion of the downtown project in the Model Cities area would not increase the amount of federal funds for which the project would be eligible and, thus, had no incentive to submit even employment plans (as West Oakland leaders subsequently requested) to WOPC review. The Port may previously have been included in the Model Cities area because West Oakland fronts on the Port and Model Cities boundaries had been drawn down to the water. However, these boundaries took on a new significance after the West Oakland Planning Committee won veto power.

With the issue still unresolved, events following the assassination of Dr. Martin Luther King had consequences for the Model Cities negotiations. As the militance of Oakland's black community increased in the aftermath of the assassination, so did the adamance of city officials against including the Port and the downtown project in the Model Cities area. On April 6th, a shoot-out between some Black Panthers and the Oakland police took place, raising the salient issue of police brutality. In response to King's death, a group of black leaders, composed primarily of black professionals and civil rights activists, formed the Black Strike for Justice Committee and organized a boycott of a market serving the black community. They demanded that the Downtown Retail Merchants Association petition the city council in support of their proposals to change the nature of police–community relations in Oakland.

Black strike activities angered the mayor (and the editor of the *Oakland Tribune*) and temporarily divided the West Oakland leaders, who became less tenacious in pursuing their boundary demands in negotiations with the city. After May 1st, the date when the boycott began, WOPC leaders were unable to change the city's position. In August, after fruitless negotiations held at irregular intervals, the WOPC withdrew its request to include the downtown project; and they declared that they would deal directly with the Planning Commission on matters concerning the Port. With these acts, the major differences between the city and the West Oakland Planning Committee were resolved.[20] However, the disposition of the final papers took several more months. (It was rumored that the city officials hoped that a Republican administration would take office and radically revise the Model Cities guidelines affecting citizen participation.)

Conclusion

Legitimacy Based upon Procedures Rather than Performance

West Oakland residents felt oppressed by the results of city policies and were prevented by the existing structural arrangements from changing them through normal political processes. Oakland's political institutions do meet standard democratic criteria for determining who should rule: each elected official, in fact, represents a majority of the total Oakland electorate. Unfortunately, each city official represents the same majority. The classic problem in democratic theory, that of the relationship between a majority and an intense minority, has substantive content in Oakland. When West Oakland residents designed the structure of their subgovernment, they incorporated the lessons that experience with the existing institutions had taught them. The structure they created included representatives of all groups and opinions rather than just the majority group and its opinions. They accepted the inevitability of conflict and created a structure that encouraged the resolution of conflict within the community rather than with the intervention of outside assistance. Self-consciously they created incentives for leaders to be responsive to the wishes of their constituents and to take responsibility for their continuing political education. These leaders were placed in the position of having to reconcile interests of the whole community with the particular desires of portions of the community; in order to do so, they were encouraged to create identification with the interests of the whole community while reducing disproportions in the costs of particular policies borne by segments of the community. Thus, West Oakland residents revealed their aspirations and their program for achieving government more responsive to their needs as they defined them. What are the lessons of their experience for social scientists?

In recent years, students of American government have focused on the question of who rules and have tended to ignore the related question of who benefits. Support for particular institutional arrangements depends upon the institution's ability to produce acceptable outcomes, not only upon its conformance with procedural norms; this fact suggests that institutional arrangements should be evaluated by performance as well as by process criteria. A political scientist must, of course, pay attention to behavior and process criteria within political structure—to who has a right to be heard in the political process and to who the winners and losers are in a particular contest. But, as the Oakland experience indicates, willingness to enter a contest and the content of the demands are influenced by assessments of the likelihood of winning. The more valid criteria for evaluating structures may well be some measure of their distribution of outcomes. Political behavior has certain universal characteristics. The relationship between characteristics of political structures and a desirable distribution of outcomes varies, however, with the situation. Investigation of the latter forces the political scientist to visualize and assess a series of desirable alternatives to assess the appropriateness of a particular structure—an activity distinguishable from, but accessory to, political decision making. When he engages in this activity, the political scientist is involved in work significant for public policy.

Political Authority Delegated to Experts

When West Oakland residents sought authority to make decisions affecting their lives, they found that they had to compete for this right with experts who wanted to "help" or "serve" them. In the course of their struggle to define the role of the West Oakland Planning Committee as a decision maker, whether for an agency or a community, they acknowledged that the city manager and his administrators exercised a preponderance of power under a weak-mayor–council-manager form of government, but they risked the loss of the Model Cities Program in order to deal directly with the city council. They underscored repeatedly their insistence that the city manager confine his role to the technical tasks compatible with a strict interpretation of the politics–administration dichotomy. For themselves, they reserved the role of citizens rather than subjects. Within their subgovernment, too, they subordinated technical assistance to political controls. Their preference for responsiveness over administrative efficiency had roots in their experience with previous social reform programs and professionalized public service.

Expertise is one kind of authority. Increasingly, it threatens to displace political authority. The determination of priorities and the allocation of scarce resources are political decisions. Experts speak of coordination, advocacy, planning, or a host of other terms in such a way that the intrinsic political nature of prioritie and allocation decisions are obscured. So long as these vital decisions are based on technical criteria to which only trained experts have access, there can be no parity between the city's professional representatives and the community's amateur representatives. The West Oakland leaders struggled to redefine administration. The scope of technical questions was narrowed and allocative decisions were reclaimed for politics. As they explored the substantive possibilities of their newly won authority, the West Oakland leaders could formulate their redistributive aims.

Economic Growth at the Expense of Redistribution

In Oakland, both the city government and West Oakland residents regard control over outside funds as vital to their economic development strategies. As a consequence of the Model Cities negotiations, they will share authority over some federal funds. The struggle between the magistracy and the people has brought into opposition differing conceptions of the solutions to the city's problems—one that places the primary emphasis upon economic expansion and one that emphasizes economic redistribution: one that expects economic benefits to percolate down to West Oakland residents and one that demands that government actively seek to change the economic status of West Oakland residents.

The Oakland case study reveals that the interests of the contestants are not far apart on all issues. In some instances, West Oakland residents castigate officials for their failure to carry out stated objectives rather than criticize the objectives themselves. Residents not opposed to increasing employment opportunities for West Oakland residents by attracting private enterprises to Oakland but they are opposed to the abandonment of the goal of increasing employment opportunities when it increases the difficulty of attracting private capital. Some objectives, of course, genuinely conflict and are less susceptible to integrative solutions. West Oakland residents explicitly reject the condition that change is permissible only insofar as the result is compatible with the status quo. They insist upon owning some of the new enterprises as well as working in them. West Oakland's veto power over matters in which outsiders have vital concern (e.g., construction and labor contracts, the location and uses of public facilities) means that in each case, the various parties must create mutually agreeable solutions or suffer an impasse.

In Oakland, the contention of the sovereignty of the magistracy and the sovereignty of the people during the negotiations over the Model Cities Program resulted in the creation of a structure in the future of the West Oakland community that acknowledged both the secessionist mood of West Oakland residents and the interests of the city as a whole and which provided the framework within which mutual interests might be negotiated. This structure may not survive for long or function as its authors hoped. However, in the absence of such a structure, the fundamental differences between the West Oakland community and the city will undoubtedly find other forms of expression. The value of an institutionalized political form seems evident. Political institutions are our principal mechanisms for reconciling the whole and the part. It is only political institutions that have the particular responsibility of integrating a community and advancing the interests of the whole. It is only political institutions that can pursue policies that assure acceptable processes and outcomes, that assure expertise and responsiveness, and that assure productivity and equality.

NOTES

This essay is based upon three years of observation of the Oakland poverty and Model Cities meetings, interaction with the participants, and examination of available records, correspondence, and newspaper reports. This research was conducted under the auspices of the Oakland Project headed by Aaron Wildavsky and funded by the National Aeronautics and Space Administration and the Urban Institute. I am grateful to Professors Wildavsky and Matthew Stolz for unfailing support and stimulation, to Michael Lipsky, Paul Cobb, Percy Moore, Mel Mogulof, Ralph Williams, and John A. Martin for their valuable comments on an earlier draft, and to Caroline Helfer for editorial assistance.

1   In arriving at these conclusions I found the following sources helpful: James Weinstein, *The Corporate Ideal in the Liberal State, 1900–1918* (Boston: Beacon Press, 1968). Gabriel Kolko, *The Triumph of Conservatism: A Reinterpretation of American History, 1900–1916*, (Chicago: Quadrangle Books, 1963,1967). Barton J. Bernstein, "The New Deal: The Conservative Achievements of Liberal Reform," in *Towards a New Past: Dissenting Essays in American History*, Barton J. Bernstein (ed.), (New York: Random House, 1967). Andrew Shonfield, *Modern Capitalism: The Changing Balance of Public and Private Power*, (New York: Oxford University Press,1965). John Kenneth Galbraith, *The New Industrial State*, (New York: Signet Books, 1967). Herman P. Miller, *Rich Man, Poor Man* (New York: Signet Books, 1964). John C. Donovan, *The Politics of Poverty* (New York: Pegasus, 1967), pp. 93–110.

2   Jeffrey L. Pressman, *Digest of Current Federal Programs in the City of Oakland*, paper prepared for Mayor John H. Reading with the assistance of the Redevelopment Agency of the City of Oakland (October, 1968).

3   William L. Nicholls II, *Tables on Employment and Unemployment from the 701 Household Survey in Oakland* (Berkeley: University of California Survey Research Center, August 1, 1968), Table R-3, p. 19. In 1966, eight and four tenths percent of Oakland's total civilian labor force was unemployed; in West Oakland the figure was fourteen and three-tenths percent.

4   *Oakland: A Demonstration City*, Report prepared by City of Oakland Redevelopment Agency (May, 1966).

5   Marshall Kaplan, *An Analysis of Federal Decision-Making and Impact: The Federal Government in Oakland*, Vol. II (Washington, D.C.: Economic Development Administration, U. S. Department of Commerce, January, 1969). He opposed the addition of the two residents to the task force because it destroyed the pure advocacy model. This addition transformed the task force from an executive committee for the city into a policy-making body, where city and community representatives would interact directly, and shifted attention from the quality of advocates possessed by each side to the parity of voting strength on the policy-making body. Kaplan feared that direct interaction would increase the severity of the conflict between public officials and West Oakland residents.

6   *Application for Planning Grant, Model Cities Program*, City of Oakland (April 3, 1967).

7   Detailed discussion of this organization occurs in a later section.

8   With the advent of the poverty program in Oakland, in December, 1964, the citizens advisory committee of the Ford Foundation's grey areas program (which had been operating in Oakland since early 1962) was transformed into the OEDC. The Mayor appointed additional members, creating a body broadly representative of the total community. At the first meeting the council approved fourteen programs for poverty funding. The first direct representatives of the poor were added four months later.

9   How willingly the city would surrender sovereignty to get federal dollars was not known, according to Percy Moore in a memo to the author, October 31, 1969 to West Oakland leaders at the time they formulated their negotiating strategy. During one particularly trying period, the City Council threatened to move the Model Cities area from West Oakland to another section of the city where the leaders might be more grateful for the benefits of the program. However, West Oakland leaders refused to take this threat seriously, since they realized the city would be unable to rapidly complete the preliminary work for another Model Cities application.

10   Warren Ilchman and Norman Uphoff, *The Political Economy of Change* (Berkeley: University of California Press, 1969), and Michael Lipsky, "Protest as a Political Resource," *American Political Science Review*, 62 (December 1968), 1144–58. See for discussion of political resources.

11   It was established less than a month before the Model Cities organization, but West Oakland residents experienced its effectiveness as a planning body prior to the conclusion of the Model Cities negotiations.

12   Members included: two clergymen, one Catholic and one Protestant; the chairman of the West Oakland Advisory Committee; the chairman of Western-End Model Cities Organization; two political entrepreneurs, the moderate chairman of Blacks Unified to Motivate Progress (BUMP); the militant proprietor of the Western-End Help Center; the chairman of the McClymonds Youth Council; the chairman of the United Voters and Taxpayers Association, an organization formed to fight the first urban redevelopment project in Oakland (this man was also a member of the board of the NAACP); and the public relations director of the Concentrated Employment Program. Among the four alternates were the chairman of the Prescott Neighborhood Council; the chairman of an association of West Oakland small businessmen; a neighborhood organizer for the West Oakland Advisory Committee; and a member of the Oak Center Neighborhood Association. Four of those selected were currently serving on the Oakland Economic Development Council.

13   These actions to secure support actually increased the delegate assembly's control over their executive. The executive committee had called for several important votes during the negotiations, but once the negotiations were completed, the leaders attempted to revert to their West Oakland Advisory Committee practice of controlling access to scarce resources. At issue in the April 14, 1969, meeting of the West Oakland Planning Committee was the use that would be made of OEO Title 1-D Special Impact Funds. The delegate assembly asserted its authority by reversing an action taken by several members of the executive committee; the assembly's reasons for the reversal were partly substantive and partly procedural—the delegates had not been adequately consulted in advance.

14   Informed observers consistently applaud Melvin B. Mogulof's refusal to step in and dictate the shape of the citizen participation structure in Oakland. Mogulof was federal regional Model Cities administrator during the time of these negotiations. Mogulof and John A. Williams, former OEO regional administrator, both have pointed out to me, after reading an earlier draft of this paper, that conflicts paralleling those described here were simultaneously occurring among the federal administrators responsible for the program.

15   After reading an earlier draft, Ralph Williams, chairman of the West Oakland Planning Committee, objected to the amount of space given to the statements of Moore and Cobb. Pointing out that Moore and Cobb, as employees of the Oakland Economic Development Council and the Neighborhood Services Project, respectively, were unable to take independent action, he recommended that, in every place where Cobb's name appears in this section, executive committee should be inserted and where Moore's name appears, Oakland Economic Development Council. I have given his recommendation serious consider-

ation and have decided that describing the positions articulated by Moore and Cobb in public meeting does not conflict with attributing responsibility to the West Oakland Planning Committee and its executive committee for making the ultimate determination on these important policy matters. I did not attend executive committee meetings and so cannot report the contribution of individual members to the final product. Thus, I treat Moore and Cobb only as spokesmen for positions which divided the whole community.

16 The distinction is between setting priorities within an agency (administrative) and setting priorities between agencies, political.

17 If professional representatives were seated, Moore or his representative would become a member of the steering committee; if lay representatives, McCullum or another of the OEDC members whom Moore characterized as black brokers would. Moore supported seating administrators because he feared that "traditional 'brokers' would be designated and would gladly assume the role of 'leader' and generate internal conflicts within WOPC to maintain status and value to City Hall." (Memo to the author, October 31, 1969.) Some West Oakland leaders may have been influenced in deciding the issue by their resentment toward Moore who insisted upon reserving a high degree of autonomy for himself as OEDC executive director. Even if made on this basis, their decision turned, nevertheless, upon the issue to the proper relationship between laymen and administrators.

18 "Report of Meeting of 10 April with the West Oakland Planning Committee," Memorandum from Mike Kenney, Model Cities specialist, to Carl Shaw, CAP regional administrator (April 16, 1968).

19 *Ibid.* Of further interest in the same memorandum is the following:

Examples of the kinds of issues WOPC raises concerning the use of Federal funds are:
a. Major public works projects such as the Bay Area Rapid Transit System station, the Oakland Stadium, highways, etc., which require demolition of residential sections and the destruction of the neighborhood and community.

b. According to the WOPC, EDA has put $23,000,000 into the Port of Oakland, and the Oakland Airport, yet this money has created no jobs for the people of West Oakland. Part of this development will mean a public recreation pier with concessions, restaurants, and small shops. WOPC points out that the EDA regulations requiring a substantial percent of local bank capital before EDA help is available to small businessmen assures that there will be no black owners of ventures in this complex since local banks will not lend to black people.

c. Difficulties of getting insurance and bank loans for homes and businesses in the ghetto.

d. Police brutality. WOPC wants to be able to stop Federal money from going to the Oakland Police Department because of a bitter and profound distrust of the Oakland Police Department for alleged police brutality.

20 The Model Cities contract was signed April 23, 1969, according to Maurice Dawson, Oakland Model Cities administrator. (Telephone interview, March 2, 1970).

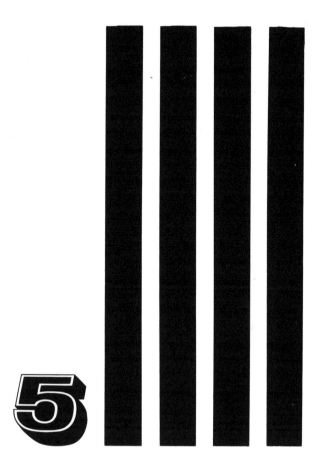

Minorities,
Neighborhood Control,
and Citizen
Participation

Neighborhood Control and Urban Governance

Charles V. Hamilton

The purpose of this essay is to deal with some problems related to the question of what has come to be called neighborhood control. Across the country, many people—particularly black Americans—in the latter years of the 1960s began to talk in terms of becoming involved in new decision-making institutions at the community, neighborhood level. Neighborhood control has become a major item on the agenda of many local groups that, at one time, were associated primarily with traditional civil rights demands: school integration, busing, open occupancy, and the like.

In a three block area on Chicago's southside, there is a five hundred forty-unit housing complex being built. It is designed as low-cost housing for local residents displaced by the expansion plans of the nearby University of Chicago. A large sign on the site reads: "Woodlawn Gardens—Planned by the Residents of Woodlawn." Reverend Arthur Brazier of The Woodlawn Organization, in his book, *Black Self-Determination: The Story of The Woodlawn Organization,* discusses the political struggles waged by that community group over the urban renewal issue on Chicago's southside. The problem involved the University of Chicago, city and federal governmental agencies, as well as a private foundation.

In Washington, D.C., Mr. Kenneth W. Haskins stated: "I am the principal of the Morgan Community School in Washington, D.C., a school that is now neighborhood controlled. . . . If a neighborhood school is to have any meaning, it must take its character from the nature of the people living in the neighborhood and from the children utilizing the school rather than

249

rigidly defining itself as an institution that accepts only those people who fit into a preconceived definition."

In April, 1969, Illinois State Senator Charles Chew, a black legislator from Chicago, sent a telegram to the Chicago Police Superintendent calling for the removal of all white policemen from Chicago's black neighborhoods in order to prevent disorders. Senator Chew stated: "The truth of the matter is that white cops feel superior to black people and use their power to harass and beat Negroes, instead of keeping the peace. . . . The white cops know nothing of black culture and the black mood and often this ignorance sparks violence in the ghetto."

At a conference in Detroit in the Spring of 1969, black spokesmen met to discuss economic development plans for black neighborhoods around the country. Don Simmons of the Harlem Commonwealth, at the conference, is reported to have said: "Obviously the Nixon Administration doesn't understand what we're talking about" when black people say they want control of their own communities. "When we say control, we mean control of health services, education and police in our communities," as well as black business.

And on and on the discussion goes, and more and more people—particularly black Americans—are talking about and pushing for neighborhood control.

"If community control is going to mean anything," Mr. Leon Finney, Director of the Woodlawn Organization (TWO) in Chicago, said, "it has to mean more than having a principal of a high school. It must mean control over the curriculum, over who supplies milk to the school. It might mean that Dean Milk Company will not supply the milk, but that the Joe Louis Milk Company will. It means deciding who gets the contracts to do work. We must be able to do more than just approve or disapprove plans. We must be in at every stage of the planning process itself."

There is a tendency today to see all this as a new thrust on the part of black people, but that is not so. Rather, it is more properly the restatement of a theme that has been advocated for more than one hundred years: a theme of self-determination. A Harvard-trained black doctor, orator, and writer, Martin R. Delaney, said on April 1, 1853, that black people, not whites, must make plans for blacks. He stated that "no enterprise, institution, or anything else, should be commenced *for us,* or our general benefit, without first consulting us."

But one hundred seven years later, Professor James Q. Wilson, in his book, *Negro Politics,* could say, accurately: "Negroes are, in a very real sense, the objects rather than the subjects of civic action. Things are often done for, or about, or to, or because of Negroes, but they are less frequently done *by* Negroes."[1]

The present emphasis on neighborhood control must be seen as an attempt on the part of many black people to overcome this situation. There are at least three important points to deal with: (1) neighborhood control as an effort to overcome alienation; (2) the problem of trying to

determine with some degree of preciseness what constitutes a representative neighborhood group; (3) the problem of working out managea-
ble forms of neighborhood control within the context of a national, state,
and city federal structure, especially when sources of revenue will ultimately come from outside the community.

Neighborhood Control to Overcome Alienation

A great deal of social-science literature recognizes that, as a result of
rapid industrialization and rapid urbanization, there is the possibility that
large numbers of people will become alienated, develop a sense of root-
lessness and not feel a part of any established institutions or structures.
Such people are prone to be attracted by appeals of those who offer
panaceas of various sorts. Such people will grope for relevant intermediary groups, that is, the groups that have meaning in their lives, as they
define that meaning. They no longer have faith in the established structures, so they move to create their own. These new structures are local,
immediate, and close at hand. In today's context, they may take the form
of newly developed Concerned Black Parents' groups, because those
parents do not feel a part of the established PTAs. And the former will
likely put high on their agenda some form of neighborhood control of the
schools. They have come to believe that the schools no longer serve the
interest of their children, so they must move to challenge the existing
power structure.

This is what Mr. Haskins meant when he said: "The term 'racism' is
often used in discussions of community control, and people recoil from
it. But racism doesn't always mean racism of, say, the George Wallace
type. It means, for example, that a public school system that fails poor
black children can be tolerated, while a public school system that fails
white middle-class children cannot. The black community, therefore, has
decided that it has to make the decisions about what can and cannot be
tolerated for its children because society as a whole has largely failed the
black community in this respect."

Neighborhood control must be understood, therefore, as a response
to a crisis of legitimacy. Very many people simply no longer believe in the
existing structures. They do not believe that urban renewal managed exclusively from city hall is for their benefit but that it is, in fact, a form of
"Negro removal." The demand today is not new: it clearly has the backing
of reams and volumes of studies and reports documenting the fact that
black people have had decisions made for them, not by them. Thus, they
advocate neighborhood control as a way to reinstitute legitimacy, as a
way to have public policy making more responsive to the needs of a
previously excluded group. As they succeed, it is believed they will overcome their feelings of alienation.

Indeed, State Senator Charles Chew believes that as the black community is policed by black policemen more sensitive to the ethos of that community, more responsive to their neighbors (many, if not most, of the black policemen live in the black neighborhoods), there is the great possibility that the crime rate will go down.

The black city councilman in Boston, Thomas Adkins, calling for a form of neighborhood control in that city over the order–maintenance functions of the police told the council: "You (whites) can't stop the rising crime in black communities, but we can."

Senator Chew (neither he nor Adkins can be considered, in the popular jargon, extremists or revolutionaries) said that the argument that there simply are not enough black policemen to patrol black areas is not valid. "First of all, fewer policemen would be needed, because—as I said—the crime rate would drop."

This may be wishful thinking, but the fact remains that the existing structures have not done the job. Therefore, when forces begin to move to institute new forms, it may well be that the status quo people or those who are hesitant about change have lost the initiative. It may well be that such people can no longer direct the pace and path of change. And if they try, they might be contributing to further alienation and discord. They will have to develop enough enlightened self-interest to understand that in some matters other people will insist on calling the shots—a difficult, if not impossible, thing for vested interests to accept. But the emphasis of the new demand makers is on viability and legitimacy, not on how to protect existing, vested interests. This has to be understood as an inevitable function of rapid politicization, which is something most American social scientists apparently know very little about, and understandably so.

What one frequently hears is that changes toward neighborhood control perhaps will not lead to the anticipated, hoped for results. For instance, there is no guarantee that community control of schools will lead to increased learning abilities for black children. In fact, one must be cautious of unanticipated consequences. One who advocates neighborhood control of schools and firmly predicts that this will lead to greater quality education is concluding more than the data permit. It is far too soon to say. How could such results be known? But the process of social change always has these inevitable unknowns. We have not made certainty of results a precondition to change for the larger society; we must not demand it of black people.

What Constitutes a Neighborhood?

A very serious problem in the neighborhood control issue involves trying to determine which community groups, in fact, represent the community. In these times of new opportunities, new rewards (public and private grants of money, prestige, influence), it is understandable that many groups and individuals will come forth as the true leaders of the community. Internal fights develop. Some groups try to out-black or out-militant each other. Charges and countercharges of sellout, being an outsider or newcomer are made. This is the period of the "politics of spokesmanship," in which a person is able to gather a few followers, hold a press conference, capture a dramatic issue, hold a rally or two and immediately be catapulted into leadership. Credentials are measured frequently by the ability to maintain visibility. This person forms the XYZ organization and proceeds to speak in the name of "the people." We are not unfamiliar in social movements with this mixture of elitism and populism, aided by the mass media. This phenomenon is also used to speak to the fact that many of those officials elected to public office in the black neighborhood have long since proved their worthlessness for dealing with the neighborhood's problems. Thus, in some instances, electoral politics gives way to the politics of spokesmanship.

We can list any number of instances around the country where local groups are now contending for the title of being "the" representative group in the neighborhood. On Chicago's westside, the Lawndale People's Planning Committee fought with the Greater Lawndale Conservation Committee for recognition as the representative group on the local Model Area Council. In Milwaukee, a local group accused the Triple-O (Organization of Organizations) of not being representative. The Triple-O claimed to represent thirty-nine groups (of approximately five hundred in the area). However, Mayor Henry Maier of Milwaukee, in a television broadcast on May 8, 1969, stated: "Of the ninety-five identifiable delegates, officers, and paid staff of this so-called 'grass-roots' organization, seventy-three percent live outside the Model Cities area, including four of Triple-O's five officers, one of them its president. Effective control seems to be in the hands of eight people."

Some are disheartened by all this. They are disappointed that there is not a united, monolithic black community with which to deal when, in fact, such has never been the case, nor should it be expected. There are many different levels of style, temperament, and talent in the black neighborhoods, and any view to the contrary probably reflects a stereotyped impression of these communities. Rather than chaotic, the diversity should be seen as the result of a political awakening. During this period of the politics of spokesmanship, it may well be that in some neighborhoods these various groups will have to take time to engage in the fruitful, healthy political process of vying for a constituency.

Some would argue that, while this politicking is going on, many of the crucial problems of the community go unsettled. True. But it is better to let the various neighborhoods work out this problem of legitimate representation themselves than to have some outside force intervene prematurely and impose its own conception of legitimacy on them. We cannot have it both ways: true representation on the one hand and immediate resolution of problems on the other. The various contentious groups should compete with each other for the loyalty of the local residents. The neighborhood will, in this manner, develop its own relevant political style. Thus, when the winner does proceed to speak for the neighborhood, there will be greater certainty that that group can deliver its constituency. If there is no appreciable opposition to a group, either because of indifference or genuine acceptance, then that group is the one with which to deal. There must be a point beyond which it is not necessary to wait for fifty percent plus one.

A sophisticated understanding of the dynamism of this period would have us know that the process of elections as a mechanism for determining representativeness might be premature in some instances. Shortly after the OEO programs started—1965–1966—elections to local community action program boards were held in some places. The turn-out was very low: two percent, five percent, etc. Many concluded from this: apathy. This was not necessarily the case. Many local residents simply were alienated from the electoral process. They had never seen elections make a difference in their lives, so why this time. The rhetoric was the same, even if the offices were different. But elections have been the traditional way to determine public leadership in this country. Now, however—in the process of becoming politicized—some communities may have to work out their own method of legitimizing leaders from the crop of spokesmen. This is what political scientists and decision makers should try to investigate.

I see the potential for new forms of politics in the black neighborhoods—just as uncertain in outcome and just as contentious—if only we do not panic and hastily conclude that it really is all a matter of maximum feasible misunderstanding.

Federalism Finances and Neighborhood Control

A discussion of the forms neighborhood control would take has to deal with a number of imperatives. To begin, we must recognize that ultimate power will reside in the national government, whether we are talking about neighborhood control, power at city hall, or in the state capitol. The central government has, and will continue to have, the monopoly of financial resources and military power. In the present constitutional and political order, the states and cities have vested authority they are not likely to give up easily. Any move for neighborhood control, which means the neighborhood must assume some of the functions the cities now perform, will have to confront this. Thus, in April, 1969, HUD Secretary George Romney told community spokesmen in Chicago that Model Cities would be run by the elected (city, county, or state) officials, and ten mayors met with President Nixon and with the Urban Affairs

Council to push their interests vis-à-vis the states.

Neighborhood control, in the next few years, will probably mean some form of decentralization of some municipal functions with ultimate responsibility resting in the city agency. This is close to what the legislators in Albany, New York did with school decentralization in New York City. There, the local neighborhoods will be given authority to perform certain functions and to make certain decisions and, in most instances, they will have to be accountable to authorities downtown. This is not the form of neighborhood control most advocates want. It is, however, the form that will probably be meted out at this stage. Indeed, there are those who would not call this neighborhood control at all, but decentralization of functions, at best, and co-optation of local forces, at worst.

At no place do we find the form of neighborhood control whereby the local community has ultimate authority over raising and allocating public funds. This does not occur with the schools, police, or any other public function. If it were to happen, one would find a new, distinct political entity which would have its sanction either in statutory law or in an amended constitution. Milton Kotler, in his book, *Neighborhood Government,* argues forcefully for a neighborhood corporation that would ultimately acquire legal, constitutional power. He describes the East Central Citizens Organization (ECCO) in Columbus, Ohio as the beginning of such a model.[2] ECCO is a neighborhood corporation owned and operated by residents of a low-income area in Columbus, Ohio. The neighborhood encompasses forty blocks of deteriorating houses, crowded schools, and crime and delinquency. Anyone sixteen years or older who lives or works in the area may become a member of ECCO at no cost. The organization operates day-care centers, credit unions, legal and medical services, restaurants, and business enterprises. General James Gavin believes neighborhood corporations such as ECCO have "shown strength in liberating and mobilizing the energies of the ghetto to solve urban problems." In his book, *Crisis Now,* General Gavin describes ECCO as an "economic force in Columbus."[3]

The National Advisory Council on Economic Opportunity, in December, 1968, issued a thoughtful study, *Decentralization: A Conceptual Analysis.* It suggests that we might begin to think in terms of at least four different kinds of delegation of authority to local communities.[4]

1 Standing delegations of authority. Here a neighborhood would operate a specified function indefinitely, subject to revocation only in case of a massive failure by the neighborhood group to perform the function. Such functions could be trash removal, street cleaning, rat control, and determination of neighborhood parking regulations.

2 Periodic delegation of authority. This authority would be renewed periodically (perhaps annually) and could include such functions as neighborhood service centers, head start programs, day-care centers, and remedial education programs.

3 Interruptible delegation of authority. This would be a grant of authority that would be renewable periodically but which could be terminated at any time if an inspection or evaluation showed that certain standards were not being followed. Here we could include neighborhood health centers. 4 Reversible delegation of authority. This would permit the city or county governing body, by a two-thirds vote, to overturn individual case decisions and would include such functions as neighborhood zoning, housing code inspection, and condemnation of abandoned buildings.

The list of functions for each category could be enlarged or restricted depending on the function and the neighborhoods.

Another imaginative suggestion of the Council was to apply the principle in international relations of *persona non grata* to neighborhoods. If a particular neighborhood found a particular public official (school principal, police commander, draft board official, or welfare official) not acceptable, through some representative process that protected civil liberites, to that neighborhood, then that official would be transferred out of the neighborhood.

The Council had other significant observations about functions which could become the subject of negotiation between the neighborhood and such larger interests as public school curriculum—some neighborhoods might want certain ethnic studies—and police operations—some neighborhoods might prefer intensive patrolling during certain hours. All these ideas are tentative, but they provide topics that could serve as fruitful subjects for discussion and possible implementation.

On the matter of money, it is clear that no local neighborhood— especially the urban poor nieghborhoods—has a sufficient tax base to support the many needed public services. This means that neighborhood control groups will have to look to outside, larger sources for revenue. It is quite unlikely that this problem will be solved until the problems related to the shrinking tax base in the cities are met. This means more equitable revenue sharing from the state capitols and more direct block grants from the federal government. It could mean the implementation of a use tax by the cities—and, after a point, even by neighborhoods. One must accept the fact, however, that the future holds a greater likelihood for the centralization of the taxing power rather than its decentralization.

Problems that appear insoluble might not be such if we begin to sift out and see precisely what social units are best fitted to perform what social functions. Understandably, many black people are worried about the political future of black voters in the cities if there is a concerted drive for metropolitan government. The fact is that metropolitan government might well be a desirable thing if we confine it to certain functions. There is no sense in talking about neighborhood, or even city, control of air or water pollution problems or of mass urban–suburban transit or of neighborhood control of the allocation of corporate property taxes. Can we begin to think about metropolitan or even regional government that would deal with certain problems? At the same time, we could identify those functions that lend themselves to performance and control at the neighborhood community level. This is the sort of restructuring of neighborhood, regional, and national government that modernizing societies should face up to.

A conference of five hundred black elected officials was held in September, 1969, in Washington, D.C., sponsored by the Metropolitan Applied Research Center. The Center brought public officials together—most of whom, of course, were local office holders ranging from school board members, justices of the peace, city councilmen, and county supervisors to state legislators and congressmen—to discuss various issues and to meet national cabinet members. Very prominent on the agenda was President Nixon's "new federalism" program. At one panel discussion, a county supervisor from San Francisco County, Terry Francois, asked Secretary of Labor George Schultz if he believed that a federal policy of funneling money through some state capitols and city halls was a useful policy in terms of actually reaching many local communities (especially, but not exclusively, in the South). Mr. Francois, and many of his colleagues at the conference, expressed the hope that it was possible to develop wholly relationships between the federal government and local urban communities—even if it meant ultimately thinking in terms of constitutional revision.

The matter of standards, understandably, concerns many. If we talk about neighborhood control of schools for Harlem, does this not mean the same for a predominantly white southern community? And does this not raise problems of racial segregation that took years of court battles to overcome? It is possible to talk about a central authority (possibly HEW) which would exercise minimal standards for all communities to meet. For example, the central government should insist on a firm (not just stated) practice of open institutions with access not restricted on the basis of racial identity. If black children want to attend a predominantly white school, they should be permitted to do so; the same applies to whites who choose to attend a predominantly black school. Some form of government subsidies might be made available to assist those parents who want to transport their children to other schools for the purpose of achieving integrated education. Qualification for teaching in particular schools should be based on substantive ability to relate to the students and to the neighborhood. Under no circumstances should the curriculum reflect a derogation of racial and ethnic groups, even though recognizing that some curricula might emphasize the culture and heritage of some groups over others. There are other standards of performance that can be applied nationally and will likely be adhered to by communities that recognize that basically the local system should prepare its constituents to maximize their political, economic, and social options on an open market. If we accept the reality that neighborhood control does not mean autonomous authority over any function, then we can get beyond this hang-up of standards.

Neighborhood control of certain police functions, such as community service and order–maintenance, does not mean a loss of continued function of law enforcement by more centralized agencies. The resources for fingerprinting and crime detection, for example, are more suitably marshalled at a level larger than the neighborhood. The same is true of medical care. Some neighborhood health services can be performed and controlled at the community level. But no one would want to confine major medical research or medical training to that level. It is unrealistic, if only in terms of cost. Each community could not have a major institution of higher education, but each neighborhood could have a considerable degree of control over community colleges.

Neighborhood control must be a kind whereby people do not feel they are mere appendages or puppets of a downtown system. And at the same time, there must be the recognition that final, unreviewable power cannot rest at the community level, unless one wants to talk about a distinct, autonomous political unit. Ultimately, a desirable goal would be the legal delegation of some functions to the neighborhood. This, of course, must be preceded by a protracted political struggle waged between organized local groups on the one hand and city halls, state capitols, and national interests, as well as vested local interests (unions, prefessional associations, etc.) on the other.

Finally, neighborhood control is not a panacea. It will not solve the vast problems of unemployment of millions of people, poor education, malnutrition, and the like. Neighborhood control is not anticentrist. It is an attempt to create a new consensual society, an attempt to create a reasonable approach toward overcoming alienation, toward giving meaning to the lives of large numbers of people who are not only politically apathetic but, worse, also politically traumatized. The process of system transformation begins where people are—on those streets, sitting on those stoops, in those tenements, fighting those rats and trying to survive. Many of those people are willing to move in a meaningful way. They will move to create relevant intermediary groupings in their day-to-day lives and, in many instances, that means their control of certain functions.

We must begin to work out the problems posed by increasing centralization on the one hand and by moves for meaningful local involvement on the other. This is the move and the meaning of political modernity in this country in the latter third of the twentieth century.

NOTES

1   James Q. Wilson, *Negro Politics* (New York: Free Press, 1960), p. 133.

2   Milton Kotler, *Neighborhood Government* (New York: Bobbs-Merrill, 1969), pp. 45–50.

3   James M. Gavin, *Crisis Now* (New York: Ranson Hanse, 1968), p. 130

4   National Advisory Council on Economic Opportunity, *Decentralization: A Conceptual Analysis* (Staff Paper, 1968), pp. 6–11.

Mexican Feasible Participation

Pepe Lucero

In a Model Cities meeting to discuss some new and surely earthshaking development or pronouncement from its funding source, an elderly Mexican-American man, more frustrated than angered, got up and said, "I don't know who this Mr. Hud is, but I don't think his heart is in the right place . . ."

Daniel P. Moynihan

The participation of Mexican-Americans on boards and committees that have been established as legal adjuncts to the various programs funded by the federal government continues to be minimal and generally ineffective, even eight years after the passage of the Economic Opportunity Act of 1964 and its provisions for "maximum feasible participation," that noble experiment in citizen, resident, and client participation. "No one seems to recall for certain just who was responsible for the phrase," says Daniel P. Moynihan,[1] but it is patently clear that Mexican participation has not been maximum. Why?

What was Feasible?

It is essential to examine briefly what degree and quality of participation was probable in the Mexican-American communities of the Southwest United States when War on Poverty was declared. The Mexican-

259

American citizens, for whom the war was being waged, were not steeped in a long history of cooperative efforts, either among themselves or with groups possessing wealth or resources in the community. Theirs was a history of going at it alone. More affluent Mexican-Americans have already discovered the chummy settings of the P.T.A., Boy Scouts, and Little League; but the poor Mexican-American was, and perhaps still is, a long way from this.

The social service agencies and organizations created out of and funded through such structures as United Fund, Community Chest, and Red Feather had operated in the poor areas for some time and had created constituencies of the poor. It would have seemed, at the beginning of the War on Poverty, that Mexican-American participation would come from them. But it did not. These agencies viewed the federal programs with suspicion and assumed that they were certainly something to stay away from. The feeling was that the federal programs asked for too many changes to be instituted and carried no guarantee of continued funding to sustain the changes. And, as it turned out, both of these concerns were well-founded. Thus, the Mexican-American poor who should have been the most ready for the War on Poverty stayed out.

this necessarily led to the overnight creation of poor Mexican-American groups who could satisfy the letter of the law; the spirit would be treated later or perhaps never. So, the cry went out for "good, safe Mexicans." They were desperately needed to bring in the rich federal programs. In the Southwest no Mexican-American participation spelled no participation of the poor, and, certainly, no program was possible without them. And so the poor Mexican-American was drafted into the War on Poverty, theoretically to sit on the councils of war but, in reality, to be a *soldado razo* (buck private). He was to remain a private, first, because the battle being fought (on his behalf, remember) was a strange and new one. Secondly, those selected to help him make those momentous decisions were strangers to him. The poor Mexican-American had not participated in unions or local government councils. Who were these people that now asked him for his opinions? Our man knew poverty but he did not recognize his newly designated allies, so he often went AWOL, or worse, deserted.

Early Mexican-American Participation

Still, the need for Mexican-American participation was a requirement that had to be fulfilled as different communities aggressively sought programs for the poor. Because they were having difficulty producing the poor Mexican-American who works as a domestic or as a migrant or seasonal farm worker, those responsible for initiating poverty programs found in the legislation the answer to their problem. They would seek "representatives of the poor." The ideal representative of the poor would be one that was, of course, Mexican-American, not too far removed from the barrio, and yet who had some experience in the governing of his social club or church and might even have participated in some council or organization such as a labor union or local government. It must be said that these representatives of the poor, in most instances, did yeoman duty in seeing that programs did come to different communities. Their failings were to be shown later when they refused to give way as the poor became more ready to serve on Community Action Agency boards and other decision-making panels.

The real poor would, in time, be criticized for their mismanagement and their misspending of public funds while many of the decision-making bodies contained no real poor people. The poor had yet to learn how to get in, stay in, and influence programs that affected their lives. But when the War on Poverty began to fail, the poor were forced to absorb some of the blame.

The lessons learned were many and varied from community to community.

—The programs needed the poor more than the poor needed the programs.

—The delegate–agencies or subcontractors to the Community Action Program agencies, jockeying for the coveted title of "the voice of the poor," eagerly courted the poor and even promised to train them in the process of citizen participation.

—The local subdivisions of government involved in the War on Poverty were willing to make concessions rather than have a public issue embarrass them.

—Public bodies could not stand public pressures.

—Poverty administrators did not have a firm footing anywhere when they tried to walk both sides of the street.

—It did not matter where the phrase had originated nor exactly how it was to be carried out, but "maximum feasible participation," while no more than a program edict, could be used as a technique in the democratic process to gain access to many other things.

What EOA Has Given

Just as the Mexican-American poor were learning rules and techniques to make their participation meaningful, things were changed by the federal agencies. The Green Amendment to the EOA gave local government subdivisions the right to take over poverty war operations. When they did, poverty boards were reduced to an advisory capacity because the prime contractors were the local governments. It must be pointed out that few local city–county governments made use of the Green Amendment and assumed control of Community Action Agencies operations. But the message was not lost on the poverty boards, especially the poor. The message was that maximum feasible participation could easily be relegated to an advisory capacity. Poverty boards were also aware that the control exerted by them was on program operations that were being financially deemphasized. The big money was going to Model Cities. And, in that set-up, the citizen and poor people participation was advisiory. The mayors were in charge—nothing was clearer.

Participation as a Means to Effect Change and Control

The participation of the client class, whether poor white, Indian, black, Puerto Rican, or Mexican-American was greatly assisted by the EOA edict of maximum feasible participation. The Mexican-American community or communities of the Southwest have been able to make use of their newly found skills in participation with varying degrees of success. But the matter of participation and involvement is no longer viewed as an end. Many began to believe that to sit on a board was to serve, but this is not the case. The agencies administering the federal funds at the local level were most often to blame for this belief. Board training was a necessary evil, poorly conducted and attended. Orientation sessions with citizen participants became gripe sessions rather than learning seminars. Participation for its own sake is now understood as a device for training but not necessarily as a vehicle for influence.

The frequent changes in program philosophy and funding priority made participation a farce. It was too often coincidental that when client, i.e., poor, participation was at its peak, programs would be reduced in funds or completely de-funded.

There is no direct correlation found, by this writer, between the watered down Mexican-American participation and the rise of groups in the Mexican-American, now Chicano, community who sought control rather than participation. But it happened. The participation element is by and large an older, more reserved group. The power element is composed of the young people of the Chicano movement. Both forces are still in existence and at work in their own style and pace. It is time that the two groups discover the worth of each other's contribution and begin to complement their efforts.

Recognizing that some institutions in the community are impervious to power plays, Mexican-Americans should participate to bring about the needed changes. By the same token, recognizing that some institutions will not and cannot change, they should be challenged, and control should be wrested from them.

To learn this combination and two work it well will be a major step towards maximum Mexican participation.

NOTES

1   Daniel P. Moynihan, *Maximum Feasible Misunderstanding* (New York: Free Press, 1969), p. xvi.

Epilogue

George Frederickson

Introduction

Three themes run through this collection of essays. All three—administrative decentralization, citizen participation, and neighborhood control—are closely coupled in reality and part of the same theoretical family. Because they are usually found bundled together theoretically and practically, it is important to make them conceptually distinct so as to indicate the points at which they are the same and the points at which they differ. This essay will attempt a brief explication of the similarities and dissimilarities between administrative decentralization, citizen participation, and neighborhood control. There are two central hypotheses here: first, when any one of administrative decentralization, citizen participation, or neighborhood control is put forward as a potential reform without the other two, little reform will ensue and the result will likely be economically and politically counterproductive for the areas that are presumed to be helped by such reforms. Real political and administrative reform in the 1970s can result only from the full development of all three of these concepts together. Second, a federated system of government that maintains tension between its greater and lesser jurisdictions will, in the long run, be politically and economically more productive for the inner city than would completely autonomous and self-supporting neighborhood governments.

Administrative decentralization, citizen participation, and neighborhood control are all put forward as solutions to our urban condition. There seems to be a shared, although not well-articulated, assessment of our urban condition, a kind of commonsense political and intellectual agreement that our condition results from a concentration of political and administrative power clusters made up of interest groups, congressional committees, and public service professions.[1] The defense cluster (military–industrial complex) insists on policing the world. The police control law enforcement and the learning force runs education.[2] The concentration of economic forces in major corporations and labor unions results in the gross maldistribution of resources, and the distribution of political services is an almost exact mirror of economic distribution; that is, the higher one's economic status, the greater the quality and quantity of public services that he receives.[3] The Balkanization of our big cities with black and brown centers and jurisdictionally distinct suburbs, in tandem with the dependency of these separate jurisdictions on the property tax, results in gross disparities in living conditions, on the one hand, and in the quantity and quality of the public services on the other. In these great cities there are so many layers of government in such complex mazes and patterns that the fixing of responsibility and the concentration of resources is difficult if not impossible. Much of what was formerly regarded as fundamentally political in the city is now regarded as part of administrative routines, such as budgeting, personnel procedures, and policy implementation. Finally, the political system is apparently unable to shift its resources from the conditions that troubled America in the Depression and in World War II, and the public service we erected to deal with those conditions, to the conditions that trouble us today. The inability of the political system to refocus its resources on contemporary problems has resulted in sharp increases in frustration for those who are being severely disadvantaged. This frustration has two distinct manifestations: such aggressive political activities as riots and a kind of political apathy or despair.

Although this is a highly simplified caricature of contemporary political, economic, and social conditions, it does nonetheless portray the general mood, particularly among social scientists. There are variations of this mood, and the agreement is by no means unanimous. But there is a surprising absence of modern social analysis challenging the above critique. We see then a kind of shared assessment of the situation and a loose intellectual coalition around these views.

Not only is there a common sense agreement as to the nature of our urban condition, but also there is a similar agreement, albeit less certain, as to the means by which urban problems can be solved. It is important to recognize that social scientists are always better at and more likely to agree on a diagnosis of a situation than they are on a prescription. So it is not uncommon to find social scientists agreeing that we are going to hell in a handbasket and telling us all the reasons why. Social scientists are also capable of clustering around idealized solutions to their shared assessment of the situation. Today this loose concensus of what needs to be done takes the form described below. It is a simplified caricature of more sophisticated suggested solutions to our social ills. There are detractors to administrative decentralization, neighborhood control, and citizen participation, and James Davis' essay in this volume catalogues well the arguments of those who see little hope in these movements. It is my position that these views are presently in the minority.

Because of the pronounced tendency of bureaucracies to evaluate their results on the basis of instrumental or functional tests versus measures of social effectiveness or productivity, it is important to determine who the clients of particular public services are, or could be, and to assess effectiveness from the client perspective.[4] This argues then that while an organization may be generally effective it can also be specifically highly effective for certain clients and highly ineffective for others. Hence the argument for client involvement and client participation. This requires a capacity on the part of governments to identify clients in the specific rather than the general sense. Decentralized forms of organization or government are a means by which evaluations of effectiveness can be made more specific. Thus we witness the development of the neighborhood as a collective of citizens with specific needs that are not being met.

The capacity of a central government to help a poverty neighborhood is now seriously in question. There is much support for fostering local definitions of problems and arguments for the development of local capacities to solve problems as they are locally defined. Finally, the dominance of public services by particular professionals, such as educators or policemen, can be lessened by the development of either citizen participation, neighborhood control, or administrative decentralization. The vague set of agreements and conclusions around this set of ideas resulted in "maximum feasible participation" without aggressive challenges.

The loose conclusion or mood supporting administrative decentralization, citizen participation, and neighborhood control is having its effect. It is evident that all three are being rapidly developed in American government.[5] For this reason, it is important that they be more fully described and compared. The idea that they are good and that they will in some fashion or another help us solve our urban problems, plus the fact that they are being widely touted and adopted, suggests the need for greater explication.

A comparison of citizen participation, neighborhood control, and administrative decentralization can be facilitated by a two-column table. (See Table I.) The first column describes the presumed values that each maximizes, and the second column sets out some of the real characteristics of each. By setting out the values and characteristics of each, we hope to sustain the argument that they must be adopted in combination if they are to have any real effect.

Table 1

	Presumed Values to Maximize	Real Characteristics
Administrative Decentralization	Central control with some local variation. Closer contacts with clients. Ability to maintain economies of scale. Capacity to accommodate graphic dispersion. Meet local needs but still be strong enough to provide general services. Facilitates participation within the organization, organizational democracy.	Maintenance of bureaucratic state. Professional dominance. Local control by élite. Gross disparities in service distribution. Productivity is administratively defined. Participative management.
Citizen Participation	Maximum feasible participation. Process of government is perforce worth being involved in. The healthy citizen participates.	Selective representation. tyranny by the majority. Very slow. A maximum amount of participation can recreate the confusion and Babel. Pluralism equals selective participation for there are citizens and there are citizens. Citizen review boards. Ombudsmen.
Neighborhood Control	Self determination Home rule. Government close to the people. The demand for human community.	Protectionist. Inefficient. Overly dependent on economic base. Presently responsible for Balkanization and the use of the suburbs as exclusive and protectant neighborhoods.

Administrative Decentralization

First there should be a distinction between administrative decentralization, political decentralization, and political fragmentation. Political decentralization is taken to mean autonomous or semiautonomous units of governments, customarily with their own elected officials, charters, and revenue-raising capacities as well as their own administrative apparatus. An example of a highly decentralized political system would be the Los Angeles–Long Beach Standard Metropolitan Statistical Area (SMSA) with its hundreds of autonomous local government units. A politically centralized system could be illustrated by the metropolitan form of government in which one jurisdiction subsumes the SMSA. Political fragmentation is taken to mean the packaging out of particular government services into autonomous or semiautonomous governing agencies, usually special district governments. Political fragmentation then is illustrated by the dramatic growth of air and water pollution control districts, school districts, weed-abatement control districts, *ad infinitum.* Administrative decentralization is taken here to mean the delegation of authority to subordinate units of a single administrative apparatus of a single jurisdiction, a delegation that can be withdrawn. This delegation can take either an areal or territorial form, or a functional or specialist form, the most typical examples being field offices or functionally distinct bureaus or agencies, such as the Forest Service in the Department of Agriculture. Administrative decentralization is much like the bureaucratic model of decentralization described by Henry J. Schmandt in this volume. It does not customarily include separate jurisdictional status, separate revenue-raising powers, or political autonomy or semiautonomy.

There is a small but rather good literature on administrative decentralization, the subject being a popular theme in public administration for decades.[6] The turbulence of the 1960s however, has resulted in a sharply renewed interest in the subject. Indeed there is a good deal of administrative decentralization underway in direct response to this renewed interest. While administrative decentralization is an honorable and often tried pattern of public administration reform, it is contended here that administrative decentralization standing alone does not meet our present needs.[7] While administrative decentralization is necessary, it is far from sufficient. Here is why:

If one can accept the characterization of our present form of government as an administrative state or bureaucratic state, then arguments for decentralized administration make little sense. The values attributed to administrative decentralization include the maintenance of administrative norms such as appointment on the basis of merit, political neutrality, highly developed specialization or professionalization (hierarchy, impersonality, and control via auxiliary staff functions such as budgeting and personnel procedures). All of these values can be accommodated by administrative decentralization. The traditions of public administration are not greatly disturbed by the development of field offices as a form of decentralization or the utilization of highly specialized and separate administrative subunits.[8] The bureau or the agency can be decentralized and can still be dominated by the narrow concerns of either administrators or functional specialists. We argue, then, that when administrative reorganization is put forward as a reform it may be a reform in the administrative sense but it is certainly not a reform in the political sense.

The U. S. Department of Agriculture is decentralized in that it has an elaborate field-office structure. The same can be said for most of the departments in the national government. Police and fire departments are customarily geographically decentralized, and most large public agencies now have such high levels of specialization that they can divide up the work into subunits which are to some degree or another decentralized.

This process of decentralization does have its positive aspects, to be sure. An agency can continue to be strong and therefore able to implement its programs but at the same time accommodate local needs and demands. It can facilitate direct contact with clients at the line level. Decentralization can accommodate economies of scale, and a decentralized organization can be a receptive environment for participative forms of management. If all these things can happen, what, then, are the problems with administrative decentralization?

The first problem has been identified by Frederick Mosher as the dominance of certain sectors of government by the "public service professions."[9] If basic decisions about law enforcement are to be made by the police, then whether or not those police are administratively decentralized is not very important. The control of defense by the military, the domination of the schools by educators, etc., is not really affected by administrative decentralization. It can be argued that each public service profession is not homogeneous, that there is disagreement among educators as to the best way to educate, disagreement among attorneys as to the best way to administer justice, and so forth. This argument is perhaps more reasonable in the light of recent events, primarily because each public service profession has its Young Turks seeking to reform it from within. To be sure, young attorneys, young medical doctors, young social workers are attempting to radicalize their professions, and some movement can be discerned. But, while the Young Turks in education might argue for more improved and innovative teaching methods and better education services for the poor, rarely does one hear a Young Turk professional argue the need for a dramatic diminution of control over education by educators, health by medical doctors, or justice by attorneys. There is a much stronger segment of each profession bent on furthering its insulation from the evils of politics. Then there is the development of public service unions to mobilize and put in concrete the dominance of public service professions. And finally there is the general mood of defensiveness on the part of most public administrators. All of this argues that the hope for fundamental reform from within or by administrative decentralization is misplaced.

The essential homogeneity of the training of most public service professionals is such that any radical departure from customary ways of carrying out public business is simply precluded.[10] While Ivan Illich may argue for deschooling society, we hear most educators talking about their efforts at administrative decentralization.[11] Why? Because the deschooling society argument gets at the heart of the domination of schools by persons trained in education and, customarily, with fairly narrow definitions of what constitutes the schooling process. Administrative decentralization allows the schooling process to continue to be controlled by educators and yet can accommodate some variations (although not very many).

The second problem with administrative decentralization has to do with the question of productivity. While it must be acknowledged that the measurement of productivity in the public sector is difficult, the difficulty is doubled because of the domination of the public service professions. The most telling example of this can be seen in the movement toward program-planning budgeting. This form of budgeting is designed to get at the question of productivity both in the general sense and in the specific sense. What has and is happening is a remarkable example of the definition of productivity by administrative agencies in such a way as to escape assessing or evaluating the real consequences of public program. Virtually every case in the Heinrichs and Taylor case book on PBS is a fascinating example of the capacity of public service agencies to avoid the question of productivity.[12] Productivity is defined as administrative productivity, not social or political productivity. As a consequence, the resultant hodge-podge is essentially the rationalization and justification of business as usual. While the Office of Management and Budget, or comparable units in state houses or city halls, are still trying to get at the question of productivity, it is patently clear that when agencies are left to define their program objectives, to draft their program papers, and to sketch the implications of the implementation of multi-year plans they simply do not get at either the question of general social productivity or of specific productivity, that is productivity for whom.

It is likely, in my judgment, that productivity will be one of the big issues in public administration in the 1970s and 1980s. It is destined to become the soft underbelly of the public service professions. The quality of public services is so generally low, the professionalization and unionization of public employees has so isolated public administrators, and public agencies appear to be so unwilling to consider the productivity issue that we are likely to experience a stong anti-administrative or anti-bureaucratic wave in politics at the national, state, and local levels. While we have experienced anti-administrative waves in the past, the upcoming one will likely be of tidal proportions. The old questions will be put more sharply: why, with so many highly trained and highly paid public servants, are we unable to improve substantially our education, our law enforcement, our health, our housing? The old administrative answer—give us more and better trained officials—is already beginning to wear thin. The search for alternatives is already underway. Can we contract out our education? Can we sharply cut the size and quality of the bureaucracy and not see any diminution in productivity?

The third problem with administrative decentralization has to do not with the general question of productivity but rather with the question expressed specifically and particularly by socio-economic class. There appears to be an alarmingly wide variation in both the quantity and quality of public services. This variation generally reflects social and economic categories: that is to say, the higher one's socioeconomic category, the more and better public services one receives. While this is not primarily a result of administrative decentralization but rather of political decentralization and fragmentation, gross disparities in services certainly are not solved nor are they likely to be solved by administrative decentralization. If service disparities are an important issue, and most contemporary students of government believe that they are, then administrative decentralization, at least on the basis of present experiences with it, cannot be put forward as a remedy. In sum then, administrative decentralization can facilitate getting government somewhat closer to the people and provide for local variations while maintaining a general capacity to get the job done. At the same time administrative decentralization, standing alone, does not facilitate the redistribution of political power. In an era in which public services were not dominated by isolated career professional groupings, administrative decentralization may have been a more fundamental reform, but not in our time. Only when administrative decentralization is coupled with height levels of citizen participation and neighborhood controls can there be hope for the redistribution of political power.

Citizen Participation

Classic forms of citizen participation have long been accepted in American government. Indeed, legislative bodies, review boards, advisory commissions, and the like usually reflect the inclusion of trusted participants. Managements must be represented as should labor, the political parties, and other representatives of easily identified interest groups. We do, then, have participation. The problem is that that participation is highly selective. Not only is participation selective, it takes a variety of forms. Broadly defined it can include that participation which occurs in the voting booth (again relatively selective), that participation which occurs in the potential for either public or private employment (again highly selective), that participation which includes access to education (again selective), as well as participation in traditional forms of representation such as legislative bodies and advisory commissions. Our preference here is to define participation broadly to include all of the forms listed above. But more important, the phrase citizen participation is today taken to mean especially the participation or participative potential of the poor, the undereducated, and the objects of racial and sexual discrimination, so when the phrase citizen participation is used it really means the special processes of participation that include those who have heretofore been excluded.

Two points are critical here. First, public service agencies—the bureaucracy—are the target of the poor because these agencies are their chief contact point with government. It is no wonder then that the participative battlefield in American government has been around education, law enforcement, social services, and health care, for it is these public service professions that bear most directly on the lives of citizens and particularly poor citizens. The second point is Dwight Waldo's contention that citizen participation is or at least should be regarded as contextual: that is to say good in one context and bad in another.[13] No doubt it makes little sense to have widespread citizen participation in every level and for every function of government. But there is an important context in which citizen participation, as defined here, should be central—the context Michael Lipsky labels street-level bureaucracies. It is in the street-level context—in education, in law enforcement, in health, in social service, in employment, and in housing—that citizen participation is being discussed.

It is now clear that traditional definitions of democratic participation are woefully inadequate. The voting process, even when it is fairly and equitably designed, can and does result in the tyranny of the majority. When the majority of the voters is made up of those who "have"—the so-called broad middle class—the policies of their representatives can be an expression of tyrannizing over the "have-nots." So, other forms of participation are urged, many of which are classic participatory forms, recognized by any student of American politics. The participation of the poor in public employment has gradually withered, in part because of the emergence of the public service professions and their utilization of the civil service procedures and in part because of the withering away of political parties at the local level. The recent Supreme Court decision, *Griggs v. Duke Power*, is an eloquent statement of the importance of a fair and equal access to employment.[14] It is also an example of the fundamental concern of the courts for minority rights in the face of majority rule. Public employment is a form of participation that is not necessarily included in the definition of political participation, but it is without doubt that form of participation customarily denied the black, the brown, and the female. While maximum feasible participation of the democratic sort, that is involvement in policy making in community action programs, may not have been very successful, there can be little doubt that the employment potential of black and brown Americans was substantially enhanced as a result of the activities of the Office of Economic Opportunity. If public service bureaucracies are the locus not only of administrative but political power, to participate in the utilization of that power might well mean employment in those bureaucracies. The problem is that the public employment customarily available for the citizens who are the subject of the participation described here has usually been at the lowest possible level. So, while participation through employment has been on the increase, most of that employment has been at very low levels of administration and has hardly made a dent in the control of policy, particularly in patterns of public service distribution. Still, public employment is a basic form of citizen participation.

When citizen participation is considered in a democratic context, the notion is that the healthy citizen participates. Participation is an indication of the absense of alienation and of the belief that by participating the citizen can see the connection between public policies and his own political, economic, or social situation. These are laudable values. The sad fact is that there is little evidence to the effect that traditional forms of political participation do result in improved circumstances for all citizens, for too often such participation is not really power altering.

High levels of participation in day-to-day policy making and implementation is simply not workable, and no one is seriously arguing a return to the town meeting. Public services must continue to be delivered promptly and effectively. But the participative question is who determines the character of a public service and the pattern of its distribution? Who determines the criteria for selecting and promoting the public employees who deliver that service? And who assesses the consequences of the public agencies' work? It does not require the resurrection of the town meeting to contend that participation in the decisions that determine who gets what should be a fundamental right of every citizen.

Why then has not citizen participation, as defined here, worked very effectively? The first reason is the control of policy and service distribution by public service professions. Administrative decentralization has been linked, customarily, with citizen participation. When administrative agencies decentralize, as in the case of the Department of Agriculture or the Selective Service, the citizens who participate in policy making at the local level are almost always the dominant elite.[15] This allows the administrative agency to develop grass roots political power on the part of local elite while claiming to be decentralized. Second, citizen participation has not worked because it has not been the tradition in either our education process, in industry or government employment, or in policy making. In short, many of our citizens have never learned to participate and many of them have had valid experiences that indicate to them that participation as it is presently designed (voting, low level employment, advisory boards, etc.) does not bring results that are beneficial to them. So why participate?

A very thorough analysis of the subject is provided in Carole Pateman's *Participation and Democratic Theory.*[16] Pateman argues that contemporary political theorists have seriously distorted the notion of political participation developed by the classic theorists, particularly Rousseau, Mill, and Cole. Among her contemporary democratic theorists, Pateman includes Schumpeter, Dahl, Berelson, Sartori, and Eckstein, and she summarizes their work in the following way:

> In the theory, "democracy" refers to a political method or set of institutional arrangements at national level. The characteristically democratic element in the method is the competition of leaders (elite) for the votes of the people at periodic free elections. Elections are crucial to the democratic method, for it is primarily through elections that the majority can exercise control over their leaders. Responsibleness of leaders to non-elite demands or "control" over leaders is insured primarily through the sanction of loss of office at elections; the decisions of leaders can also be influenced by active groups bringing pressure to bear during inter-election periods. "Political equality" in the theory refers to universal suffrage and to the existence of the equality of opportunity of access to channels of influence over leaders. Finally, "participation" so far as the majority is concerned, is participation in the choice of decision makers. Therefore, the function of participation in the theory is solely a protective one. The protection of the individual from arbitrary decisions by elected leaders and the protection of his private interest. It is in the achievement of this aim that the justification for the democratic method lies.
>
> Certain conditions are necessary if the democratic system is to remain stable. The level of participation by the majority should not rise much above the minimum necessary to keep the democratic method (electoral machinery) working; that is, it should remain at about the level that exists at present in the Anglo-American democracies. The fact that non-democratic attitudes are relatively more common among the inactive means that any increase in participation by the apathetic would weaken the concensus on the norms of the democratic method, which is a further necessary condition. Although there is no definite "democratic" character required of all citizens, the social training or socialization in the democratic method that is necessary can take place inside existing, diverse, non-governmental authority structures providing that there is some degree of congruency between the structure of authority in government and the non-governmental structure close to it, then stability can be maintained. As Bachrach has noted, such a model of democracy can be seen as one where the majority (non-elites) gain maximum output (policy decisions) from leaders with the minimum input (participation) on their part.[17]

Pateman then summarizes the criticisms of the contemporary theorists, criticisms which have come to be known as the "critique of democratic theory." The contemporary theorists, while claiming to be empirical, have, as Walker has put it, "fundamentally changed the normative significance of democracy."[18] Pateman argues that one of the fundamental changes has been in contemporary concepts of participation as they relate to democracy. She argues that the classic theorists held participation to be a central tenent to a democracy. "The existence of representative institutions at national level is not sufficient for democracy; for maximum participation by all the people at that level of socialization, or 'social training' for democracy must take place in other spheres in order that the necessary individual attitudes and psychological qualities can be developed." To Pateman, the notion of self-government includes at its base the concept of participation, but participation will always be selective if only a certain segment of society is educated and socialized to believe themselves capable of self-government. Pateman's central thesis then is:

> The major function of participation in the theory in participatory democracy is therefore an educative one, educative in the very widest sense, including both the psychological aspect and the gaining of practice and democratic skills and procedures. Thus there is no special problem about the stability of the participatory system; it is self-sustaining through the educative impact of the participatory process. Participation develops and fosters the very qualities necessary for it. The more individuals participate the better able they become to do so. Subsidiary hypotheses about participation are that it has an integrative effect and that it aids the acceptance of collective decisions.[19]

For participation to be effective, the citizenry must be broadly educated to understand and utilize participatory processes. Such a pattern of education, Pateman argues, would greatly heighten political efficacy and reduce alienation. Further, it would not result in the development of servile or passive political behavior, but rather result in the development of psychological qualities that cause one to believe that he can be self-governing and be confident in his abililty to participate responsibly and effectively and to control his own life and environment. She argues that this kind of education can occur most effectively in the workplace and at the local level of government. She then describes the research of Almond and Verba and Easton and Dennis and summarizes it with the conclusion that political efficacy or high participation is primarily a function of social and economic class; the higher social and economic classes do develop skills at participation and those psychological characteristics which cause them to believe that they can be self-governing or at least can influence the processes and consequences of government.

The concept of participation in policy making in the workplace is now fundamental to both American and British organization research and theory. Pateman summarizes this research with the conclusion that widespread and real participation in policy making in the workplace can be learned and, when learned, can have a highly politive effect on efficacy, on the workers level of commitment to the organization, and on the productivity of that organization. Rather than threatening organizational stability, worker participation in organizational policy making enhances that stability by fostering processes of organizational change or self-correction. Miss Pateman then goes on to discuss workers self-management in Yugoslavia. She observes in her research on the subject that participation and the capacity to effect decisions is widespread in the Yugoslavian experience, with positive effects on both productivity and citizen efficacy.

Carole Pateman is optimistic about the potential for citizens of local government and employees in their workplace to be self-governing yet effective even in highly complex processes. But effective participation will require educational processes and reinforcing experiences leading to the conclusion that participation is productive not only among the middle and upper classes but also among us all. Still, participation, standing alone, cannot redistribute power. Where policy making is centralized and professionally dominated, participation can become wasted motion. If the resources and skills necessary to effectively carry out government programs are lacking, then participation is a cruel hoax. So administrative decentralization must be tied to citizen participation by the democratization of the workplace and by the capacity of citizens to cause bureaucrats to deliver local government services as local citizens wish them to be delivered. This brings us to neighborhood control.

Neighborhood Control

Neighborhood control is the idealized setting for a combination of administrative decentralization and citizen participation. Although far from perfect, the suburban city, when large enough and when blessed with a strong revenue base, is the best example of the potentialities of neighborhood control. As David Perry says in his essay, the suburb, despite our criticisms of it, is an idealized state, a dream for the working class family (particularly if it is white) to attempt to realize and an isolated and protected enclave for those who have made it. The suburban city has its own government, its own revenue base (however meager), its own schools, its own civil servants, and many forms of control by citizens over their government. This is not to suggest that the contemporary American suburb constitutes either an adequate model of or definition of neighborhood control; rather, the suburbs are, as Perry suggests, an interesting analogue to neighborhood control.

Neighborhood control is almost always considered in an urban and often inner city urban context rather than a suburban context. And, the usual definition and description of neighborhood control is to the effect that the residents of a specifically designated sector or region of the city have forms of control over those public services and public servants that most directly impinge on their lives. In its idealized form neighborhood control would involve actual governments-within-governments, that is a neighborhood government that controls neighborhood schools, police, social services, housing, zoning, much as a suburban government does. The neighborhood then becomes a political jurisdiction with boundaries and powers. But, the city continues to be the revenue gathering jurisdiction, and the provider of areawide functions. Revenues are disbursed to the neighborhood governments on the basis of some formula but left to the neighborhood to spend.

This idealized form of neighborhood control is not in vogue. Some modified versions of this model are found in federally funded multi-service agencies and in the consolidation of federal moneys in inner city community action programs such as the Oakland situation described in Judith V. May's essay. The important distinction is that the city itself has not had to really shift its priorities or alter very dramatically its patterns of resource allocation. The "hard money" taken from the city general fund and coming from locally or state provided revenues continues to go to such standard functions of local government as education, police, public works, and the like. The "soft money" from the national government can be controlled (although not always) by people at the neighborhood level and used for purposes that the federal granting agency and the neighborhood leaders find agreeable. Mayors and governors have generally opposed this "dual sovereignty," to use May's phrase, and have pressed the national government to cause all grant money to pass through their offices and be approved and dispensed by them. It is for this reason that many friends of the neighborhood control that has grown up around federal grants, well described by both Judith May and Jeffrey Pressman, regard revenue sharing and block or noncategorical federal grants as the fundamental device by which governors and mayors hope to wrest greater control over federal money. The likely result will be reduced support for inner city programs and a diminution in neighborhood control.

While the control of fiscal resources is essential to any definition of neighborhood control, so are the other political characteristics of local government that have come to be regarded as primarily administrative. The modification of personnel procedures and requirements so that public employment will be more accessible to the poor and to minorities is a form of control, a form of control that was especially important in the Ocean-hill–Brownsville case described in Norman I. and Susan S. Fainstein's essay. Purchasing controls are important. When the neighborhood can determine which firms get printing contracts, fuel contracts, the sale of police cars, and capitol construction contracts, they have a form of control which is as central to American politics as the ballot. But the most important form of local control is, or should be, over the quantity, quality, and distribution of public services. This requires a fundamental recognition that public service quantity, quality, and distribution decisions are not the sole preserve of the public service professions. They are fundamentally political decisions that belong in the political arena. When the neighborhood controls, or at least shares the control, these things, it has achieved some level of self-government. Without some of these controls, citizen participation is meaningless.

Although political systems move gradually, they do move. The movement toward neighborhood control in local government is incremental, as has been the movement toward metropolitan government. On the metropolitan government side we find dramatic increases in the utilization of areawide planning and zoning activities. Air and water pollution control are almost always handled at the county or regional level. Patterns of vertical drift in social services, health services, and transportation systems are apparent. So while few metropolitan areas have opted for full tilt metro-government, almost all are experiencing vertical drift or functional centralization. At the same time these areas are witnessing decentralization, increased levels of citizen participation, and some primitive forms of neighborhood control. This is particularly the case in the education function, as the Fainsteins and Charles V. Hamilton describe, in law enforcement, and medical services. So while we see few examples of full tilt metro-government we do see rather systematic growth in centralization; and likewise while there are, to my knowledge, no examples of full tilt neighborhood control, we see many examples of the movement toward decentralization coupled with some forms of neighborhood control over the street level bureaucracies.

The types of neighborhood control now in use are by no means as complete as the ideal model. They are, however, the early evidence of the move toward decentralization. Many cities are now utilizing little city halls.[20] There is a dramatic increase in the availability of such neighborhood facilities as storefront legal services, neighborhood health centers, and the like.[21] Citizen advisory boards for neighborhoods are on the increase. The use of ombudsmen is clearly on the rise. So, while this movement is incremental and hardly full tilt, neighborhood control is a reflection of what Henry J. Schmandt in his essay rightly calls a contemporary "structural imperative."

A Tension Model

The most telling argument against neighborhood control is this: why divide up our huge cities into self-governing neighborhoods at the same time we find them decaying, weakened by a shrinking fiscal base, the habitat of the poor, the undereducated, the unemployed, the lawless, and the addicted? What is there left to control? How could a division of this problem into neighborhoods possibly be put forward as a potential solution? How can neighborhood control amass enough power and resources to make government effective under such conditions?

The only real answer is the obvious one: by a federated system. The power, resources, the facilities, and the manpower of the central government must always be the base of neighborhood control. Neighborhood governments should be pursuing their objectives attempting to get the schools to hire more black teachers and to prepare and implement curricula that are more relevant to needs as they are defined at the neighborhood level. The central city government, and particularly the public service professions, will continue to attempt to pursue their needs, that is meritized and probably unionized bureaucracy, policy control, and the like. This brings us to a concept of neighborhood control based on a notion of productive tension.

Two conditions appear necessary to a functioning tension model. First a tension model could work when there are contrasting values, that is to say, when tensions are real and not contrived. Second, both the greater and the lesser jurisdictions in the model should have separate areas of autonomy and control. This implies that the lesser jurisdictions must have definitive geographic boundaries. An example of such a model would be the tension between the national government and the governments of the southern states around the so-called states' rights issue. While this tension was at one point out of control—the Civil War—it has in many ways been highly productive. The expansion of voting rights for black Americans, the integration of school systems, the expansion of civil liberties reflect values being pursued by the national government. At the same time southern states have pursued different values but are now in a position of coming around. Further, the states are now significantly different than they were thirty years ago. Because they have their own governments they can accommodate to change. If those states were simply administered units of the national government, the accommodation to change would likely be slower and based less on public support. One might argue that the states' rights issue as an example of tension is not an appropriate analogue for the tension between the general government of a large city and its neighborhood governments. That may be, but this does not mean the tension theory in a federated system is without merit.

Paul Ylvisaker, in his seminal essay on decentralization, "Some Criteria for a 'Proper' Areal Division of Governmental Powers," argued that the first maxim of decentralization should be the power to govern. He argues that "the assignment of powers to component areas should in each case be a general one, governing the whole range of governmental functions, rather than a partial one relating only to a particular function."[22] While this conforms to the neat and clean symmetry that is common in classic organization theory, it is simply not politically feasible. Even if it were feasible, it might prove to be disastrous for those subdivisions too weak to govern. To be sure, it would be desirable if, say, Ocean Hill–Brownsville could have general power covering the whole range of governmental functions. But where would Ocean Hill–Brownsville get the resources? While the resources question may be a practical one, there is also an important theoretical question. Are not the values held by the public service professions of some validity and, similarly, are not the values of the neighborhood of some validity? Is it not possible, then, to design a pattern of urban federalism that manages the tension between these values rather than attempting to eliminate the tension on the assumption that one or the other set of values should be victorious? Tension theory presumes that it is possible to put these values into productive juxtaposition.

There is some possibility that modern theories of organization will eventually take hold in large city government. These theories of organization are difficult to summarize briefly, but, in greatly oversimplified terms they involve administrative decentralization, distribution of services on the basis of need rather than the basis of economic status, a matrix organizational structure, or at least highly modified and more flexible forms of hierarchy, and much greater participation in policy making both by public employees and by the recipients of their services.[23] The theory derived from the conclusion that our traditional concepts of reform are no longer useful. Social mobility and technological change is now so widespread that the notion of reform is less useful than it once was. Reform suggests that it is possible to put things right. In a society as fluid as ours the question is no longer one of reform but one of the degree of lag. How can we design government forms that are capable of shorter rather than larger lags between what the people need and what the government provides?

Much of this theory also derives from a contemporary concern over the seeming inability of people to control their governments. At great epic moments in history governments are changed, such as the New Deal programs mounted to get us out of the Depression and the elaborate military machinery created to get us through World War II and keep us in the Cold War. What we now recognize is our remarkable capacity to create massive public agencies to carry out public programs. We know how to build public agencies and meet obvious and generally agreed upon needs. We seem, however, to be unable to dismount these programs when it appears that they are no longer needed. Because of their guaranteed share of the budget, their merit bureaucracy, etc., these programs ultimately become as great a problem as the problems they were originally designed to solve. So the present mood in organization theory is not a reform mood.

Neighborhood control is not urged because it will put things right. The organization theorist suspects that what is put right today will, in the not too distant future, need to be put right again. So the theorist searches for forms of government and systems of organization that are as easy to dismount as they are to mount and are as flexible as possible. The theorist, then, is brought to a fundamental respect for the creative potential of tension or conflict. Tension can give the policy makers some sense of what is appropriate to do at a particular point in time. So long as a real political conflict is nurtured, then it is always possible to listen to the warp and woof of contrasting values. When the neighborhood is able to press its preferences on a central government in such a way that these preferences are regarded as legitimate because the neighborhood has a kind of legal standing, then the central government must in some fashion accommodate to neighborhood needs. For this reason then, neighborhood control is critical. Administrative decentralization does not impart sufficient legitimacy to the needs of the neighborhood as they are defined by the citizens in the neighborhood. And without some form of neighborhood jurisdiction or para-jurisdiction the hope of citizen participation is lost. The citizen has reason to believe that by working in a pattern of tensions between the neighborhood and the central government he can enhance his values and he will participate productively.

In any federated system there are problems of umpiring the clash of values and the problems of resource allocation. The courts have become the umpires of federal relations and are, at the moment, wrestling with the question of poor versus rich local government jurisdictions. It appears that they are moving in the direction of areawide revenue gathering jurisdictions coupled with formulae for distribution based on either equity or need. The gross disparities between the fiscal base of separate jurisdictions will likely be changed by the courts. Similarly, the gross disparities in state aid will be repaired. All of this suggests the practical importance of setting up neighborhoods with some kind of jurisdictional status. With this status, these jurisdictions can compete for resources raised on an areawide basis with some promise of a greater slice of the fiscal pie than they would get if they were fully autonomous or not federated. The theoretical point here is the capacity of the neighborhood jurisdiction to negotiate with the central government for the kinds of services they want and in the proportion they want. As the local jurisdictions' needs change, they can have some control over public services, so those services can be made to change. The second theoretical point here is the umpiring capacity of the courts. They are dealing with the critical issues of balancing the powers of majority rule and the rights of minorities. In many ways these are the same issues that are being handled politically and administratively in the movement toward decentralization and neighborhood control.

Herbert Kaufman has observed that we move in cycles on the design of government and the values associated with design. The values he identifies are representativeness, politically neutral competence, and executive leadership. He argues that while we are now witnessing reforms that seek to enhance the value of representativeness we will soon swing back to competence, then to executive leadership, and ultimately back to representativeness. He identifies this movement as a process of reform, followed by reform, and that customarily these reforms are put in terms of centralization and decentralization, the cycle moving from one to another and back. Empirically, Kaufman is correct, and describes accurately what has occurred. But, as argued earlier, the whole notion of reform, of putting things right, is now under serious attack. Contemporary theory is very processual, that is if a process such as designed tension management can be maintained, the cycles between reforms can be shorter or less inclined to lag. If the system is open to the clash of values, can be more flexible in the utilization of its resources, and can still rely on a skilled and well-developed administrative apparatus, the cycles should be shorter and smoother. A combination of administrative decentralization, citizen participation, and neighborhood control in a federated local setting could bring the combination of flexibility, equity, and excellence needed to recreate our great cities.

NOTES

1   J. P. Leiper Freeman, *The Political Process: Executive Bureau-Legislative Committee Relations*, rev. ed. (New York: Random House, Inc., 1965).

2   Frederick C. Mosher, *Democracy and the Public Service* (New York: Oxford University Press, 1968).

3   See especially John Coons, William Clune, and Stephen Sugarman, *Private Wealth and Public Education* (Cambridge, Massachusetts: The Belknap Press of Harvard University Press, 1970); and James W. Guthrie and Associates, *Schools and Inequalities* (Washington, D.C.: The Urban Coalition, 1969).

4   James Thompson, *Organizations In Action* (New York: McGraw-Hill, 1967).

5   See especially George J. Washnis, "Neighborhood Facilities and Municipal Decentralization," *Comparative Analysis and Case Studies of Twelve Cities* (Washington, D.C.: Center for Governmental Studies, March, 1971), I and II.

6   James W. Fesler, *Area and Administration* (University, Alabama: University of Alabama Press, 1949); Arthur Maass (ed.), *Area and Power: A Theory of Local Government* (Glencoe, Illinois: The Free Press, 1959); Herbert Kaufman, "Administrative Decentralization and Political Power," *Public Administration Review* XXIX: 1 (January/February, 1969), pp. 3–15.

7   See especially Dwight Waldo, "Some Thoughts on Alternatives, Dilemmas and Paradoxes in a Time of Turbulence," *Public Administration in a Time of Turbulence*, Dwight Waldo (ed.) (New York and London: Chandler, 1971), pp. 258–264.

8 Dwight Ink and Alan L. Dean, "A Concept of Decentralization," *Public Administration Review* XXX: 1 (January/February, 1970), pp. 60–63.

9 Frederick C. Mosher, *op. cit.*

10 See especially Herbert Kaufman, *The Forest Ranger* (Baltimore: The Johns Hopkins Press, 1960).

11 Ivan Illich, *Deschooling Society* (New York: Harper and Row, 1970).

12 Heinrichs and Taylor, *Program Budgeting and Benefit-Cost Analysis* (Los Angeles: Good Year Publishing, 1969).

13 Dwight Waldo, *op. cit.*

14 *Griggs* vs. *Duke Power* Supreme Court Report, No. 124, October 10,1970, issued March 8, 1971.

15 Charles M. Hardin, *Food and Fiber in the Nation's Politics* National Advisory Commission on Food and Fiber, Technical Papers. (Washington D.C.: August 1967, U.S. Government Printing Office), III. James David and Kenneth Dolbere, *Little Groups of Neighborhoods*.

16 Carole Pateman, *Participation and Democratic Theory* (London: Cambridge University Press).

17 *Ibid.,* p.14.

18 Jack L. Walker, "A Critique of the Elitist Theory of Democracy," *American Political Science Review,* LX: 2, pp. 285–95.

19 Pateman, *op. cit.,* pp. 42–43.

20 George J. Washnis, *Little City Halls* (Washington, D.C.: Center For Governmental Studies, January, 1971).

21 George J. Washnis, *Neighborhood Facilities and Decentralization, op. cit.*

22 Paul Ylvisaker, "Some Criteria for a 'Proper' Areal Division of Governmental Powers," *Area and Power,* Arthur Maass (ed.) *op. cit.,* pp. 27–49.

23 See especially Frank Marini, *Toward a New Public Administration* (New York and London: Chandler, 1970); Dwight Waldo, (ed.), *Public Administration In a Time of Turbulence* (New York and London: Chandler, 1971); *Public Management* (November).

Index

Boldface numbers indicate pages on which authors' contribution begins. Italic numbers indicate pages on which complete reference appears and numbers in parenthesis indicate note numbers.